THE healthy family cookbook

ALSO BY

Hope Ricciotti, M.D.

AND

Vincent Connelly

THE PREGNANCY COOKBOOK

THE MENOPAUSE COOKBOOK

THE BREAST CANCER PREVENTION COOKBOOK

THE healthy family cookbook

Hope Ricciotti, M.D.

AND

Vincent Connelly

**Scripps Miramar Ranch
Library Center**

 W. W. NORTON & COMPANY • NEW YORK • LONDON

The Healthy Eating Pyramid is reprinted with the
permission of Simon & Schuster
Source from *Eat, Drink, and Be Healthy* by Walter C. Willett, M.D.
Copyright © 2001 by President and Fellows of Harvard College.

Illustrations by ArtParts
Manufacturing by The Maple-Vail Book Manufacturing Group
Book design by Rubina Yeh
Production manager: Amanda Morrison

LIBRARY OF CONGRESS CATALOGING-IN-PUBLICATION DATA
Ricciotti, Hope.
The healthy family cookbook / Hope Ricciotti and Vincent Connelly.—1st ed.
p. cm.
Includes bibliographical references and index.
ISBN 0-393-32419-2 (pbk.)
1. Nutrition. 2. Family—Health and hygiene. 3. Cookery. I. Connelly, Vincent. II. Title.
RA784.R53 2004
641.5′63—dc22
2004006500

W. W. Norton & Company, Inc.
500 Fifth Avenue, New York, N.Y. 10110
www.wwnorton.com

W. W. Norton & Company Ltd.
Castle House, 75/76 Wells Street, London W1T 3QT

1 2 3 4 5 6 7 8 9 0

contents

introduction

The Healthy Family Cookbook is based upon how we actually live: bringing up children while juggling careers; trying to maintain a healthy weight while feeding our children; staying fit and active together. As a physician and a chef, it represents our collective experience and knowledge based upon the latest scientific evidence about diet and a healthy lifestyle for you and your children. They are surprisingly similar. As well-done scientific evidence has emerged in the last few years, the components of a healthy diet have changed dramatically. But we don't want to simply inform you of this new data; we want to help you implement it. We want to help you get started by giving you our techniques, tips, opinions, and favorite recipes in this hands-on guide. Whether your family has toddlers or high-school-age children, you can eat the same foods together in order to maximize your health and wellness. You can stay active together. You can enjoy a household where you gather around delicious meals and share your daily lives together.

Families Today Are in a Hurry You race to get the children to school and yourself off to work or to your household duties in the morning. But you want to provide a healthful breakfast and to pack a nutritious lunch. You want to eat dinner together; yet everyone doesn't like the same foods, and you don't want to become a short-order cook. You want to maintain or lose weight, but the rest of your family's not on a diet. We'll give you tips on organizing your life, your shopping, your kitchen, your cooking techniques, and how to prepare one meal that will satisfy the entire family. We'll teach you the basics of nutrition for your children and yourselves so you can plow through the confusing maze of information that is out there. We'll give you some basic information and tips for losing and maintaining weight. We'll inform you of the latest information about exercise for you and your family. This should all be fun, exciting, family centered, quick, and easy. It should be your lifestyle—not a diet.

Sound too good to be true? We don't think so. We live this lifestyle every day. We savor our meals and food yet maintain healthy weights and lifestyles. We spend quality time with our children and involve them in food preparation and shopping in fun and educational ways. We have firsthand experience. As a uniquely qualified husband-and-wife team of chef and physician, we'd like to share our ideas and expertise from our research and experiences. Come join us.

Hope and Vince

PART ONE

health
and
nutrition

how to eat now and for the rest of your life

Understanding the modern concepts of what constitutes a healthy diet can be very confusing. Every day we hear in the media about new ideas and research on what we should be eating. One day we are told to eat beef and bacon, and the next day that they'll give you a heart attack. On another day the food pyramid is out and potatoes are no longer a vegetable. This information ranges from high-protein/low-carbohydrate to low-fat/high-carbohydrate recommendations, and everything in between. The myriad of reports makes it very difficult and confusing to know what is best for our families, even for those who are motivated and trying to make healthy food choices. We'll try to sift through this information to help you better understand how to provide what the latest research has shown to be the healthiest style of eating for you and your family.

Many of the latest theories on diet and health have some truth to them and some scientific evidence to support their contentions.

The problem is that some of this information gets distorted, hyped, and turned into extreme diet fads that are restrictive and impossible to stick to in the long run. The simple fact is that you need a varied diet which contains a wide array of foods so that it contains the nutrients needed for health and so that you and your family can maintain this diet for a lifetime. You need to feed yourself and your family in healthy, practical, simple, and economical ways. This can be done, with a little background knowledge, some basic cooking skills, and some attention to shopping and stocking your pantry with the correct foods. We'll give you some recipes where you can apply this knowledge and these skills, and you will be rolling.

New Ideas on the Basics of Nutrition The first step in providing a healthy family diet is to understand the latest dietary recommendations. Recent research has taught us that a healthy diet consists of a moderate amount of unrefined carbohydrate, a moderate amount of protein, and a moderate amount of unsaturated fat. Many of these basic principles of good nutrition are the same whether or not you are a child, an adolescent, or an adult, in midlife, or beyond.

With the increasing recognition of the role of diet in preventing chronic diseases, new dietary recommendations and guidelines reflect current beliefs about how nutrients, such as excess calories and saturated fat, or foods such as fruits and vegetables, relate to our health. While it is critically important for your diet to contain a variety of healthy nutrients and foods, too much of a good thing is also a very bad thing. Many of us have made the mistake of eating too many calories. Even when the source of these calories is healthy foods, being overweight is unhealthy. In this day and age, nutrient and dietary excesses are far more of a problem for us than deficiencies.

Current Food Guide Pyramid The food pyramid was the classic basis for dietary guidelines from the United States Department of

Agriculture. The government issued the following dietary guidelines in the form of the Food Guide Pyramid:

- 6 to 11 servings of rice, bread, cereal, and pastas
- 3 to 5 servings of vegetables
- 2 to 4 servings of fruits
- 2 to 3 servings of milk, yogurt, cheese
- 2 to 3 servings of meat, poultry, fish, dry beans, eggs, nuts
- fats, oils, and sweets: use sparingly

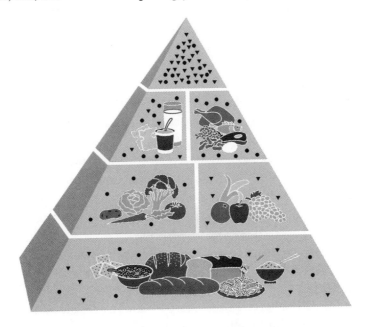

As reasonable as the food pyramid recommendations may sound, the findings from recent research from the Harvard School of Public Health and Harvard Medical School indicate that they may not be the best dietary guidelines for maintaining health, and that it is time to change this classic thinking.[1]

Problems with the Old Food Pyramid Some believe that it was politicians and not scientists, doctors, or nutritionists who came up with the food pyramid in the first place. These outside influences on the contents of the pyramid may have caused some distortions in the recommendations. The primary problem with the American diet is that we are consuming too many calories, whether from fat or carbohydrates, in relation to our level of physical activity. The old food pyramid does not have a way to account for our overconsumption of calories. In addition, the old pyramid does not distinguish between good fats and bad fats. Finally, there is no distinction made between refined and unrefined carbohydrates.

Based upon the new Harvard data, problems with the current food pyramid include that it[2]

- is out of sync with the most current scientific evidence.
- gives people a license to overeat.
- assumes that only fat calories can make people fat. In reality, it's too many calories from any source, whether they derive from carbohydrates or from fat.
- emphasizes large amounts of carbohydrates, and does not differentiate between refined and unrefined sources of carbohydrates.
- does not make a distinction between types of fat or protein.
- mixes red meat, chicken, nuts, and legumes together.

The Harvard scientists believe that the deficiencies in the food pyramid may have spawned the notion that low-fat eating is low-calorie eating, and this misconception may have led to the increase in weight we have seen over the last decade in the United States. This thinking has helped to spawn a lucrative low-fat food industry. Foods like fat-free brownies, fat-free ice cream, and fat-free cookies are not low in calories and may be contributing to the misconception that they can be consumed with abandon, leading to an increase in obesity.

The low-fat and fat-free versions of foods are not the nutritional bargains we have been led to believe. Sometimes the nutrient gains you make for the sacrifice in taste just aren't worth it when it comes to calories. For example, a reduced-fat blueberry muffin from Dunkin' Donuts has 450 calories, while the regular version has 490 calories.[3] Five reduced-fat Ritz crackers have 70 calories, while five regular Ritz crackers have 80 calories.[4] These marketing strategies in the guise of healthy eating have fooled many of us into eating too many calories in the form of so-called low-fat foods, with a subsequent increase in the quantity of food we have consumed. This has translated into weight gain.

The Healthy Eating Pyramid Scientists from the Harvard School of Public Health have introduced a new pyramid, the Healthy Eating Pyramid, to address the deficiencies in the old food pyramid. The new pyramid is based upon many different lines of research, and is the end result of over twenty years of investigation by a variety of groups of scientists in different fields. The scientific data behind the Healthy Eating Pyramid is the strongest underlying any dietary recommendations to date. It has not been influenced by lobbyists or politicians, but rather has been based strictly upon scientific data. This is in marked contrast to many of the popular diets used by millions of people today, for which the evidence is very limited. These dietary guidelines are the first ones that are truly evidence based. We use this data as the basis for our recommendations in this cookbook.

Summary of the Healthy Eating Pyramid Several important points should be gleaned from the Healthy Eating Pyramid. At the base of the pyramid is a recommendation for daily exercise and weight control. When it comes to long-term health, keeping your weight in a healthy range is far more important than the exact ratio of fats to protein to carbohydrates in your food. Thus, the underlying basic tenet of the Healthy Eating Pyramid is that you should work to maintain or regain a healthy weight through limiting caloric intake and exercising regularly.

With regard to diet content, the Healthy Eating Pyramid tells us the basis should be whole-grain foods and healthy oils such as olive oil and other vegetable oils. It is important to realize that the latest data shows that not all fats are bad and, in fact, some should be required in any diet. Monounsaturated and polyunsaturated fats found in such foods as nuts, avocados, fish, olives, and vegetable oils help lower bad cholesterol levels without affecting good cholesterol levels.

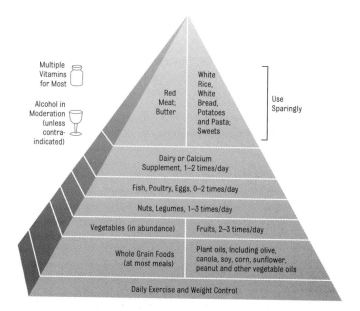

Multiple
Vitamins
for Most

Alcohol in
Moderation
(unless
contra-
indicated)

Red
Meat;
Butter

White
Rice,
White
Bread,
Potatoes
and Pasta;
Sweets

Use
Sparingly

Dairy or Calcium
Supplement, 1–2 times/day

Fish, Poultry, Eggs, 0–2 times/day

Nuts, Legumes, 1–3 times/day

Vegetables (in abundance)

Fruits, 2–3 times/day

Whole Grain Foods
(at most meals)

Plant oils, Including olive,
canola, soy, corn, sunflower,
peanut and other vegetable oils

Daily Exercise and Weight Control

From *Eat, Drink, and
Be Healthy* by Walter C.
Willett, M.D. Copyright
Simon & Schuster 2001.

The dietary guidelines for the Healthy Eating Pyramid include:

- There is no limit on vegetables; you can eat them in abundance.
- Fruits should be eaten 2–3 times per day.
- Nuts and legumes should be eaten 1–3 times per day.
- Fish, poultry, and eggs are grouped together and recommended 0–2 times per day.
- The "use sparingly" category consists of red meat, butter, white rice, white bread, potatoes, pasta, and sweets.
- A daily multivitamin or calcium supplement is recommended.
- Choose healthier sources of proteins—limit red meat and choose beans, nuts, fish, poultry, and eggs.
- Eat plenty of vegetables and fruits, but hold the potatoes.

New versus Old Pyramid In a landmark study done by the Harvard School of Public Health, the health of those who followed the new Healthy Eating Pyramid was compared to the health of those who followed the traditional Food Guide Pyramid. The study assessed the diets of more than one hundred thousand men and women and assessed their health for eight to twelve years.[5]

Questionnaires were used to capture detailed information about food consumption patterns. These questionnaires assessed the quality of food choices, such as white meat over red meat, whole grains over refined grains, oils high in unsaturated fat over ones with saturated fat, as well as multivitamin use.

With such a large number of participants, along with the rigorous study design, the results from this study are highly reliable scientific evidence in favor of the eating patterns espoused in the Healthy Eating Pyramid. This study found individuals following the Healthy Eating Pyramid had many major health benefits. Among those who followed the revised food pyramid, the following was found:

- Men lowered their risk of cardiovascular disease by 39 percent.
- Women lowered their risk of cardiovascular disease by 28 percent.
- Men lowered their overall risk of major chronic disease by 20 percent compared with those whose diets least followed the revised guidelines.
- Women lowered their overall risk by 11 percent compared with those whose diets least followed the revised guidelines.
- This type of diet has an impact that is just as powerful as the best cholesterol-lowering drugs in preventing heart disease.

Decrease portion size One particularly important principle in a healthy diet is portion size. You may be eating a diet that is exactly what the Healthy Eating Pyramid recommends, but if your portions are too large, and you are gaining weight, then you are negating all your efforts toward health through diet. When determining portion size, the overall emphasis should be on the word *moderate*. Virtually anything you eat in moderate amounts is okay. However, large amounts of even the healthiest foods will add too many calories to your diet. You may be eating an extremely healthy diet in terms of the quality of the foods you eat—whole grains, fruits, fish and other lean protein sources. But if you are eating too much of these foods, you will still be overweight, and being overweight is unhealthy.

Examples of Serving Sizes

WHOLE GRAINS
½ cup brown rice
½ cup bran cereal
½ cup oatmeal
1 slice whole-grain bread or pita
½ cup whole-wheat pasta

NUTS AND LEGUMES
1 ounce nuts, any variety
½ cup cooked beans or legumes
2 tablespoons peanut butter

FISH, POULTRY, EGGS
2–3 ounces fish
2–3 ounces poultry
1 egg

DAIRY
1 cup skim milk
1 cup nonfat yogurt
1½ ounces cheese
½ cup part-skim ricotta cheese
1 cup nonfat frozen yogurt

Control of portion size is absolutely critical to any diet. In the United States, our portion sizes have been growing along with our waistlines. We have supersized our fries, made our muffins giant, and added 30 percent more to virtually anything you can think of. This expansion has to stop, and we need to exercise some restraint in our portion sizes. You need to pay attention to quantity and exercise a philosophy of restrained eating, both in your home and when you eat out. Make certain to limit quantities, discourage frequent snacking, and encourage daily physical activity.

Body Mass Index Body Mass Index, or BMI (wt/ht²), provides a guideline based on weight and height to determine whether your weight is appropriate for your height. The mathematical formula is:

$$\text{Weight (kg)/height squared (m}^2)$$

BMI is the most commonly used approach to determine if adults are overweight or obese and is also the recommended measure to determine if children are overweight. In children, BMI growth charts can be used clinically beginning at two years of age, when an accurate height can be obtained.

For adults, numerous studies have found that keeping your body mass index (BMI) under 25 will decrease your risk of dying early, mainly from heart disease and cancer. The BMI chart may be used for both men and women. Most experts agree that BMIs from 25 to 30 should be considered overweight and over 30 obese. Keeping your family's weight in the healthy range is the most important measure of your health. Almost one-fourth of Americans are now in the obese range. Obesity among children is rising at an alarming rate. You can make a huge difference in your family's health by controlling weight in all members of your family.

It is not clear where underweight on the BMI chart should be defined. Most experts agree that healthy weights are between 18.5 and 25. However, if smokers and others with chronic illness are factored out, then BMIs as low as 17 have been shown to be healthy in physically active individuals.[6] The issue of eating disorders is complex, and BMI alone cannot be used directly to diagnose them.

Adult—Body Mass Index Chart[7]

BMI	19	20	21	22	23	24	25	26	27	28	29	30
HEIGHT (INCHES)					BODY WEIGHT (POUNDS)							
58	91	96	100	105	110	115	119	124	129	134	138	143
59	94	99	104	109	114	119	124	128	133	138	143	148
60	97	102	107	112	118	123	128	133	143	148	153	158
61	100	106	111	116	122	127	132	137	143	148	153	158
62	104	109	115	120	126	131	136	142	147	153	158	164
63	107	113	118	124	130	135	141	146	152	158	163	169
64	110	116	122	128	134	140	145	151	157	163	169	174
65	114	120	126	132	138	144	150	156	162	168	174	180
66	118	124	130	136	142	148	155	161	167	173	179	186
67	121	127	134	140	146	153	159	166	172	178	185	191
68	125	131	138	144	151	158	164	171	177	184	190	197
69	128	135	142	149	155	162	169	176	182	189	196	203
70	132	139	146	153	160	167	174	181	188	195	202	209
71	136	143	150	157	165	172	179	186	193	200	208	215
72	140	147	154	162	169	177	184	191	199	206	213	221
73	144	151	159	166	174	182	189	197	204	212	219	227
74	148	155	163	171	179	186	194	202	210	218	225	233
75	152	160	168	176	184	192	200	208	216	224	232	240
76	156	164	172	180	189	197	205	213	221	230	238	246

Children—Body Mass Index Chart[8]

BMI	13	14	15	16	17	18	19	20	21	22	23	24	25	26	27
HEIGHT (INCHES)					BODY WEIGHT (POUNDS)									
30	17	18	19	20	21	23	24	26	27	28	29	31	32	33	34
31	18	19	20	22	24	25	26	27	29	30	31	33	34	35	37
32	19	20	22	23	25	26	28	29	31	32	33	35	36	38	39
33	20	22	23	25	26	28	29	31	32	34	36	37	39	40	42
34	21	23	25	26	28	30	31	33	34	36	38	39	41	43	44
35	23	25	26	28	30	31	33	35	37	38	40	42	43	45	47
36	24	26	28	29	31	33	35	37	39	40	42	44	46	48	50
37	25	27	29	31	33	35	37	39	41	43	45	47	49	51	52
38	27	29	31	33	35	37	39	41	43	45	47	49	51	53	55
39	28	30	32	35	37	39	41	43	45	47	50	52	54	56	58
40	30	32	34	36	39	41	43	45	48	50	52	55	57	59	62
41	31	33	36	38	41	43	45	48	50	52	55	57	60	63	65
42	33	35	38	40	43	45	48	50	53	55	58	61	63	66	68
43	34	37	39	42	45	47	50	52	55	58	61	63	66	69	71
44	36	38	41	44	47	49	52	55	58	61	64	66	69	72	75
45	37	40	43	46	49	53	56	59	62	65	68	71	74	77	78
46	39	42	45	48	51	54	57	61	64	67	70	73	76	79	82
47	41	44	47	50	53	56	60	63	66	69	73	76	79	82	85
48	43	46	49	52	56	59	63	66	69	72	76	79	82	86	89
49	44	48	51	54	58	62	65	69	72	75	79	82	86	89	93
50	46	50	53	57	61	64	68	71	75	79	82	86	89	93	96
51	48	52	55	59	63	67	71	74	78	82	85	89	93	97	100
52	50	54	57	62	66	70	73	77	81	85	89	93	96	100	104
53	52	56	60	64	68	72	76	80	84	88	92	96	100	104	108
54	54	58	63	67	71	75	79	83	87	92	96	100	104	108	112
55	56	61	65	69	73	78	82	86	91	95	99	104	108	112	116
56	58	63	67	72	76	81	85	89	94	98	103	107	112	116	122
57	61	65	70	74	79	83	88	93	97	102	107	112	116	120	126

While BMI does not directly measure percent of body fat, it provides a more accurate measure of overweight and obesity than relying on weight alone. Calculating BMI is simple and useful for monitoring trends in populations but by itself is not diagnostic of an individual's health status, and it does have some limitations. For example, very muscular people may fall into the overweight category when they are actually healthy and fit. In addition, individuals who have lost muscle mass, such as the elderly, may be in the healthy weight category according to their BMI, when they actually have reduced nutritional reserves.

CDC Growth Charts: United States

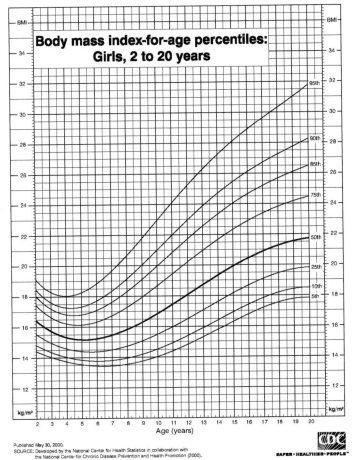

Body mass index-for-age percentiles:
Girls, 2 to 20 years

Published May 30, 2000.
SOURCE: Developed by the National Center for Health Statistics in collaboration with
the National Center for Chronic Disease Prevention and Health Promotion (2000).

SAFER · HEALTHIER · PEOPLE™

BMI was only recently recommended as a measurement for children. Doctors have been using the weight-for-height charts to assess the appropriateness of a child's weight, but that measurement is of limited value because it can only be used in boys younger than eleven and a half years and girls younger than ten years. Doctors have found BMI to be a better indicator of body "fatness" and potential weight problems. BMI is particularly helpful for identifying children and adolescents who are at risk for being overweight as they get older. In older children and teens, there is a strong correlation between BMI and the amount of body fat.

Therefore, those with high BMI readings—and probably high levels of fat—are most likely to have weight problems when they are older. Although BMI is not a direct or perfect measure of body fat, children with BMI values at or above the 95th percentile of the sex-specific BMI growth charts are categorized as overweight, and those with a BMI between the 85th and 95th percentile are classified as at risk of becoming overweight.

CDC Growth Charts: United States

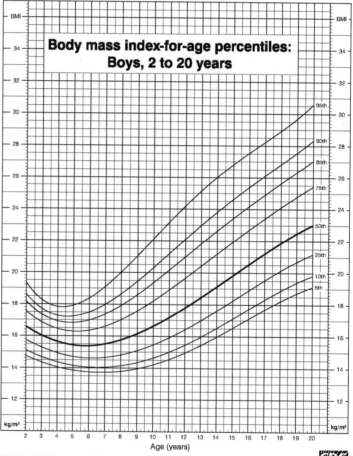

Published May 30, 2000.
SOURCE: Developed by the National Center for Health Statistics in collaboration with the National Center for Chronic Disease Prevention and Health Promotion (2000).

SAFER · HEALTHIER · PEOPLE™

Fiber Dietary fiber is the indigestible portion of plant foods and an important nutrient for health. Most Americans do not have enough fiber in their diet. Fiber reduces the risk of heart disease, diabetes, diverticular disease, and constipation. However, fiber provides many benefits beyond reducing the risk of cancer. A high-dietary-fiber intake has been linked to a lower risk of heart disease in several large studies that followed people for six years.

FIBER AND HEALTH BENEFITS In a Harvard study of over forty thousand male health professionals, researchers found that a high-total-dietary-fiber intake was linked to a 40 percent lower risk of coronary heart disease, compared to a low-fiber intake.[9] Cereal fiber, the fiber found in grains such as oatmeal or whole-wheat bread, was particularly beneficial. In a related Harvard study of female nurses, the findings were quite similar.[10] Another health benefit of a high-fiber diet is a lower risk of diabetes. Finally, fiber has long been used in the prevention of diverticulitis, an inflammation of the intestine that is one of the most common disorders of the colon among the elderly in Western societies. In North America, this painful disease is estimated to occur in one-third of all persons over forty-five years of age and in two-thirds of all persons over age eighty-five. The Harvard study of male health professionals found that eating dietary fiber, specifically insoluble fiber, was associated with about a 40 percent lower risk of diverticular disease. Another benefit of this type of diet is the full feeling fiber can create, which often prevents overeating.

Daily Dietary Fiber Recommendations

AGE	MINIMUM DAILY GRAMS OF FIBER
3	8
4	9
5	10
6	11
7	12
8	13
9	14
10	15
11	16
12	17
Adolescents and Adults	20–35

REDUCING CONSTIPATION WITH FIBER Constipation is a problem for many individuals eating our typical Western diet, which can be low in fiber. Fiber in the diet is the best way to naturally manage constipation. The fiber provides bulk for stool formation and helps move wastes more quickly through the colon. Low-fiber diets have caused Americans to become big consumers of laxative and stool-softening agents. Most of these agents would not be needed if people added more fiber to their diets.

FIBER AND COLON CANCER RISK—NO REDUCTION Fiber has little, if any, effect on the risk of colon cancer. For many years, scientists thought that a high-fiber diet reduced the risk of colon cancer.

However, recent studies that were better designed have failed to show a link between fiber and reduced colon cancer risk. One Harvard study that followed over eighty thousand female nurses for sixteen years found that dietary fiber was not strongly associated with a reduced risk for either colon cancer or polyps (a colon cancer precursor).[11]

TYPES OF FIBER There are two forms of fiber: soluble and insoluble. Both confer health benefits. Soluble fiber attracts water and turns to gel during digestion. This slows digestion and the rate of nutrient absorption from the stomach and intestine. It is found in oat bran, barley, nuts, seeds, beans, lentils, peas, and some fruits and vegetables. Insoluble fiber is not digested by the body and is found in foods such as wheat bran, all vegetables, and whole grains. It appears to speed the passage of foods through the stomach and intestines and adds bulk to the stool.

People over twelve years old should aim for a minimum of twenty to thirty-five grams of fiber (soluble or insoluble) daily, as recommended by the National Cancer Institute for all adults. The average American adult consumes only ten to twelve grams of fiber each day. Children from the ages of two to twelve years old should consume an amount equal to or greater than their age plus five grams per day.

Tips for Enhancing Fiber in Your Diet

- Eat whole fruits instead of drinking fruit juices.
- Eat a variety of vegetables daily.
- Substitute brown rice for white rice.
- Substitute whole-wheat bread for white bread.
- Substitute whole-wheat pasta for white pasta.
- Eat whole-grain cereals for breakfast.
- Snack on raw vegetables.
- Substitute legumes and nuts for meat two to three times per week.

Fresh fruits and vegetables are excellent sources of fiber as are whole-grain breads, cereals, pastas, brown rice, and beans. Peeling can reduce the amount of fiber in a food, so leave the skin on fruits such as apples to increase the quantity of fiber you consume. Flaxseed provides another rich source of fiber—you can simply grind it and sprinkle it on your yogurt or cereal for a quick boost. The fiber content of foods is the same whether they are cooked or raw.

Some Sources of Fiber

	SERVING SIZE	GRAMS OF FIBER
Bread, Grains, Rice, and Crackers		
Bran muffin	1 medium	2.50
Cracked-wheat bread	1 slice	2.34
Graham cracker	2½″ square	0.70
French bread	1 slice	0.70
Oatmeal (rolled oats)	1 cup	2.50
Popcorn, popped	1 cup	1.45
Rice, brown	1 cup	3.32
Rice, white	1 cup	0.74
Wheat Thins	4	1.47
White bread, enriched	1 slice	0.74
Whole-wheat bread	1 slice	1.75
Fruit		
Apple, with peel	1 medium	4.28
Applesauce, unsweetened	1 cup	5.12
Banana	1 medium	3.85
Blueberries	1 cup	4.93
Cantaloupe	½ medium	2.65
Cherries	20	3
Grapefruit	½ medium	1.46
Grapes, with skin	1 cup	3.2
Nectarine	1 medium	3.26
Peach	1 medium	2.3
Pear	1 medium	3.82
Pineapple, fresh	1 cup diced	2.95
Strawberries	1 cup	3.38

Raspberries	1 cup	9.10
Watermelon	1 slice, 10″ diameter	9.60

Legumes

Black beans, cooked	½ cup	9.7
Chickpeas, cooked	½ cup	5.5
Kidney beans, cooked	½ cup	9.7
Pinto beans, cooked	½ cup	9.39
Tofu	3 ounces	0.1

Nuts

Almonds	12 nuts	2.53
Cashews	11 medium	1.06
Peanut butter	1 tablespoon	0.29
Peanuts	18 medium	1.51
Pine nuts	1 ounce	0.25
Sunflower seeds	2 tablespoons	0.69
Walnuts	10 halves	0.78

Vegetables

Avocado	1 medium	7.94
Broccoli	1 cup cooked	9.39
Carrots	1 medium	3.6
Celery	1 cup diced	7
Collard greens	1 cup cooked	7
Eggplant	1 cup cooked	4.5
Peas	1 cup cooked	17
Pepper, sweet green	1 medium	1.04
Pepper, sweet red	1 medium	2.46
Potato, white in peel	1 medium	4.4
Potato, white peeled	1 medium	3
Romaine lettuce	2 cups chopped	1.65
Spinach	¾ cup cooked	8.47
Squash, summer	1 cup cooked	3.5
Squash, winter	1 cup cooked	6.88
Swiss chard	1 cup cooked	6.8
Tomato, raw	1 medium	2.03
Tomato, canned	1 cup	2.2

Salt Salt added in cooking or at the table makes up just 15 percent of the salt in the average diet. It is in processed, ready-to-eat, and restaurant foods that we get most of our salt—about 75 percent. In our home, we do use salt in our recipes. We are all at a healthy weight and do not have high blood pressure. However, we do not eat many prepared foods and rarely eat fast food. For most individuals, the vast majority of salt in their diet comes from these "hidden" sources. The best way to eat less salt is to cut the amount of chips, prepared dinners, and other processed and ready-to-eat foods. You can't always go by taste in judging the salt content of an item, particularly in restaurants where food doesn't have an ingredient label. A small order of McDonald's French fries, which taste salty, have 135 milligrams of salt, compared with a McDonald's Quarter Pounder with cheese, which doesn't taste obviously salty but which has 1,250 milligrams of salt.[12]

Studies on the effects of salt on hypertension largely come from one famous diet—the DASH diet—Dietary Approaches to Stop Hypertension. This diet is heavy on fruits, vegetables, and low-fat dairy foods. It was developed to test if diet alone could markedly decrease blood pressure. In 1997 investigators reported that the DASH diet could reduce blood pressure as much as blood-pressure medications. There is a great deal of individual variation, though, on how salt sensitive your body is. Some individuals are, on average, much more salt sensitive than others.

Research indicates that Americans' high salt intake is a leading cause of high blood pressure. The research has also shown that reducing the amount of salt we eat will not only help those who already have a problem, but also reduce the natural slow increase in blood pressure as we age. For some (but not all), limiting salt in the diet can replace or reduce the amount of blood pressure medication needed to control blood pressure. However, several studies show that a reduction in salt in the diet may not help everyone lower their blood pressure, due to this individual variation in salt sensitivity. The best approach to controlling blood pressure includes limiting salt, eating a diet rich in fruits and vegetables, keeping weight under control, and exercising regularly. While salt is important, it is only one factor in blood pressure control and general health.

Most of the recipes in this book use salt "to taste." For those with hypertension, the amount of salt you use should be kept to a minimum, since salt in the diet is an important issue for your health.

Alcohol New research has changed our thinking about alcohol. This change began when researchers and doctors noticed that the French, despite a diet high in fat, have low heart disease rates. We thought that drinking all that red wine with meals must be the reason. When we looked closely, we found that in addition to the red wine, overall, French people's diet and lifestyle is actually quite heart healthy. They use healthy oils, and many different fruits and vegetables. Since then, research has now supported that, for most adults, alcohol in moderate amounts is considered part of an overall heart-healthy lifestyle. As we did more research, we learned that the benefits from alcohol are not limited to just red wine. When the effects of drinking red and white wine, beer, and spirits are compared, all appear to cut the risk of heart attacks to a similar degree. The problem with recommending alcohol as part of a healthy lifestyle is that the exact definition of what constitutes moderate drinking is still not totally clear. Some people are unable to restrict their drinking to one or two drinks. And this ends up being an extremely important issue, since crossing the line into heavier drinking brings a host of other ills.

IN MEN In men, multiple studies have found that men who have one or two alcoholic drinks a day, three or more times a week, are 30 to 40 percent less likely to have heart attacks than men who don't drink alcohol at all.[13] To give you an idea of the magnitude of this effect, it is about the same as if you took one of the cholesterol-lowering drugs known as statins. Increasing alcohol consumption beyond this level brings on more of the negative effects of alcohol. If you are a man and you already drink alcohol, keep it moderate. If you don't drink, you don't need to start. You can get similar benefits by exercising.

IN WOMEN A recent report in the *Archives of Internal Medicine* found that women who drink in moderation are 78 percent less likely to develop high blood pressure. In this study, moderate drinkers consumed two or three alcoholic drinks per week: either 4 ounces of wine, 12 ounces of beer, or a shot of spirits. The mechanism of this blood-pressure-lowering effect is not currently known. It is possible that alcohol has a relaxing effect on blood vessels that accounts for the blood pressure effect. Critics say that perhaps these women didn't get high blood pressure for various lifestyle factors that may accompany the tendency to drink in moderation, since the mechanism of action of alcohol on blood pressure is not known. Nonetheless, there is evidence that alcohol can be heart-healthy in women. It's just that we also need to balance this benefit with the increased risk of cancer with even moderate intake.

In women, what constitutes moderate alcohol intake is a bit fuzzier than with men. The problem is that moderate alcohol intake—one to two drinks a day—has been shown to increase a woman's breast and colon cancer risk. Thankfully, new evidence has found that this increased risk of cancer is seen mostly in women who do not get sufficient amounts of folic acid in their diets.[14] Some studies show that if you get enough folic acid, either from your diet or from a supplement, the cancer risk is not increased with moderate alcohol intake.

TOO MUCH IS A VERY BAD THING It is very important to realize that with alcohol, more is not better, and too much can cause a multitude of ill effects. For instance, it can poison heart cells, kidney cells, and brain cells. And, of course, alcohol is an addictive substance. Overindulging in alcohol can cause liver cancer, and it can increase a woman's risk for breast cancer and colon cancer. Alcohol consumed by pregnant women causes birth defects, cognitive defects in babies exposed in utero, and other serious pregnancy complications.

WHAT DO I RECOMMEND? If you are a woman in her reproductive years who is not using birth control, avoid alcohol. Anyone with a history of addiction or family history of alcohol should be very wary of alcohol. And anyone taking any medication with which alcohol can interact, or with any disease process in which alcohol can cause additional problems, should avoid it. Remember, too, that alcohol contains calories, and any heart-healthy benefits will be negated by your weight gain if you just add on calories from alcohol to your daily total without some compensatory decrease in intake or extra energy burned. But for healthy adults, one drink a day for women and one to two drinks a day for men can be part of a healthy lifestyle.

Caffeine Most major health organizations, including the American Medical Association and the U.S. Food and Drug Administration, have stated that moderate coffee or tea drinkers likely have no need for concern about their health relative to their caffeine consumption provided other lifestyle habits (diet, alcohol) are moderate. Moderate consumption is considered to be about 300 milligrams of caffeine, which is equal to about three cups of coffee. A cup of coffee is considered an 8-ounce drink.

Caffeine may increase your alertness when you are tired and enhance the performance of certain tasks. Individuals differ greatly in their sensitivity to caffeine. Caffeine temporarily stimulates the central nervous and cardiovascular systems, increasing heart rate and blood pressure, stimulating muscles, and increasing urination. Some people can drink several cups of coffee within an hour and not notice any effect, whereas others will feel stimulating effects after one cup. Caffeine does not accumulate in the bloodstream and is excreted within several hours following consumption. Some individuals find they are very sensitive to caffeine and have trouble sleeping even if they drink it early in the day.

There are side effects to consuming too much caffeine. Caffeine at doses higher than someone is accustomed to may cause jitters, anxiety, and diarrhea. In addition, if you consume caffeine regularly and suddenly stop, you may experience withdrawal symptoms, including jitters and headache.

Caffeine has been shown to aggravate fibrocystic breast disease, a condition that includes benign fibrous lumps in the breast which can be painful, but is not precancerous. Caffeine has been implicated in stomach distress and increased calcium loss from bone. But moderate amounts of caffeine, 300 milligrams per day, seem to have little influence on bone health. There is no evidence that caffeine increases the risk of developing cancer or is connected to the development of heart disease. In fact, some studies show that deaths from heart disease are highest in those who do not drink coffee.[15] This is probably not due to any protective effect of coffee, but possibly because those who do not drink it may have stopped because of illness. Another study showed that caffeine drinkers have a lower risk of developing Parkinson's disease.[16]

Research indicates there is no difference in the way that children and adults handle caffeine. These studies have shown that caffeine-containing foods and beverages do not have an effect on hyperactivity or the attention span of children.

For now, the current recommendation is in moderation, two or three cups a day. You should be wary of specialty coffee drinks since many are oversized or made with whole milk and cream, which can quickly boost calories and saturated-fat content.

Our Family's Dietary Evolution It is interesting to reflect on our own experience in this dietary evolution. As children, we were brought up on meat and potatoes. We then changed our diet as young adults to a high-carbohydrate, moderate-protein, low-fat version. We frequently ate white pasta and white bread. Today, we are moderate in all three categories. We have switched to largely unrefined carbohydrates such as whole-grain breads and brown rice, and we consume a bit more fat mostly in the form of olive oil and nuts. We have wine with meals a bit more often. We drink one to two cups of coffee daily. We reserve white pasta and white bread for once-in-a-while treats. It was an easy transition. The whole grains add substance and flavor to many of our favorite meals. But we still delight in the occasional plate of white pasta or a loaf of light, crusty French bread. You don't need to be extreme to be healthy.

Eating for a Lifetime Together The information from the Healthy Eating Pyramid from the Harvard School of Public Health has been used as the basis for our recommendations in this cookbook. While the basic components of diet—carbohydrates, protein, and fat—are the same, what constitutes healthy choices in each of these areas has undergone dramatic changes. We'll review them one at a time and discuss the latest evidence for the best types of each for you and your family in chapters 2, 3, and 4.

Your interest in diet and nutrition can serve to alter positively your and your family's eating habits. All the recipes in this book are healthy—that is, they are balanced in nutrient content, moderate in carbohydrates and protein, and utilize healthy fats. They are rich in unrefined grains. They will leave you feeling full and satisfied while keeping your family's weight under control. Best of all, the meals are delicious and simple to prepare. Eating well is a joy and something that you can all do together to build a healthy family.

1. W.C. Willett, P. J. Skerrett, and E.L. Giovannucci, *Eat, Drink, and Be Healthy: The Harvard Medical School Guide to Healthy Eating* (New York: Simon & Schuster, 2001).

2. M.J. Stampfer, F.B. Hu, J.E. Manson, E.B. Rimm, and W.C. Willett, "Primary Prevention of Coronary Heart Disease in Women Through Diet and Lifestyle," *New England Journal of Medicine* 343 (2000):16–22; M. McCullough, D. Feskanich, M.J. Stampfer, E.L. Giovannucci, E.B. Rimm, F.B. Hu, D. Spiegelman, D.J. Hunter, G.A. Colditz, and W.C. Willett, "Diet Quality and Major Chronic Disease Risk in Men and Women: Moving Toward Improved Dietary Guidance," *American Journal of Clinical Nutrition* 76 (2000): 1261–71.

3. Dunkin' Donuts Nutrition Information, www.dunkindonuts.com/nutrition.

4. U.S. Food and Drug Administration Food Label Nutrition Facts.

5. M. McCullough, D. Feskanich, M.J. Stampfer, E.L. Giovannucci, E.B. Rimm, F.B. Hu, D. Spiegelman, D.J. Hunter, G.A. Colditz, and W.C. Willett, "Diet Quality and Major Chronic Disease Risk in Men and Women: Moving Toward Improved Dietary Guidance," *American Journal of Clinical Nutrition* 76 (2002): 1261–71.

6. W.C. Willett, "Guidelines for Healthy Weight," *New England Journal of Medicine* 341 (1999):427–34.

7. Table for Calculated Body Mass Index Values for Selected Heights and Weights, Department of Health and Human Services, Centers for Disease Control, USA, 2000.

8. Ibid.

9. E.B. Rimm, A. Ascherio, E. Biovannucci, D. Spiegelman, M.J. Stampfer, and W.C. Willett, "Vegetable, Fruit, and Cereal Fiber Intake and Risk of Coronary

Heart Disease among Men." *Journal of the American Medical Association* 275 (1996):447–51.

10. S. Liu, J.E. Buring, H.D. Sesso, E.B. Rimm, W.C. Willett, and J.E. Manson, "A Prospective Study of Dietary Fiber Intake and Risk of Cardiovascular Disease among Women," *Journal of the American College of Cardiology* 39 (2002):49–56.

11. C.S. Fuchs et al., "Dietary Fiber and the Risk of Colorectal Cancer and Adenoma in Women," *New England Journal of Medicine* 340 (1999):169–76.

12. McDonald's Nutrition Information, www.mcdonalds.com.

13. E.B. Rimm, "Alcohol Consumption and Coronary Heart Disease: Good Habits May Be More Important Than Just Good Wine," *American Journal of Epidemiology* 143 (1996):1094–98; K.J. Mukamal, K.M. Conigrave, M.A. Mittleman, C.A. Camargo Jr., M.J. Stampfer, W.C. Willett, and E.B. Rimm, "Roles of Drinking Pattern and Type of Alcohol Consumed in Coronary Heart Disease in Men," *New England Journal of Medicine* 348 (2003):109–18.

14. W.Y. Chen, G.A. Colditz, B. Rosner, S.E. Hankinson, D.J. Hunter, J.E. Manson, M.J. Stampfer, W.C. Willett, and F.E. Speizer, "Use of Postmenopausal Hormones, Alcohol, and Risk for Invasive Breast Cancer," *Annals of Internal Medicine* 137 (2002).

15. P. Kleemola, P. Jousilahti, and P. Pietinen, "Coffee Consumption and the Risk of Coronary Heart Disease and Death," *Archives of Internal Medicine* 160 (2000):3383–400.

16. G.W. Ross, R.D. Abbott, H. Petrovich, et al., "Association of Coffee and Caffeine Intake with the Risk of Parkinson's Disease," *Journal of the American Medical Association* 283 (2000):2674–79.

CHAPTER 2

carbohydrates— the good, the bad, and the ugly

Our thinking about carbohydrates in the diet has undergone dramatic changes in recent years. In the past, we were encouraged to eat an abundance of complex carbohydrates, along with a subsequent reduction in the percent of calories in our diet from fat. Complex carbohydrates in the current food pyramid are grouped together at the base—bread, cereal, rice, and pasta. However, there is no differentiation between unrefined and refined carbohydrates. White bread, potatoes, pasta, and white rice are all liberally allowed. In contrast, the Healthy Eating Pyramid groups refined carbohydrates at the tip, in the "use sparingly" area. Instead, whole grains, which are unrefined carbohydrates, are recommended in abundance.

Good and Bad Carbohydrates The only differentiation in the old pyramid in types of carbohydrates is between simple and complex.

At the chemical level, this differentiation is technically correct; however, from a health standpoint, not all complex carbohydrates are equal, and new evidence shows that our previous view of simple carbohydrates as bad and complex carbohydrates as good was not correct. Simple carbohydrates are found in fruits, juice, sugar, candy, and soda. Complex carbohydrates are found in bread, rice, vegetables, pasta, and cereals. In your body, it matters more whether the carbohydrates are refined or unrefined, rather than simple or complex. New data has shown that the majority of carbohydrates in the diet should be unrefined whole grains instead of refined carbohydrates—brown rice instead of white rice; whole-grain pasta instead of white pasta; whole-grain bread instead of white bread.

Chemistry of Carbohydrates In the body, all carbohydrates are broken down into glucose, whether simple or complex, refined or unrefined. Glucose enters the bloodstream and serves as fuel. Many so-called complex carbohydrates, such as potatoes and white bread, are converted rapidly to glucose once we eat them. In fact, these refined carbohydrates are even worse than sugar in causing a rapid rise in blood glucose, since recent studies show that they actually result in a more rapid rise in glucose than even pure sugar. The body does not handle large quantities of refined carbohydrates well. They are quickly digested and pass immediately as glucose into the bloodstream, where their rapid rise places great demands on the regulatory system. These changes in blood glucose have been associated with many health conditions, including heart disease and diabetes.

In contrast, unrefined carbohydrates, such as brown rice and whole grains, are broken down more slowly by the body, resulting in a more stable release of fuel into the bloodstream. This more level supply avoids the rapid ups and downs of blood glucose one sees after consuming refined carbohydrates.

New Evidence about Carbohydrates, Glucose, and Insulin Your body responds to this rapid infusion of glucose by a rise in the hormone insulin, produced by your pancreas. Insulin is regulated in response to blood glucose and functions to drive glucose into the cells in your body to provide energy for those cells. When glucose is high, your body increases the level of insulin available. This then triggers your liver to increase triglyceride levels (associated with poor health) and decrease HDL cholesterol levels–the "good" cholesterol. Insulin also works to push the glucose into your muscle and fat cells and out of the bloodstream. This results in a rapid fall in blood glucose levels.

Recent studies have shown that these high levels of glucose and insulin can lead to diabetes and heart disease, and are particularly harmful to sedentary and overweight individuals. In these individuals, the body's tissues do not respond to insulin as they should. This resistance to insulin keeps higher levels of sugar in the bloodstream for longer periods of time. Your body sees these higher levels of glucose in the bloodstream and keeps producing more insulin. Eventually, your body can't keep up and the insulin production in the pancreas falters. This leads to type II diabetes, a condition of insulin resistance and high blood sugar levels.

High Body Mass Index, Sedentary Lifestyle, and Insulin Resistance Weight and exercise seem to matter here, as high-carbohydrate diets do not have the same detrimental effects on lean, active people that they do on overweight, sedentary people. So if you are lean and active, you can afford a few more unrefined carbohydrates in your diet. But everyone can benefit from increasing the percentage of carbohydrates in their diet that come from unrefined grains.

The further you get from a healthy body mass index, the more resistant to insulin your body becomes. In addition, the less active you are, the more fat relative to muscle you have, even if you are in a healthy body mass index range. Fat cells, unlike muscle cells, do not handle glucose and insulin very well. Muscle handles glucose especially well when it has been exercised. So the less muscle or the more fat you have in your body, the harder it is to clear glucose from the bloodstream. People who are overweight and not physically active and eat a diet high in refined carbohydrates have an increased chance of having a heart attack. Some people are genetically predisposed to more insulin resistance than others. But all people can improve their situation through weight control, staying physically active, and eating a healthy diet. Even if you are in a healthy body mass index range, this switch from refined to whole grains will be healthier for you because you will be taking in micronutrients that would have been processed away.

Brown Rice and Whole Grains Taken together, this data shows that we should obtain the majority of our carbohydrates from whole grains, and put potatoes and white bread on an "occasional" list in order to minimize sharp rises in blood glucose. The complex carbohydrates that are a better choice for your diet are the unrefined ones that contain high-fiber, intact grains. Once the germ and bran from the grain are removed from the wheat and it is ground into a fine powder, such as occurs in the processing of wheat flour for white bread, the body can then rapidly absorb the carbohydrates. Keeping the kernels of grain intact slows down their absorption in the body and results in a delayed and sustained release of glucose into your bloodstream. This avoids the sharp spike in blood glucose seen after consuming refined carbohydrates.

In order to implement these recommendations in your diet, you should switch to whole-grain pasta, brown rice, and whole-grain breads and cereals for the majority of your carbohydrates. Once you get used to this change, you will enjoy these foods as another way to vary your diet. And your children, if you start them on these foods right from the start, will not even notice the difference.

Shopping for Unrefined Carbohydrates—Read the Label

When choosing cereals, check the ingredients and choose those that list whole wheat, oats, barley, or other grains. Choose breads made from whole grains. Make certain the first ingredient has the word *whole* in it. Choose brown rice instead of white.

We Did It We made this change in recent years in our home, since our 1990s diet was low in fat and high in refined carbohydrates. We are all active and relatively lean, so it is likely that our heart disease and diabetes risks are low. Yet we felt it was time for an adjustment. When our children were six and eight, we learned about the new research on the benefits of unrefined carbohydrates, and we began substituting whole-wheat pasta for white, whole-grain bread for white, and brown rice for white. We now limit white potatoes and white pasta to once in a while (potatoes are Joe's favorite food, so we still serve them about once a week). It was not a difficult change to make, especially since we were careful about choosing recipes in which we could make the substitutions. In certain meals, such as Linguine with Peppers, Onions, and Mushrooms (see page 200), the whole-wheat pasta tastes even better than white. The earthy flavors of the wheat pasta contrast with the sweetness of the vegetables, resulting in a delectable dish. In burritos and other rice and bean dishes, whole-grain rice adds a lovely, nutty taste, which enhances the flavors. Now, when Vince bakes our bread, he substitutes whole-wheat flour for one-half of the white flour.

You Do Not Need to Be Extreme We are not absolute about this change to unrefined grains, and you do not need to be either. For example, some of our old favorites are significantly better when made in the traditional manner with white pasta, such as Scampi (see page 300) or Linguine with Smoky Scallops and Garlicky Tomatoes (see page 205). We save those recipes for our once-in-a-while treats. We still enjoy a wonderful light French baguette from our favorite bakery, especially when we are having it with a bit of good cheese. Since this is a once-in-a-while treat, it seems even more special. Remember, you do not need to be extreme and deny yourself all your favorite foods. It is not inconsistent to have the occasional white French baguette and Brie or your favorite potato dish, just as long as it is done occasionally.

Fruit—Simple Carbohydrates but Good for You Fruits, although they contain simple sugars, are also nutrient- and fiber-packed. Eating an abundance of a wide variety of fruits and vegetables has a protective effect against the development of cancer, heart disease, and stroke, among other diseases. Fruits have so many health benefits that it would be a mistake to look at them only as simple sugars. But other simple-carbohydrate foods such as candy and cookies are full of "empty" calories since they generally contain few nutrients. While it is fine to eat sweets occasionally, you don't want sweets to constitute your body's major fuel source. Fruits, on the other hand, should be plentifully consumed because of their many health properties.

Good Carbohydrates to Eat

Bulgur
Brown rice
Kasha
Oatmeal
Quinoa
Whole-wheat flour
Whole-grain cold
    cereals
Whole-grain
    couscous
Whole-grain
    crackers
Whole-grain pita
    bread
Whole-wheat or
    whole-grain bread
Whole-wheat pasta

Low Fat Is Not Low Calorie During the 1990s, a low-fat and high-carbohydrate diet was encouraged by the nutrition establishment. During this time, low-fat foods became popular and widely available in the markets. Low-fat products are usually made by substituting sugar and other carbohydrates for fat. But this type of diet and the wide availability of these low-fat products did not lead to weight loss. In fact, the opposite has happened—Americans became fatter. This is likely in part because the message became a bit distorted—we thought we could eat as much low-fat and carbohydrate-rich food as we wanted to. But in reality, a calorie is a calorie, whether it comes from carbohydrates, protein, or fat. Eating four low-fat chocolate cookies can still be a hefty amount of calories. And if you take in more than you burn, you gain weight. Keeping in mind this general principle that a calorie is a calorie whether it comes from refined or unrefined carbohydrate, table sugar, or Gummy Worms should simplify things for you.

You do not need to give up carbohydrates in your diet. A healthy diet does not need to be unduly restrictive in carbohydrates, such as in the Atkins diet, with its emphasis on very low carbohydrate eating. Rather, you should adjust the carbohydrates you consume to include unrefined grains such as brown rice, whole-wheat bread, and whole-grain cereals. When baking, substitute whole-wheat flour for part of the white flour. These grains are satisfying, intensely flavorful, healthy, and delicious.

CHAPTER 3

protein—quit beefing

There are two basic things to keep in mind when paying attention to protein in your family's diet. First, the protein sources you choose should emphasize chicken, fish, and vegetarian sources such as nuts and beans. You and your family should eat less red meat and choose low-fat or nonfat dairy products. Second, you need to make certain that you obtain adequate amounts of protein in your diets. This is especially important for your children, whose growing bodies need protein to build muscle and other body tissues.

Women need about 50 grams per day of protein, and men need about 65 grams per day. It is fairly easy to meet these protein requirements. The average adult in the United States eats much more protein than is needed—on average, from 75 to 110 grams per day. Therefore, most of us will not need to increase the amount of protein we consume to meet these requirements. Children's protein needs depend upon their age and weight (see box).

Minimum Protein Requirements in Children

AGE	CHILD'S WEIGHT (POUNDS)	RDA PROTEIN (GRAMS/DAY)
1–3	29	16
4–6	44	22
7–10	61	28
11–14 (boys)	99	45
11–14 (girls)	101	46

Vegetarians need to be aware of consuming enough protein, though, and may need to increase the amount from these recommendations since extra protein is needed if it all comes from vegetable sources. Since some vegetable proteins do not supply all eight essential amino acids, different plant foods need to be consumed in combination in order to become complete proteins. Rice and beans, for example, are each high in the essential amino acid that the other is low in. Other plant proteins, such as quinoa and soybeans, are complete proteins by themselves.

While you will have no problem filling your protein requirement, you should try to obtain protein from heart-healthy sources that are low in saturated fat and cholesterol. It is never too early for you and your family to practice heart-healthy eating habits. Atherosclerosis, hardening of the arteries that can lead to heart disease later in life, has been found even in young children, so why not start good habits early with your child's diet? Heart-healthy, low-fat protein sources include skinless chicken, fish, beans, nuts, tofu, quinoa, low- or nonfat dairy products, and soy milk. These are good choices for all of you. While beef is not forbidden, it makes good sense to limit your intake to once per week, choose lean varieties, and trim the fat before preparing. Serve chicken with the skin removed. This, too, will minimize the saturated-fat content. Try to use beans in cooking. They are heart-healthy and economical. Simple dishes like our Stewed Pinto Beans and Brown Rice (see page 225) can be served one night for dinner, and then be used the next night as the filling for burritos. Our children love our Black Bean Burritos (see page 229).

Fish Fish is an excellent choice for a protein source, since it is low in saturated fat and calories. A good goal is to try to eat fish up to two times per week. Certain fish give you an extra health boost, since they are rich in heart-healthy omega-three fatty acids—

PROTEIN SOURCE	SERVING SIZE	GRAMS OF PROTEIN
Beans, pinto	1 cup	14
Beans, black	1 cup	15
Beef	3 ounces	23
Cheese, cheddar	1 ounce	7
Cheese, feta	1 ounce	4
Cheese, mozzarella	1 ounce	7
Cheese, Parmesan	1 tablespoon	2
Chicken, thigh	1 thigh	14
Chicken, white	3 ounces	37
Chickpeas	1 cup	14
Egg	1 large	6
Egg white	1 large	3.5
Fish, haddock	3 ounces	20
Fish, cod	3 ounces	19
Fish, salmon	3 ounces	23
Lentils	1 cup	18
Milk	1 cup	8
Soy milk	1 cup	7
Turkey	3 ounces	18
Tofu	3 ounces	6.5
Yogurt	1 cup	10
Peanuts	1 ounce	7
Quinoa, dry	½ cup	11
Walnuts	1 ounce	4

salmon, mackerel (avoid king mackerel–see below), anchovies, bluefish, and striped bass. Omega-three fatty acids are natural blood thinners that are considered part of a heart-healthy diet. In addition to reducing heart disease risk, they have been shown to reduce the risk of cancer, stroke, and other diseases.

MERCURY AND FISH Mercury, a heavy metal, is widespread in the environment. Mercury has been shown to cause neurologic and kidney damage. Women who are pregnant and young children need to be particularly careful about exposure to mercury, because their developing nervous systems are more susceptible to the toxic effects of mercury than are adults. Children exposed to mercury have been found to have learning and motor development delays.

Mercury seeps into our lakes, rivers, and oceans as runoff from industrial processes. We are exposed to mercury primarily by eating fish. All fish contain some mercury. Fish consume plants containing mercury, causing mercury levels in their bodies to build up. Predator fish eat other smaller fish, causing the levels of mercury in their bodies to be higher than in the plant eaters. Those fish at the top of the underwater food chain tend to build up the highest levels of mercury.

Many authorities currently recommend that pregnant and breast-feeding women as well as young children avoid the fish that are highest in mercury: swordfish, shark, king mackerel, and tilefish. Some recommend that tuna be avoided, since this is somewhat high in mercury and can be commonly consumed. Canned tuna tends to be lower in mercury than fresh tuna steak, since younger, smaller, and lower mercury types such as albacore tuna are often used in canning. In addition, it is recommended that all freshwater fish (those that live in rivers and lakes) be avoided by these individuals, since freshwater fish in many areas tend to contain high levels of mercury and other pollutants.

A WORD ABOUT CHOLESTEROL IN FISH AND SHELLFISH In general, fish and shellfish are low in fat and cholesterol when compared to beef, chicken, and dairy products. Although shellfish have a reputation for being high in cholesterol, this is not completely accurate.

Average Mercury Levels in Seafood Species[1]

FISH WITH HIGHEST MERCURY LEVELS

Species	Mean (PPM)
Tilefish	1.45
Swordfish	1.00
Shark	0.96
King mackerel	0.73

FISH AND SHELLFISH WITH MUCH LOWER MERCURY LEVELS

Species	Mean (PPM)
Grouper (Mycteroperca)	0.43
Tuna (fresh or frozen)	0.32
Lobster (Northern American)	0.31
Grouper (Epinephelus)	0.27
Halibut	0.23
Sablefish	0.22
Pollock	0.20
Tuna (canned)	0.17
Crab, blue	0.17
Crab, king	0.09
Catfish	0.07
Scallop	0.05
Salmon (fresh, frozen, or canned)	ND
Oysters	ND
Shrimps	ND

FISH WITH METHYLMERCURY LEVELS BASED ON LIMITED SAMPLING (GREATER DEGREE OF UNCERTAINTY IN VALUES)

Species	Mean (PPM)
Red snapper	0.60
Bass, saltwater	0.49
Marlin	0.47
Trout, freshwater	0.42
Bluefish	0.30
Croaker	0.28
Trout, seawater	0.27
Cod (Atlantic)	0.19
Mahi mahi	0.19
Ocean perch	0.18
Haddock (Atlantic)	0.17
Whitefish	0.16
Herring	0.15
Spiny lobster	0.13
Perch, freshwater	0.11
Perch, saltwater	0.10
Flounder/sole	0.04
Clams	ND
Tilapia	ND

ND= none detected

Shrimp, with about 150 milligrams of cholesterol in 3 ½ ounces, are now considered an acceptable alternative to red meat by the American Heart Association. Even lobster, which many on cholesterol-limited diets have been forbidden, has only 70 to 95 milligrams of cholesterol per 3 ½ ounces. Compare an egg with about 200 milligrams of cholesterol, or 3 ½ ounces of hamburger with 100 mg. The key here is, as always, moderation.

Nuts as Protein Nuts are a terrific source of protein. An ounce of nuts contains approximately 8 grams of protein. Several recent studies have confirmed that individuals who consume nuts several times a week have a lower risk of heart disease. Nuts are rich in healthy unsaturated fats, but you need to be a little careful with nuts, as they are also high in calories. It is important, therefore, not to eat nuts in addition to what you are already eating, but rather to substitute nuts for other protein sources. Simply adding a serving of nuts a day will add too many calories, and you'll gain weight. This increase in weight will increase your risk of heart disease and offset any health benefit you obtain from consuming them. Nuts make a great quick meal-on-the-go. Even better, use nuts as the protein source in some of your favorite recipes. Nuts make a great garnish for vegetables, such as Broccoli with Oyster Sauce (see page 313), which can be sprinkled with chopped peanuts or cashews. Another of our children's favorites is Spinach with Raisins and Pine Nuts (see page 314). Nuts also add a wonderful flavor, texture, and heart-healthy protein source when sprinkled on salads, such as our Mixed Greens with Pecans and Blue Cheese (see page 319) or Red Leaf and Arugula Salad with Pine Nuts and Raisins (see page 325).

DECREASE THE RISK OF DEVELOPING PEANUT ALLERGIES Peanuts are an economical and healthy source of protein. However, peanuts and peanut butter have become one of the world's most allergenic foods. It is estimated that about one person in two hundred is allergic to peanuts, and five to seven people die each year from severe anaphylactic reactions to them.

There are some simple measures that you can take to minimize your family's risk of developing this increasingly common allergy. Pregnant women and breast-feeding mothers who have close family members with allergic reactions, asthma, hay fever, or eczema (reactions collectively called atopy) have been advised by a government report to avoid eating peanut products in a bid to reduce the numbers of children who develop peanut allergies. The advice, which comes from the government's Committee on Toxicity of Chemicals in Food, Consumer Products and the Environment, is aimed at up to a third of pregnant women. Families without a history of these types of allergic reactions can ignore the warning. The report also advises that children from families with a history of peanut allergies should not eat peanut products until they are three years old. Children under the age of five should not be given whole peanuts because of the risk of choking.

Soy as Protein Tofu, soybeans, edamame, soy milk, and other soy products are excellent and versatile protein choices for you and your family. Soy is growing in popularity and general acceptance as our knowledge about the health benefits of soy grows. Once you get used to using these soy foods in cooking and learn some basic recipes that include soy, it will feel no different to cook up a stir-fry with tofu and beef instead of just beef (see Linguine with Tofu, Flank Steak, Bok Choy, and Asparagus on page 202), or to make your mashed potatoes with soy milk and silken tofu instead of butter and cream. Our Spaghetti and Meatballs (see page 336) is prepared with a combination of tofu and beef, making the meatballs lighter, more nutritious, and just as delicious. Our Oven-Baked Tacos (see page 348) contain a combination of beef and tofu and just may become one of your children's favorite finger foods. One of our most popular recipes is "Creamy" Caesar Salad (see page 326). The creaminess in the dressing doesn't come from raw eggs or oil but rather pureed silken tofu. This salad will leave your family and friends scratching their heads trying to figure out the "secret" ingredient.

We eat a lot of tofu in our home because of its many health properties, but we also use it because it is inexpensive and convenient. We keep a block of tofu in the our refrigerator the way most people keep cheese, so that we have it on hand to use as a protein source in many of our quick favorites—Baked Tofu Parmesan (see page 238) being our once-a-week regular.

Studies indicate that consumption of soy protein instead of animal protein, such as beef, decreases cholesterol. Soy is known to lower cholesterol levels by 10 to 20 percent when you eat between 1 to 1½ ounces daily. A study published in the *New England Journal of Medicine* indicates that an average daily consumption of 1¾ ounces of soy protein results in: a 9.3 percent decrease in total cholesterol; a 12.9 percent decrease in LDL (bad) cholesterol; and a 10.5 percent decrease in triglyceride levels. These reductions are even greater if you have high cholesterol levels.

PHYTOESTROGENS IN SOY Soy is rich in a substance called phytoestrogens. Phytoestrogens are compounds found in plants with activity similar to estrogen in the body. The chemical makeup of phytoestrogens resembles the body's estrogen. Two major categories of phytoestrogens are isoflavones and lignans. Soy is the major source of isoflavones, while flaxseed is the major source of lignans.

The action of phytoestrogens in the body is complex. In some body tissues they act like a weak estrogen. But in other body tissues, such as the breast, they appear to have antiestrogenic properties. Because of this resemblance to your body's estrogen, phytoestrogens can mimic the action of your natural estrogen on some of your body's tissues and organs. They have been shown to decrease hot flashes,[2] and may have an effect on other symptoms of menopause, including mood disturbances, sleep difficulties, fatigue, and vaginal dryness. Evidence from molecular and cellular biology experiments, animal studies, and some human clinical trials suggests that phytoestrogens in the diet may confer health benefits by preventing cardiovascular diseases and cancer.

PHYTOESTROGENS AND PROTECTION AGAINST CANCER Japanese women eating a traditional diet rich in soy products have a low incidence of estrogen-dependent cancers, such as breast cancer,[3] compared to Western women. This incidence increases once Asian women Westernize their diet.[4] Breast, colon, prostate, endometrial, and ovarian cancers and coronary heart disease all have lower incidences in Asia and eastern Europe than in Western countries.[5] Japan has consistently been reported to have the lowest risk of hormone-dependent cancers.[6]

Data from studies with animals has confirmed a protective

action against breast cancer.[7] Studies in humans show that women who consume high quantities of soy products and therefore have greater urinary concentrations of their breakdown products in their urine have reduced rates of breast cancer. It appears that the higher the amount of breakdown products in the urine, the lower the risk of breast cancer.[8]

PHYTOESTROGENS AS HORMONE BLOCKERS The mechanism behind this protective effect is not yet fully understood. There are several theories that are currently being researched that may explain it. It may be that this protective effect relates to the fact that phytoestrogens are a weak estrogen and therefore compete with the body's own natural estrogen, so that the breast and other hormonally responsive tissues are not exposed to as much estrogen in the long run. This effect would likely be important in pregnancy, the premenopausal years, and in adolescence, when estrogen levels are higher. This theory suggests that the protective effect of phytoestrogens on breast cancer risk therefore needs to be started early in life.

The anticancer mechanisms of phytoestrogens are also likely to be attributable to metabolic properties that do not involve estrogen receptors. A proposed mechanism for this nonhormonal protective effect of phytoestrogens in the diet is that they have been

Phytoestrogen Content from Isoflavones[9]

FOOD	TOTAL (MILLIGRAMS/4 OUNCES)
Soybeans (edamame)	185
Texturized vegetable protein	157
Soy flour	154
Tempeh	128
Tofu	71
Soy milk	20
Tofu yogurt	20

Breast Cancer Survivors
and Phytoestrogens—Are They Safe?

Several animal studies have found that phytoestrogens retard breast cancer development, suggesting that soy foods and flaxseed may have protective effects with regard to estrogen-dependent cancers in animals.[10] In addition, human breast cancer cell lines, which are a way of studying human cells in the laboratory, show that lignans and isoflavones reduce their proliferation.[11] Finally, phytoestrogens have been shown to inhibit enzymes associated with cancer cell proliferation, especially tyrosine kinase.[12] Tyrosine kinase inhibitors have potential as anticancer agents in both the prevention and treatment of cancer.

However, one recent study shows that we should proceed with caution in women with a diagnosis of breast cancer. A one-year study of the effects of a commercial soy protein isolate on breast discharge raised some concern about an increase in cell growth in response to soy. The breast fluid showed increased secretion of overgrown cells and increased concentrations of estrogen in the discharge. These findings are considered worrisome in terms of breast cancer risk. The study was subject to several limitations, including a high rate of women dropping out of the study, and no control population for comparison. In addition, the soy used was a soy protein isolate, and not the whole foods such as tofu or soy milk. Thus, further study is warranted.

Until further study is done on women with breast cancer, my advice to women already diagnosed with breast cancer is to consume phytoestrogens only from natural sources in the diet such as soy foods and flaxseed. Do not consume commercially processed sources of phytoestrogens, such as supplement pills or powders. These may contain large doses of phytoestrogens—much larger than you would consume in your diet. It is also possible that the anticancer properties found in the diet may require dietary co-factors to work that are processed away in pills and powders. Finally, in those who are already diagnosed with breast cancer, until more is known I would limit intake to one serving of phytoestrogen-containing foods, such as a glass of soy milk or 2 to 3 ounces of tofu daily. If you are a breast cancer survivor, it is best to check with your doctor for the latest research.

shown to block an enzyme, tyrosine kinase, that is important in cancer cell growth. Blockage of this enzyme inhibits the growth of cancer cells by decreasing the action of certain cellular growth factors. Other possible explanations include influences on other enzymes, protein synthesis, cell proliferation, angiogenesis, calcium transport, growth factors, lipid oxidation, and cell differentiation.[13] Research is actively under way to further elucidate the protective effect of phytoestrogens on breast cancer.

HOW MUCH SOY IS THE RIGHT AMOUNT? No one knows the answer to this question. The average Asian woman's diet contains about 3 to 4 ounces of soy foods such as tofu a day, yielding about 50 to 70 milligrams of isoflavones. Thus, if you include soy or flaxseed in one of your meals every day, you will get roughly the same amount. Most of the recipes in this book that contain phytoestrogens have approximately this amount in a serving.

Heart-Healthy Proteins While our knowledge about protein in the diet is not nearly as extensive as carbohydrates, what is clear is that too much animal protein is not good for you and your family. It a takes a bit of practice to cook with beans, legumes, tofu, and nuts, but the results are delicious and the health benefits many. Most of the recipes in this book are from heart-healthy protein sources. By using heart-healthy protein sources in exciting and delicious ways, you will not miss daily servings of red meat. In fact, you and your children may find them preferable once you make these tasty meals.

1. EPA Mercury Study Report to Congress, *A Survey of the Occurrence of Mercury in the Fishery Resources of the Gulf of Mexico Report 2000*, U. S. Food and Drug Administration, Center for Food Safety and Applied Nutrition, Office of Seafood.

2. P. Alvertazzi, F. Pansini, and G. Bonaccorsi, "The Effect of Dietary Soy Supplementation on Hot Flushes," *Obstetrics and Gynecology* 91 (1998):6–11.

3. H. Nagasawa, "Nutrition and Breast Cancer: A Survey of Experimental and Epidemiological Evidence," *IRCS Journal of Medical Science* 8 (1980):317–25.

4. I. Kato, S. Tominaga, and T. Kuroishi, "Relationship Between Westernization

of Dietary Habits and Mortality from Breast and Ovarian Cancer in Japan," *Journal of Cancer Research* 78 (1987):349–57.

5. D.P. Rose, A.P. Boyer, and E.L. Wynder, "International Comparison of Mortality Rates for Cancer of the Breast, Ovary, Prostate, and Colon, Per Capita Fat Consumption," *Cancer* 58 (1986):2363–71.

6. D.M. Parkin, "Cancers of the Breast, Endometrium and Ovary: Geographical Correlations," *European Journal of Cancer Clinical Oncology* 25 (1989):1917–25.

7. S. Barnes, C. Grubbs, K. Setchell, and J. Carlson, "Soybeans Inhibit Mammary Tumors in Models of Breast Cancer," in *Mutagens and Carcinogens in the Diet*, ed. M. Pariza (New York: Alan R. Liss, 1990).

8. H. Aldercreutz, H. Honjo, and A. Higashi, "Urinary Excretion of Lignans and Isoflavonoid Phytoestrogens in Japanese Men and Women Consuming a Traditional Japanese Diet," *American Journal of Clinical Nutrition* 54 (1991):193–1100.

9. J. Blake, "Phytoestrogens: The Food of Menopause?" *Journal of the Society of Obstetricians and Gynecologists of Canada* (May 1998).

10. C.A. Lamartiniere, J.B. Moore, N.M. Brown, et al., "Genistein Suppresses Mammary Cancer in Rats," *Carcinogenesis* 16 (1995):2833–40.

11. F.V. So, N. Gunthrie, and A.F. Chambers, "Inhibition of Proliferation of Estrogen Receptor-Positive MCF-7 Human Breast Cancer Cells by Flavonoids in the Presence and Absence of Excess Estrogen," *Cancer Letter* 112 (1997):127–33; G. Peterson and S. Barnes, "Genistein Inhibits Both Estrogen and Growth Factor Stimulated Proliferation of Human Breast Cancer Cells," *Cell Growth and Differentiation* 7 (1996):1345–51.

12. G. Peterson, "Evaluation of the Biochemical Targets of Genistein in Tumor Cells," *Journal of Nutrition* 125 (1995):784–89S.

13. H. Adlercreutz and W. Maxur, "Phyto-oestrogens and Western Diseases," *Annals of Internal Medicine* 29 (1997):95–120. D.C. Knight and J.A. Eden, "A Review of the Clinical Effects of Phytoestrogens," *Obstetrics and Gynecology* 87 (1996):897–904.

CHAPTER 4

fat—all is not equal

When it comes to fat in the diet, the advice you hear tends to be very extreme. Popular diets range from ultra-low-fat diets, like the one Dean Ornish promotes, to the Atkins diet, which is very high in fat and protein and extremely low in carbohydrates. When information is so conflicting, the best recourse is to go back to the scientific evidence and see what the researchers have found. Many of the leaders and scientists in the nutrition field now believe that it may not be the amount of fat in the diet but the type of fat in the diet that matters in determining health. This has been a shift in our prevous view of the last two decades, when a reduction in the total percentage of calories from fat was the number-one nutritional priority.

Fat in the Diet—Change It to Unsaturated There is now clear evidence that it is not the total amount of fat in your diet but the type of fat you eat that determines your risk of heart disease. Eating unsaturated fats and monounsaturated fats has been shown to protect against the development of heart disease and is now considered part of a heart-healthy diet. To reduce your risk, you need to replace saturated fat (found mainly in animal products, such as meat, butter, and whole milk) with unsaturated fats—polyunsaturated and monounsaturated. Safflower, sunflower, corn, and soybean oils are high in polyunsaturated fats; canola and olive oils are good sources of monounsaturated fats. This substitution will substantially reduce your risk of heart disease. The latest research does not support that you need to keep these healthy fats to the former recommendation of 30 percent of total calories.

Heart-Healthy Fat Sources

Avocado
Canola oil
Corn oil
Nuts and seeds
Nut butters—
    peanut, cashew,
    almond
Olives
Olive oil
Safflower oil
Sesame tahini
Soybean oil
Soy-nut butter
Sunflower oil

Heart Disease and Your Child's Diet It is never too early or too late in life to begin to worry about the saturated fat and cholesterol levels in your family's diet. Atherosclerosis starts to develop even in children as young as toddlers. There may even be a relationship between what you consume in pregnancy and your child's risk of developing heart disease later in life. It therefore makes good sense both for your and your family's health to keep your diet low in saturated fat and cholesterol, and to include healthy mono- and polyunsaturated fats. This is equally important for adults and children.

If you start these habits early, your children will become accustomed to this style of eating. For example, our children's favorite after-school snack is bread sprinkled with olive oil. They would not even think to ask for bread and butter, since they were brought up on olive oil, and would choose it over butter. We think it is delicious, too!

Take a Dietary Inventory of the Type of Fat in Your Diet The type of fat that the typical American consumes is largely saturated fat, which has been shown to increase heart disease and other health problems. In order to keep your intake of fat largely to the unsaturated and monounsaturated types, you will need to make some different choices in types of meats, dairy products, and other

Principal Foods Contributing Cholesterol, Saturated, Hydrogenated, and Trans Fat to the Diet

Bacon

Beef shoulder, shanks, or chuck

Bologna

Butter

Cheese (full-fat versions)

Chips made with hydrogenated oil

Coconut oil

Crackers (made with hydrogenated oils)

Egg yolks

Ground beef with greater than 12 percent fat

Hot dogs—beef and pork

Ice cream—whole fat

Liver and other organ meats

Poultry skin

Mayonnaise (made with hydrogenated oil)

Palm oil

Pepperoni

Pork ribs—back, country style, spare

Pork sausage

Pork shoulder

Prime ribs of beef

Rump roast

Salami

Salt pork

Second-cut brisket

Short ribs of beef

Shortening or lard

Whole and 2 percent milk

proteins in your diet. You should choose the majority of your protein sources from fish, beans, skinless chicken, and tofu instead of beef, which is high in saturated fat. When choosing dairy products, instead of whole milk, yogurt, and cheese, switch to skim milk and yogurt, and low-fat cheeses–the nutritional benefits from protein and calcium are the same without the saturated fat. Substitute nuts for some or all of the beef or other meat in your favorite recipes. Nuts are a rich source of healthy fats. Use beans and tofu liberally as protein sources instead of, or in addition to, beef and pork. For example, in our Spice-Rubbed Pork Shoulder with Black Beans and Brown Rice (see page 279), we combine a fattier cut of meat with beans, which keeps the quantities of meat you consume, and therefore the saturated-fat content, lower. You can make delicious burritos from the leftovers with our Carnitas and Black Bean Burritos (see page 282).

The recipes in this book can give you ideas for healthy, quick, and creative ways to alter the fat content in your diet to include the healthy types and minimize the unhealthy types. This way, your whole family can enjoy good food and good health together.

CHOOSING CUTS OF BEEF. Remember that you do not need to be extreme and entirely eliminate beef from your diet in order to have a heart-healthy diet. You can serve beef approximately once a week. There are certain cuts of beef that you can choose that are lower in saturated fat than others. Leaner choices of beef include tenderloin, sirloin, flank steak, first-cut brisket, and hamburger with less than 12 percent fat. Trim all the visible fat on any beef you prepare. If you decide to serve one of the higher-fat types of beef as a treat, keep portion sizes smaller. A good rule of thumb is to have your portion size about the size of a deck of cards. Savor the taste and eat it slowly.

Omega-Three Fatty-Acid-Rich Foods

Flaxseed
Herring
Mackerel
Pumpkin seeds
Trout
Tuna
Salmon
Sardines
Soybeans and
    soybean oil
Walnuts and
    walnut oil
Wheat germ

Omega-Three Fatty Acids As we increasingly recognize that not all fats are bad, and eating a balanced diet of the right fats is the key to good health and longevity, omega-three fatty acids from fish oil and from flaxseed have emerged as a new means toward achieving health through diet. Omega-three fatty acids are increasingly being recognized as having numerous health benefits. Omega-three fatty acids are known as "essential fatty acids," which means that they cannot be manufactured in your body but need to be supplied by your diet. There are three principal omega-three fatty acids—alpha-linolenic acid (ALA), eicosapentaenoic acid (EPA), and docosahexaenoic acid (DHA). ALA is found in large amounts in flaxseed and flaxseed oil, and in smaller amounts in soybean and canola oils. EPA and DHA are found mainly in fatty, cold-water fish—salmon, tuna, swordfish, mackerel, anchovies, bluefish, and striped bass.

The health benefits from omega-three fatty acids have been well proven both for disease prevention as well as cancer prevention (including breast cancer). There is a growing body of evidence that they may also help arthritis, depression, and improve control of diabetes. Omega-three fatty acids have also been proven to decrease heart disease through their effects as natural blood thinners. The proposed mechanism for the protective effect in cancer prevention appears to be that omega-three fatty acids affect prostaglandins, which in turn modulate the immune response, blood supply, and cell membrane integrity in decreasing cancer cell growth. Studies in mice as well as human breast cancer cell lines in the laboratory have demonstrated a protective effect. In addition, a large human population study shows that the greater the consumption of fish or fish oil, the lower the incidence of death from breast cancer.[1]

Eating one to two servings of these fish a week has been shown to significantly lower cholesterol and raise HDL. Eating omega-three fatty acids can help prevent the buildup of cholesterol-laden plaques that can clog the arteries and lead to heart attack and stroke. They lower the levels of triglycerides and total cholesterol in the blood, while raising the amount of HDL (good) cholesterol.

Those who do not eat fish can obtain omega-three fatty acids by consuming flaxseed and flaxseed oil. Flaxseed and flaxseed oil are rich in the omega-three fatty acid alpha-linolenic acid (ALA). Be aware that flaxseed has a hard outer coating. Unless it is ground or thoroughly chewed, it will pass through your body undigested. Thus, to obtain the maximum benefits of the omega-three fatty acids, you should grind flaxseed prior to consuming it.

In addition to the many health benefits from omega-three fatty acids, flaxseed is an excellent source of fiber. This fiber helps to keep your bowels moving, which keeps you comfortable as well as prevents painful hemorrhoids. Similar to fiber found in oat bran, flaxseed has been found to have a cholesterol-lowering effect. A high-fiber diet also helps you to feel full sooner, making restrained eating a bit easier.

Finally, flaxseed is also an excellent source of the phytoestrogen lignan, which also has been shown to have a cancer-protecting property. Flaxseed contains no gluten, so it can be used by those with gluten allergies.

Cooking with Flaxseed and Flaxseed Oil Flaxseed oil can burn at low temperatures, so it can be difficult to cook with it. Cooking also inactivates the phytoestrogen properties of flaxseed oil. We prefer to use flaxseed itself in cooking rather than the oil. It is an inter-

esting and versatile ingredient and gives you the additional benefit of fiber. Remember to grind it before consuming it, since it will
pass through your body undigested if you do not. Flaxseed and
flaxseed oil can turn rancid quickly if stored at warm room temperatures, so they should stay refrigerated once they are opened.

Flaxseed is a tiny reddish-brown seed with a lovely nutty flavor.
In Europe, bakers frequently grind it and use it in baked goods such
as cookies, cakes, and breads. We use it in the recipe for Raspberry-
Oat Squares (see page 377), where it lends a nutty flavor and chewy
texture. You can also sprinkle it on yogurt or cereal.

Many products are made from flax and flaxseed. Be aware that
linseed oil should not be used in cooking. Linseed oil is pressed from
flaxseed to be used as industrial oil for paints and furniture. It is
pressed and extracted from flaxseed with a petroleum solvent and
is not useable for food. Fiber in the stem of flax plants is used for
producing linen cloth.

Omega-Three Fatty Acids and Brain Development There is a
good deal of evidence that omega-three fatty acids are necessary
for the complete development of the human brain during pregnancy and the first two years of a child's life. It is thought that if a
pregnant or nursing mother is deficient in omega-three fatty
acids, the deficiency can lead to the baby having a nervous system
or immune system that is not fully developed. If a pregnant or
nursing woman is well nourished, she will supply her baby with
a blend of essential fatty acids that ensure the fast-growing baby's
brain and body tissues have a rich supply of this nutrient. It is thus
recommended that you consume two or three servings a week of
fatty fish (but make sure it is one low in mercury; see page 36), or
a serving of flaxseed (2–3 tablespoons) or flaxseed oil (1–2 tablespoons) a week while you are pregnant or nursing.

How Your Diet Affects Your Cholesterol Levels There is a relationship among the saturated-fat content of your diet, your blood-
cholesterol level, and your risk of developing coronary artery
disease. Cholesterol can be deposited on the walls of your blood ves-

sels and lead to heart disease and circulatory problems. A high blood-cholesterol level (200 milligrams or more) is a well-established risk factor for heart disease. Cholesterol is uniquely found in animal products, organ meats and egg yolk being especially rich sources. Although cholesterol comes from your diet, it is also synthesized in your body in the liver. This synthesis occurs independent of your dietary intake (although it appears to be raised by the ingestion of saturated fats, such as beef and butter). Because of this synthesis, you can't completely control your cholesterol level through your diet. To a degree, one's cholesterol level is inherited, but diet can strongly affect it.

How Fats Are Handled by the Body Fats are not soluble in water and, therefore, must receive special treatment during digestion for the body to handle them. In order to be distributed to the rest of the body from the stomach, fats are carried as complexes with blood proteins for their journey in the blood to the liver or to adipose tissue (the storage form of fat in the body). These lipid-protein complexes, called lipoproteins, come in a few varieties: high-density lipoproteins (HDL) and low-density lipoproteins (LDL).

Research has found that the levels of these substances may affect the risk of heart disease. High levels of HDL, which carry cholesterol to the liver, are associated with a lower risk of heart disease, whereas high levels of LDL are associated with a higher risk of heart disease. We thus think of HDL as the "good cholesterol" and LDL as the "bad cholesterol." Most evaluations of your risk of heart disease should include both an HDL level as well as an LDL level.

Hydrogenated Fat and Trans-Fatty Acids Other types of fat found in foods as a result of chemical processing are hydrogenated fats and *trans*-fatty acids. Originally manufactured with claims that they were healthier than saturated fats, these types of fats have been found to promote heart disease as badly or worse than saturated fats. Some of the chemical bonds in unsaturated fats have hydrogen added in a process known as hydrogenation.

This changes the physical state of fat from liquid to solid by changing some unsaturated bonds to saturated. Margarine is an example of a fat that has been hydrogenated in order to convert it from a liquid to a solid. In a similar process, in trans-fatty acids, the position of the hydrogen bond is changed from its natural position (known as cis) to an unnatural position (known as trans). Trans-fatty acids are found in vegetable shortenings, margarine, and many processed cookies and crackers. You can tell by reading the ingredient list, as manufacturers are now required to list this on the label.

Products containing hydrogenated fats and trans-fatty acids, especially margarine, were heavily promoted in the past as being healthier than foods containing saturated fat. It was thought that they did not raise blood cholesterol in the same manner that saturated fats did. However, such claims were never substantiated and have recently been found to be false. Concerns have arisen because consumption of these hydrogenated vegetable fats and trans-fatty acids has been tracked closely in time with coronary heart disease. Recent evidence has shown that, gram for gram, trans-fatty acids are actually worse than saturated fat for your health because they have about the same adverse effects on LDL cholesterol, but unlike any other type of fat, trans fat also reduces HDL cholesterol (the good cholesterol) and increases triglycerides. This combination—high LDL, low HDL, and increased triglycerides—adds up to a combination that has potent adverse effects on heart disease risk.

Beware of Partially Hydrogenated Vegetable Fats Unfortunately, trans fats are a prominent part of our diet, especially in packaged foods and store-bought baked goods. These fats are hidden in many of the processed foods we eat. If you look at grocery shelves and read labels, almost everything in a package contains partially hydrogenated vegetable fat—these are trans fats. Fast food is loaded with trans fats.

Thankfully, with our increasing recognition of the health detriments of trans fats, there are some changes beginning to take place in the marketplace. We are starting to see some trans-free baked goods such as cookies from Barbara's Bakery and crackers from

Hains Kashi companies. There are several newly available trans-fatty-acid-free margarines, such as Spectrum Naturals spreads and Earth Balance Natural Margarine. But currently the majority of margarines and packaged foods still contain trans fats, so you have to really take note and read the labels to avoid these fats, in addition to limiting your and your family's intake of fast foods.

A Satisfying Diet A diet that is not ultra low in fat will keep you feeling full and satisfied. No matter how you dress it up, an ultra-low-fat diet is never tasty. Thankfully, a diet that is based upon healthy fats has also been proven to be heart-healthy. Cooking with rich olive oil, savory nuts, and delicious fish is a diet your whole family will love and savor together. This is a diet you can stick to for life.

1. C.P.J. Caygill, A. Charlett, and M.J. Hill, "Fat, Fish, Fish Oil, and Cancer," *British Journal of Cancer* 74 (1996):159–64.

CHAPTER 5

weighty matters

As a nation, we are getting fatter. Despite the proliferation of complex new diets and strategies for weight loss, we are losing the battle of the bulge. More than half of American adults are overweight or obese, and the prevalence has steadily increased over the years. Among adults, the rate of extreme or morbid obesity has nearly tripled over the past decade. The increases in overweight and obesity cut across all ages, racial and ethnic groups, and both sexes. Being overweight or obese is associated with heart disease, certain types of cancer, diabetes, stroke, arthritis, breathing problems, and psychological disorders such as depression. At a time when tobacco-related illnesses are declining, obesity is implicated in an alarming increase in diabetes cases and is a leading reason why there haven't been more advances in reducing the nation's number-one killer, heart disease.

Now, more than ever, we need an even greater emphasis on the simple message of weight control through restrained eating, good food choices, and exercise for health. The simple fact is that if you eat more calories than you burn, you will gain weight. There is no magic diet that will cure this epidemic.

Too Many Calories Although multiple factors can account for weight gain, in the end, the basic cause is taking in more calories than you expend. Many of us believe that the kind of food we eat is more important for managing weight than the amount of food we eat. Many individuals avoid certain types of food to control their weight. The messages about low-fat or low-carbohydrate eating may have caused us to lose sight of the real issue: total calorie intake. Effective weight-management strategies place equal focus on both the kind and amount of food consumed.

Studies have shown that in the past decade, physical activity patterns have not changed much. What has changed is the number of calories we take in. There has been a growing trend of increased portion size, both in the home and in restaurants. Also, we are concentrating too hard on cutting fat or restricting carbohydrates without cutting calories. Many of us think we can consume as many fat-free brownies, servings of ice cream, and cookies as we want. But fat free is far from calorie free. We are eating more and wondering why we are getting fatter.

USDA statistics show that the American total daily caloric intake has risen from 1,854 calories to 2,002 calories over the last twenty years. This theoretically works out to an extra fifteen pounds every year. Ironically, studies also show that we are unaware that the portions we consume have increased in size. We have not noticed that portions in restaurants, fast-food chains, and our own homes have grown compared to just ten years ago.

Counting Calories The regulation of weight is quite simple. To lose weight, the calories you take in from the food you eat must be fewer than the calories used up by your body's daily processes plus the amount of calories you burn when you exercise. If you burn more calories than you eat, you will lose weight. It is that simple. When the calories you eat equal the calories you use up, you will maintain your weight. And of course, when the calories you eat are more than what you use up, you will gain weight. All the fad diets operate on this principle. By restricting the types of foods you eat, ultimately you eat fewer calories since there are only so many turkey slices or cabbage soups you can consume in a day.

Super-Sized Meals In 1955, a McDonald's hamburger contained 1.5 ounces of meat, and the fries that came with it were 2.3 ounces. Today, a "super-sized" burger can have as much as eight ounces of beef, and the fries can be as large as 7.1 ounces. And the soda? A 7-ounce regular soda of 1955 is dwarfed by today's 42-ounce super-sized serving. This jug of soft drink can equate to one-half or two-thirds of a day's allotment of calories. Increasingly, we are being tempted to buy more food than is good for us. This has contributed to the misconception that the kind of food is more important than how much food we eat. You need to avoid the large-portion trap.

A recent article in the *Journal of the American Medical Association* shows that over the past twenty years, the size of food portions consumed at restaurants, fast food establishments, and at home has increased significantly.[1] Many believe this is one major factor contributing to the obesity epidemic in the United States. Fast-food establishments serve the largest portion sizes, compared to restaurants and homes, offering these larger portions for bargain prices, making it less expensive ounce for ounce to eat larger portions. We want larger portions because they are bargains. The marketing of these super-sized meals means we consume more calories.

It may come as a surprise, though, that the large-portion-size epidemic has also made it into our homes. Even when we prepare our own meals, we are serving our families larger amounts. This phenomenon is thought to represent general changes in eating behavior—we have gotten used to seeing more on our plates.

Overweight Children Life as an overweight adult often has its roots in being an overweight child. In the United States at least one child in five is overweight. Over the last two decades, this number has increased by more than 50 percent, and the number of extremely overweight children has nearly doubled. More and more children are being diagnosed with previously grown-up, obesity-linked conditions such as high cholesterol and type II diabetes.

Children become overweight for a variety of reasons. The most common causes are genetic factors, lack of physical activity, unhealthy eating patterns, or a combination of these factors. Children whose parents or siblings are overweight may be at an increased risk of becoming overweight themselves. While these genetic factors do play a role in increasing the likelihood that a child will be overweight, shared family behaviors such as eating and activity habits also influence body weight. In addition, children's activity level plays an important role in determining their weight. Today, the lure of sedentary activities such as television, computers, and electronic games contributes to an inactive lifestyle. The average American child spends approximately twenty-four hours each week watching television. You can help your child set limits on these types of activities and give him plenty of opportunities to be physically active. Finally, your child's diet may include too many high-saturated-fat snacks, soda, or calorie-dense foods. You can help your child by limiting access to snacks between meals, and by serving healthy meals containing plenty of fruits and vegetables.

Talk to Your Doctor If you think your child is overweight, it is important to talk with your child's doctor. Your child's physician will measure her weight and height to determine if she is overweight. Assessing overweight in children is difficult because children grow in unpredictable spurts. Your child's doctor can help determine whether she will naturally grow into a normal weight, or if you need to make some changes in your family's diet and physical activity to help her achieve this. Family involvement helps to teach everyone healthful habits and does not single out the overweight child. Children should never be placed on a restrictive diet to lose weight, unless a doctor supervises one for medical reasons. Having them eat the diet we suggest in this book instead of one filled with cookies and unhealthy snacks should help them achieve a healthy weight and maintain growth and development.

Don't Diet—Learn to Cook This book is not about a quick weight-loss diet. Rather, this book is about maintaining a diet and lifestyle that will allow you to achieve and maintain a healthy weight over time. There is no overnight fix. Regaining and maintaining a healthy weight is a lifetime commitment, so the emphasis in this book is not on dieting, but rather on a sustainable lifestyle approach to eating and exercise that you can maintain for life.

Learn to cook and eat in a way you can continue for a lifetime—light, healthy, and simple. There simply is no substitute. If you eat out or buy prepared foods for every meal, you will find it next to impossible to loose or maintain a healthy weight. And you'll spend a great deal of money doing so.

You Say You Don't Have Time to Cook? If you care about your health and your family's health, you need to make time to cook. With some simple recipes and organizational tips, it won't take nearly as much time as you think. Part of staying healthy is making a commitment to spend some time and energy cooking and planning your meals for you and your family. And once you get in the habit of doing so, you'll find it actually takes no more time than picking up takeout. You will then reap not only the benefits of healthy, delicious food but also the subtle benefits of a warm and cozy household. What could be a better atmosphere in which to bring up children than a warm kitchen where dinner is cooking in the oven, or the delicious aroma of fresh-baked bread is wafting through the house. Numerous studies show the benefits of eating together at dinnertime and sharing your day's accomplishments over food you cooked yourself.

Popular Weight-Loss Diets—Try Them—You Won't Like Them If you are trying to lose weight fast, go ahead and try one of the popular weight-loss diets (under your doctor's supervision). Trying to lose weight too quickly will leave you hungry and feeling deprived and may backfire. If you cut your calories too severely, your body will go into starvation mode, and will slow down its metabolic rate in order to conserve energy.

No one can stick to these restrictive diets for a lifetime. When you are ready to live a normal life again, come back and read the rest of this book. You can learn to eat in a way that is satisfying, delicious, and simple on a daily basis. We want to teach you to cook and be organized so that you can have your diet become part of your life. With a few simple cooking techniques and ideas for foods to consume, you can be eating nutritious and savory meals, while still losing weight. There needs to be room for error, room for your favorite sweets, and room to allow you to dine out. Eventually, eating this reduced-quantity but high-quality diet, you will lose weight. How much you lose depends upon how much you eat and how much you exercise.

Once you've lost the weight, you should continue this same eating and lifestyle pattern in order to maintain your weight loss. That is how it works. Your diet is for life. If you notice you are gaining some weight back, you either need to make some adjustments in your diet or exercise more. If you stop losing weight, yet are not at a weight that is appropriate for your body (see BMI index, page 11), you can again make some adjustments—eat less or exercise more.

Quick, Easy Weight Loss? Beware the diet guru who rejects scientific evidence-based medicine and professes to know better. Ask yourself—what data does this so-called expert use to make these claims? Research on diet is difficult, painstaking, and takes years to accumulate in adequate quantities to be able to make accurate statements. We are only just beginning to gather this evidence. Take caution in any diet that suggests that the key to weight loss lies not in controlling calories but in adjusting your body's level of a single hormone or simple body chemistry. Your body is a complex and integrated system of hormones, chemicals, and nutrients, and no two individuals are alike. Tinkering with these hormones and nutrients by eating extreme diets may lead to long-term health problems and may affect medications you are taking. There is currently no long-term data supporting the health claims of these extreme diets.

How the Fad Diets Work The following is a brief summary of diets to beware of. It is all too easy to become frustrated with your weight and fall prey to promises of instant success.

LOW-CARBOHYDRATE DIETS Low-carbohydrate diets are some of the most controversial yet some of the most popular today. One famous plan is the Atkins diet. Named after Dr. Atkins, this program was one of the first to popularize low-carbohydrate, high-protein diets that individuals can use on their own rather than in a medical clinic. The underlying principle is that metabolic imbalance is the cause of most obesity, and that carbohydrates in the modern diet and their effects on insulin in your body are the root of this problem. This diet abandons the balanced-diet approach in favor of a diet that contains almost no carbohydrates and therefore results in a metabolic state called ketosis. In the medical arena, this is called a protein-sparing modified fast.

Ketosis is a state in which the cells in the body produce a substance called ketones in response to a low level of glucose. Glucose is released into the bloodstream when carbohydrates are consumed, since glucose is the breakdown product of carbohydrates. When few carbohydrates are consumed, glucose levels are very low. Because of this, insulin levels are very low, since the body regulates the level of insulin in large part due to the level of glucose in the bloodstream. Insulin is a hormone that drives glucose into the cells in your body. Insulin levels rise in response to the consumption of carbohydrates and the resulting glucose in the bloodstream. When glucose levels are low, insulin levels in the body plummet. When glucose levels in the body and in the cells are low, the cells produce ketones, which are an alternative fuel for the body. These ketones, according to Atkins, have an appetite-suppressing property. Measuring ketones is an integral part of the diet plan and one of the primary indicators of success and compliance. Dr. Atkins maintains that carbohydrates and their effects on hyperinsulinemia are the reason for the increasing rates of obesity, hypertension, heart disease, and diabetes.

There is, in fact, some research supporting these theories. Several well-respected journals have evaluated these modified fasts using meat, fish, fowl, or high-protein liquid formulas. The dramatic decreases in serum glucose, serum insulin, blood pressure, cholesterol, triglycerides, and weight reported by Atkins have been confirmed by research centers all over the U.S. But missing is the fact that the individuals participating in these programs received complete physical examinations and were monitored by physicians during the weight-loss and transition periods. Ketotic diets, regardless of calorie level, bring about significant metabolic changes that can be beneficial for weight loss but may cause havoc with medications and other treatments often utilized by overweight individuals. For example, the diuretic effect of ketosis is sufficiently dramatic that high blood pressure medication may need to be adjusted. This diuretic effect is part of what accounts for the initial dramatic weight loss in these diets, since you lose water weight from your body due to the effect of ketosis.

This diet is a short-term fix for a permanent problem. The tendency to gain weight will not go away, since this diet is so unbalanced that you can't stay on it for more than a few weeks without feeling deprived and out of sync with the eating patterns of your friends and family. And the lack of balance in the long run can hurt your health. Extreme high-protein, low-carbohydrate diets can lead to vitamin deficiencies, a loss of bone density, and other problems. No one I have ever spoken to has been able to stick with this diet in the long term.

Another low-carbohydrate diet similar to the Atkins plan is Protein Power, written by husband-and-wife physicians Eades and Eades. Like Atkins, these physicians characterize obese patients as suffering from "disordered insulin metabolism." They are slightly different from Atkins in that they emphasize the role of the hormone glucagon in counterbalancing the role of insulin. They also recommend exercise, especially strength training, to enhance the release of growth hormone.

THE CARBOHYDRATE ADDICT'S DIET The Carbohydrate Addict's Diet is a mixture of the low-carbohydrate diet and a traditional diet. Written by husband-and-wife researchers Heller and Heller, this diet plan is designed to limit the number of times dieters eat carbohydrates and the amount of time in which they eat them. By doing this, dieters are reducing the insulin response and its effect on appetite regulation. This diet allows two meals in a day that are low carbohydrate and high protein, similar to the diets of Atkins and Protein Power. It differs from these diet plans in that one meal a day is considered the "reward meal." This meal can contain any amount of carbohydrates or other foods dieters would like to eat. However, this meal needs to be completed within one hour. The authors view carbohydrate addiction as a result of hyperinsulinemia, which interferes with the satiety (feeling full) signals after eating carbohydrates. By decreasing the number of times dieters eat carbohydrates and the amount of time in which they eat them, dieters are reducing the insulin response and its effect on appetite regulation.

Our interpretation of this diet is that the Hellers have found an interesting way to restrict the total number of calories you consume in the day by setting these time and meal restrictions. There is no magic here. You simply end up burning more calories than you use. You can do this just as readily by eating three balanced meals a day and being conscious of portion size.

THE ZONE Another anticarbohydrate diet is the Zone, promoted by Dr. Barry Sears. This diet recommends the 40-30-30 diet plan—40 percent of calories from carbohydrates, 30 percent from protein, and 30 percent from fat. Several nutritional products have been marketed, especially to athletes, using this nutritional profile. This diet is not significantly different from the way the U.S. population currently eats. This plan makes unsubstantiated claims such as permanent weight loss, prevention of cancer and heart disease, greater energy and physical performance, improved mental focus and productivity, and alleviation of the painful symptoms of diseases such as multiple sclerosis and HIV. Like the other diets discussed, one of the principles of this diet is the effect of excess dietary carbohydrates on the insulin-glucagon system.

The mechanics of the Zone diet involve eating every meal and snack with a composition of 40-30-30. Dieters are given a method to determine their protein needs, and this amount of protein is the limit for the day. The carbohydrate level of the diet is determined by matching the amount of protein with carbohydrate. The type of fat is restricted as well, with dieters told to limit their intake of "bad" fats such as arachidonic acid and saturated fat and instead to obtain their fat from "good" fats, such as monounsaturated fat. Dieters are directed to eat a meal or snack every four to six hours because that is as long as the meal or snack keeps them in the Zone. However, no one meal can contain more than 400 calories.

This diet is so complex and difficult to follow that few dieters will achieve much success. The time, energy, and attention paid to preparing the food is prohibitive. Achieving the 40-30-30 nutritional balance at every meal or snack is not maintainable over the long run.

THE ORNISH DIET The Ornish diet is at the other extreme from high protein/fat diets. It is an ultra-low-fat diet that Dr. Dean Ornish published as an alternative to cardiac bypass surgery as a means of potentially reversing heart disease. There is some credible evidence to support this extreme diet, and for those who have heart disease, this diet may keep them out of the operating room. But this is an extreme diet for extreme circumstances. The average person or family does not need to eat this type of a diet, and for children it may even be unhealthy to consume this little fat in the diet.

No Long-Term Benefits Research has shown that high-protein, low-carbohydrate diets, with the proper supplements, can be safe for the short term with proper medical supervision. However, no support exists for continuing this type of diet in the long term. Regardless of supplements recommended, the restrictions in carbohydrates do not allow individuals to consume the fiber and phytonutrients contained in fruits, vegetables, and whole grains necessary for health. Endurance athletes will have a difficult time with the limitations of these diets in supporting high levels of activity, such as long-distance running or intensive weight training because the low carbohydrate content of the diet does not maintain the necessary glycogen stores for intense exercise. The average person will have a hard time with this restricted diet, since it is very difficult to live in the real word eating only protein and fat. One can only eat so much steak, chicken, and fish without craving a plate of pasta, a bowl of fruit salad, or a lovely bean-based soup.

It's Not What You Eat; It Is How Much You Eat In general, it is not what you eat, but how much you eat. The main theme for your diet should be to eat foods in smaller quantities. Often, when I closely examine people's diet, they are eating healthy and nutritious foods, but they are eating quantities that are too large to allow them to lose weight. Quantity, not quality, is usually where people get into trouble. If you eat too much, no matter how low in fat and calories a particular food may be, too much will eventually add up to too many calories. By the same token, there are no forbidden foods, just limited amounts of those foods. For example, if potato chips are your downfall, allow yourself a few chips with your lunch. If you love ice cream, allow yourself a small serving for dessert once in a while. Save up your calories for these treats by exercising an extra fifteen minutes, or eating lightly at dinner to allow room for a small dessert in your diet.

Tips for Weight Loss While we have no magic regimen for helping you to lose weight, the following tips may be helpful:

- Family-style eating—Don't do it. It is a good idea to avoid "family-style" eating. Family-style eating means you put the food on the table in front of you and your family in serving bowls. It is just too easy to reach over and take another portion without even thinking. You might eat double the amount of food you would have normally. Rather, fill your plate at the stove with the desired amount of food. This allows you to visualize just how much you are eating, and also helps you to see if you are eating a balanced meal. This visualization is very important in feeling fuller. In addition, serving the food in this manner for everyone saves on dishwashing, since you don't use any serving bowls.
- Weighing and measuring—For meat, such as beef, chicken, and fish, try to keep the amount in a serving at dinner to 4 ounces, and at lunch to 3 ounces. This may seem like a very small amount if you are used to eating more, but you have to get used to eating less, and savoring it more. Limit bread at dinner to one slice, and try not to have bread with every single meal. Make cer-

tain to eat large amounts of vegetables with as many meals as you can, and you will feel more satisfied.

- Eating breakfast–It is important not to skip breakfast. It does not need to be a huge, farmer's style breakfast. It can be quick and easy. You can combine a small amount of carbohydrate, protein, and fat to make a quick and fulfilling meal. Try a small amount of peanut butter and jam on a slice of toast, with a cup of coffee or tea. Or have a small bowl of cereal with skim milk and half a banana, along with a cup of coffee or tea. This will give you energy to start your day, and will keep you from being so hungry at lunch that you overeat.

- Soup for dinner–Eating a broth-based soup as a main course will fill you up before it fills you out. Soup, a one-pot meal that can be simple to prepare and easy to store for another day, that is prepared with a small amount of meat or other protein source and lots of vegetables is nutritionally complete. The hot liquid gives you a feeling of fullness and satisfaction without consuming lots of calories. Allow yourself a slice of good bread and a large salad with a light dressing, and you'll be full and satisfied for hours. Soup for dinner is an especially good way to accelerate your postpartum weight loss.

- "Calories in the bank"–If you are planning an evening out and know you will be eating a large meal, try to eat a light lunch and breakfast that day, or try to lengthen the time you spend exercising that day. These can then become your "calories in the bank" so that you can eat a bit more that night.

- Sweets and goodies–You should not deny yourself some occasional sweets and goodies. Rather, treat yourself to a small amount of your favorites from time to time. The emphasis here is on "small." Have a piece of good chocolate, a small slice of cake, a handful of chips, a cookie or two, or a scoop of ice cream. But take time to savor it. Try having it with a cup of tea or coffee, and it will seem to last longer and you will feel fuller from the hot liquid. Also, pick lower-fat versions of cookies, ice cream, or chips. Often, there is very little difference in taste. If you would really like to indulge, and have a hot fudge sundae or a decadent dessert, then plan for it with "calories in the bank," or make up for it the next day by being a bit more strict with your diet, or by exercising a bit longer. This give-and-take will keep life interesting, and keep you content yet slim!

- Alcohol—The same principles for sweets and goodies hold for alcohol. A small amount on occasion is fine—just remember that you'll need to eat a bit less to compensate for the calories from the alcohol, or exercise a bit more. But if that glass of wine is what makes you feel fulfilled, then denying yourself completely will never work. Just have a glass from time to time, keep the quantity low, and be sure to adjust your food intake accordingly.

Eating as Art and Pleasure Go ahead and try these diets for some quick weight loss. Remember that much of the initial rapid weight loss is from reducing water. Few can continue restrictive diets for a lifetime and be fulfilled and content. Eventually you will get bored and begin to stray and then gain weight. Eating with your friends, family, and children should not be a chore with restrictions in major food groups. Eating should be varied, exciting, pleasurable, and use fresh and local foods. Your plate should have an abundance of colors and textures.

With a few skills and tricks, eating can be a pleasure and an art, and you and your family can maintain a healthy weight and lifestyle at the same time. You should set an example for your family with a healthy approach to eating and exercise. Learn to cook, eat as a family, and enjoy and savor your meals. Learn preparation and cooking techniques like the ones they use in spas, so that you do not feel deprived but rather delighted with what you are eating. Since you don't have the time that a spa chef has to plan and serve meals, we'll teach you how to organize your kitchen and shopping so that you can incorporate this pattern of eating into your daily life. Eating as a family will be pleasurable and different every day. As a parent, you have an awful lot to live for, so attain a healthy weight both for yourself and for all those who love you.

1. S.J. Nielsen and B.M. Popkin, "Patterns and Trends in Food Portion Sizes, 1977–1998," *Journal of the American Medical Association* 289 (2003):450–53.

CHAPTER 6

calcium—the whole family needs it

C alcium is a mineral that the body needs for numerous functions. Calcium is involved on the cellular level in diverse body functions: the beating of your heart, controlling your blood pressure, and even in the prevention of premenstrual syndrome. Numerous studies have now confirmed that calcium aids in the prevention of colon cancer. Calcium is vital to the maintenance of strong bones. It provides structure for the body, since 99 percent of the calcium in the human body is stored in the bones and teeth. The remaining 1 percent is found in the blood and other tissues.

Understanding the regulation of calcium in the body will help you to understand why calcium in the diet is so important. Bones consists of a matrix of collagen containing calcium and phosphate. The most significant function of bone is actually not as a supporting structure, but rather its role as a calcium reservoir for many body functions. Calcium is an essential element for all cell functions. Your heart requires calcium to beat, your muscles

69

require calcium to function, and your nervous system requires calcium to transmit messages.

Your body obtains the calcium it needs in two ways. One way is from foods that contain calcium, such as dairy products and dark green leafy vegetables. The other way is by removing it from the store of calcium in your bones. For normal cellular activity, blood calcium levels must be maintained in a very tight range. The reservoir of calcium in the skeleton is critical in allowing a steady supply of calcium for cellular functions at a moment's notice. Your body withdraws calcium from your bones when blood levels of calcium drop too low, usually when it's been awhile since eating a meal containing calcium. Ideally, the calcium that is borrowed from the bones will be replaced at a later point. However, if your diet is lacking calcium, this doesn't always happen.

How Much Calcium Do You Need? Balance studies that examine the point at which the amount of calcium consumed equals the amount of calcium excreted suggest that an adequate intake is 550 milligrams a day. To ensure that 95 percent of the population gets this much calcium, the National Academy of Sciences established the following recommended intake levels:

Recommended Calcium Intake
(National Academy of Sciences)

AGE (YEARS)	DAILY CALCIUM (MILLIGRAMS)
Birth–6 months	210
6 months–1 year	270
1–3	500
4–8	800
9–18	1,300
19–50	1,000
over 50	1,200
Pregnant/lactating	1,000

While it is clear that consuming adequate calcium, especially in youth, is one of the keys to reducing the risk of osteoporosis, the exact amount of calcium it takes to do this is not. Different scientific studies have revealed conflicting answers to this issue. Some recent studies have reported that calcium intake as an adult doesn't actually appear to lower a person's risk for osteoporosis. Harvard's large studies of male health professionals and female nurses found that individuals who drank one glass of milk or fewer per week were at no greater risk of breaking a hip or forearm than were those who drank two or more glasses per week.[1] Some additional evidence also supports the idea that adults may not need as much calcium as is currently recommended. In countries such as India, Japan, and Peru, where calcium intake is as low as 300 milligrams a day, the incidence of osteoporosis-related fractures is low. However, there are differences in other important bone-health factors in these countries, such as higher levels of physical activity and greater levels of sunlight, which could explain their lower fracture rates. Until we have more information, it makes sense to continue to follow the National Academy of Science recommendations for your and your family's intake of calcium.

Vitamin D Your body needs vitamin D in order to absorb calcium. When blood levels of calcium begin to drop, the body responds in several ways. It promotes the conversion of vitamin D into its active form, which then travels to the intestines, where it encourages greater calcium absorption into the bloodstream. It also goes to the kidneys, where it aids in minimizing calcium loss in the urine. For bone health, an adequate intake of vitamin D is no less important than calcium. Most experts recommend a daily intake between 400 and 800 IU. This amount can be obtained from fortified dairy products, egg yolks, saltwater fish, liver, and vitamin supplements. Some calcium supplements and most multivitamins contain vitamin D, so it is important to check the labels to determine how much each contains. Vitamin D can also be made in your skin when it is exposed to sunlight. The amount of vitamin D produced in the skin varies depending on the time of day, season, latitude, and skin pigmentation. Usually ten to fifteen minutes exposure two to three times a week of the hands, arms, and face is enough to satisfy the body's vitamin D requirement. Use of sunscreen markedly diminishes the manufacture of vitamin D in the skin, as do window glass, clothing, and air pollution. Skin color also affects vitamin D production; the fairer you are, the more vitamin D you make. As we age, our ability to make vitamin D through the skin decreases. People who are housebound and experience no sunlight exposure are unable to make vitamin D.

But not all sunlight is equal in allowing vitamin D production in the skin. Above 40 degrees latitude (north of San Francisco, Denver, Indianapolis, and Philadelphia), the winter sunlight isn't strong enough to promote vitamin D formation. Sunscreens also prevent the formation of vitamin D, although they are still recommended to reduce risk of sun-induced skin cancer and skin damage. Those who don't spend much time outdoors, or who live in these areas, should consider supplementing their vitamin D intake.

Achieving Your Maximum Peak Bone Density Bone is living tissue that is always being regenerated. Bone cells called osteoblasts build bone, while other bone cells, called osteoclasts, remove bone. Throughout your life, your bones are constantly being broken down and built up, a process called "remodeling."

One of the most important principles to keep in mind when considering calcium and the health of your skeleton is the fact that your maximum bone density is determined by about age thirty. After this time you are simply working on maintaining your skeleton and preventing bone loss. Thus, the issue of adequate dietary calcium and physical exercise is most important in children and young adults. Bone development begins before birth and proceeds at its fastest rate during adolescence. Up to about age thirty, in a healthy individual with adequate calcium intake and physical activity, bone production exceeds bone destruction. After that, destruction exceeds production. So to stem the tide of osteoporosis, it's important to do two things. First, do whatever you can to make the strongest, densest bones possible during the first thirty years of life. Second, limit the amount of bone loss in adulthood.

Osteoporosis Osteoporosis, or "porous bones," is the weakening of bones caused by a reduction in the actual amount of bone matter. Currently, over 25 million Americans have osteoporosis. People typically lose bone as they age, despite consuming the recommended intake of calcium necessary to maintain optimal bone health. Each year, osteoporosis leads to more than 1.5 million fractures, including 300,000 broken hips. The loss of bone with aging is due to several reasons, including genetic factors, physical inactivity, and lower levels of circulating hormones (estrogen in women and testosterone in men).

Postmenopausal women account for 80 percent of all cases of osteoporosis because estrogen production declines rapidly at menopause. Men are also at risk of developing osteoporosis, but they tend to do so five to ten years later than women, since testosterone levels do not fall abruptly the way estrogen does in women. Twenty percent of cases of osteoporosis are in men. It is estimated that osteoporosis will cause half of all women over age fifty to suffer a fracture of the hip, wrist, or vertebra.

Lifestyle Factors Can Lower Risk of Osteoporosis There are a number of lifestyle factors that can lower the risk of osteoporosis, including:

- growing healthy bones in youth and early adulthood
- getting regular exercise, especially weight-bearing and muscle strengthening exercise
- getting adequate vitamin D, whether through diet, exposure to sunshine, or supplements
- consuming enough calcium so as to reduce the amount the body has to borrow from bone
- consuming adequate vitamin K, found in leafy green vegetables

Risk Factors for Osteoporosis Certain individuals are more likely to develop osteoporosis than others. Factors that increase the likelihood of developing osteoporosis are called "risk factors." The following risk factors have been identified:

personal history of fracture after age fifty
low bone density
history of fracture in a first-degree relative
being female
being thin and/or having a small frame
advanced age
family history of osteoporosis
estrogen deficiency as a result of menopause, especially early
    or surgically induced
absence of menstrual periods for prolonged times (amenorrhea)
anorexia nervosa
low lifetime calcium intake
use of certain medications such as corticosteroids and anti-
    convulsants
low testosterone levels in men
inactive lifestyle
cigarette smoking
excessive alcohol
Caucasian or Asian race

Exercise Physical activity that puts some strain or stress on
bones causes the bones to retain and possibly even gain density
throughout life. Cells within the bone sense this stress and
respond by making the bone stronger and denser. Such "weight-
bearing" exercises include walking, dancing, jogging, weight lifting, stair climbing, racquet sports, and hiking. Swimming is a
useful form of exercise for the heart and cardiovascular system.
But because water supports the bones, rather than putting stress
on them, it's not considered a good "weight-bearing" exercise for
bone strength. In addition, physical activity doesn't strengthen all
bones, just those that are stressed, so you need a variety of exercises or activities to keep all your bones healthy. The benefits of
activity are most pronounced in those areas of the skeleton that
bear the most weight, such as the hips during walking and running and the arms during gymnastics and upper-body weight
lifting.

Another function of physical activity, probably at least as important as its direct effect on bone mass, is its role in increasing muscle strength and coordination. With greater muscle strength, one can often avoid falls and situations that cause fractures. Making physical activity a habit can help maintain balance and avoid falls.

Kids and Their Bones Helping your children to meet the proper nutritional requirements for optimal bone health needs to start in childhood. Osteoporosis has been called "a pediatric disease with geriatric consequences," because the bone mass attained in childhood and adolescence is a very important determinant of lifelong skeletal health. Bones are living tissues that are constantly changing. Old bone is removed and remodeled and replaced by new bone. During childhood and adolescence, much more bone is deposited than removed, as the skeleton grows in size and density. Children's peak bone mass occurs in the mid-twenties. Up to 90 percent of bone mass is acquired by age eighteen in girls and by age twenty in boys. Through a combination of diet and exercise, you can help your children reach their genetically programmed peak bone density.

Peak bone mass in children is influenced by a number of factors. Some you can change, such as nutrition and physical activity. Others you can't, such as those influenced by genetics, race, and gender. Bone mass is generally higher in men than in women. Before puberty, boys and girls develop bone mass at similar rates. After puberty, however, boys acquire greater bone mass than girls. African-American girls tend to achieve higher peak bone mass than Caucasian girls, and African-American women are at lower risk for osteoporosis later in life. More research is needed to understand the differences in bone density between the various racial and ethnic groups. However, because all women, regardless of race, are at significant risk for osteoporosis, girls of all races need to build as much bone as possible to protect themselves. Hormonal factors, including the production of estrogen, affect the development of bone mass. Girls who start to menstruate at an early age typically have greater bone density. Those who frequently miss their menstrual periods sometimes have lower bone density.

Calcium is an essential nutrient for bone health. In fact, calcium deficiencies in young people can account for a 5 to 10 percent lower peak bone mass and may increase the risk of bone fracture later in life. A well-balanced diet including adequate amounts of other vitamins and minerals such as vitamin D, vitamin C, and phosphorus is also important for bone health. Finally, physical activity is crucial for building healthy bones.

Your children's diet needs to include enough vitamin D from sunlight or foods such as egg yolks or fortified milk. Young children, ages two to eight are more likely to obtain adequate dietary calcium, but among older children from ages nine to nineteen, only 19 percent of girls and 52 percent of boys obtain enough calcium to ensure optimal peak bone mass.

Men and Osteoporosis Many think of osteoporosis as a woman's disease only. While it is more common in women, men do get osteoporosis. One in four men over age fifty will have an osteoporosis-related fracture in their lifetime (compared to one in two women). And the one-year mortality following a hip fracture is nearly twice as high for men as for women.

One note of caution for men: A diet high in calcium has been implicated as a potential risk factor for prostate cancer. In a Harvard study of male health professionals, men who drank two or more glasses of milk a day were almost twice as likely to develop advanced prostate cancer as those who didn't drink milk at all. Moreover, the association appears to be with calcium itself, rather than with dairy products in general. Although more research is needed, we cannot be confident that high milk intake in men is safe. Right now, a moderate intake of calcium seems to be the right course.

Bottom-Line Recommendations for Calcium Intake and Bone Health Adequate, lifelong dietary calcium intake is necessary to reduce the risk of osteoporosis. Consuming adequate calcium and vitamin D and performing regular, weight-bearing exercise are also important to build maximum bone density and strength. After age thirty, these factors help slow bone loss, although they cannot completely prevent bone loss due to aging.

Milk and dairy products are a convenient source of calcium for many people. They are also a good source of protein and are fortified with vitamins D and A. At this time, however, the optimal intake of calcium as well as the optimal sources of calcium are not clear. As noted earlier, the National Academy of Sciences currently recommends that people ages nineteen to fifty consume 1,000 milligrams of calcium per day, and that those age fifty or over consume 1,200 milligrams per day. Reaching 1,200 milligrams per day would usually require drinking two to three glasses of milk per day over and above an overall healthy diet.

However, these recommendations are based on very short-term studies, and are likely to be higher than what people really need. Consumption of calcium and dairy products has been shown to have benefits beyond bone health, possibly lowering the risk of high blood pressure as well as colon cancer. While the blood pressure benefits appear fairly small, the protection against colon cancer seems somewhat larger, and most of the latter benefit comes from having just one glass of milk per day. Getting more than this does not seem to lower risk any further.

Sources of Calcium Food is nearly always a better source of calcium than supplements, if for no other reason than food provides more nutritional benefits than a supplement, and less risk of side effects. Dairy products are a well-known and rich source of calcium. In addition, tofu and certain vegetables are excellent nondairy sources of calcium. Achieving the recommended daily amounts of calcium is not difficult for people whose diets are rich in dairy products. Drinking three or four glasses of skim milk a day, for example, will get you close to your daily requirement through milk alone. But other sources of calcium, as well as calcium supplements, can provide a nondairy source.

Sources of Calcium

FOOD	QUANTITY	CALCIUM (MILLIGRAMS)
Dairy Products		
Blue cheese	1 ounce	183
Ice cream, soft vanilla	1 cup	236
Milk, whole	1 cup	291
Milk, skim	1 cup	302
Mozzarella	1 ounce	147
Parmesan	1 ounce	336
Riccotta, part skim	½ cup	337
Romano	1 ounce	330
Yogurt, frozen	½ cup	147
Yogurt, nonfat	1 cup	415
Beans and Legumes		
Black beans	½ cup cooked	30
Chickpeas	½ cup cooked	45
Soybeans	½ cup cooked	131
Soybeans, dry roasted	½ cup	232
Soy milk	1 cup	46
Tempeh	2 ounces	47
Tofu	2 ounces	154
Vegetables and Fruits		
Boy choy	1 cup	116
Broccoli, cooked	1 cup	132
Collard greens	1 cup	357
Dandelion greens	1 cup	147
Fortified juices	1 cup	300
Kale	1 cup	206
Mustard greens	1 cup	193
Romaine lettuce	1 cup	37
Sea vegetables (wakame)	¼ cup dry	67
Spinach	1 cup	56
Swiss chard	1 cup	128
Turnip greens	1 cup	252
Nuts and Seeds		
Almonds	2 tablespoons	42
Pine nuts	1 ounce	38
Sesame seeds	2 teaspoons	218
Tahini	2 tablespoons	139

Dairy Products Milk is one of the best dietary sources of calcium for two reasons: The lactose (milk sugar) that occurs naturally in milk and the vitamin D added to it enhance calcium absorption through the intestine. This maximizes the amount of calcium your body obtains from each glass you drink. Dairy products have the highest concentration per serving of a highly absorbable form of calcium.

Because whole milk is high in saturated fat, we recommend drinking nonfat milk, which retains all the calcium content and none of the fat. You should also choose skim over reduced-fat (2 percent) and even low-fat (1 percent) milk, unless you really dislike the taste of skim milk. Even low-fat milk (1 percent) has some saturated fat, so you should aim for skim milk as your goal. You can switch gradually, and even blend low-fat and skim milk, gradually decreasing the amount of low-fat milk until you get used to drinking skim milk. Most individuals find that once they switch to skim milk, after a few weeks they do not miss the flavor of whole or low-fat milk.

When consuming other types of dairy products, try to choose non-fat over low-fat or whole-milk yogurt, as it is very similar in taste and texture, yet much healthier. When choosing cheeses, try to find low-fat or part-skim cheeses. For example, when buying mozarella cheese, buy the part-skim version. We doubt you can tell the difference between the whole-milk and the part-skim mozarella. These easy substitutions can make a big difference in the saturated-fat content in your diet.

Nutrition Comparison of Whole, Low-Fat, and Skim Milk

1 CUP	FAT (GRAMS)	CALCIUM (MILLIGRAMS)	CALORIES (CALORIES)
Whole milk	9	276	150
Reduced-fat milk (2%)	5	317	140
Low-fat milk (1%)	2	348	120
nonfat milk	0	285	90

Dairy Products and Lactose Intolerance For some, dairy products are a problem because of lactose intolerance. Millions of Americans are lactose intolerant—they are unable to digest the sugar in milk. Consuming dairy products often causes them physical discomfort—cramping, bloating, gas, and diarrhea. Lactose intolerance is a condition that results from a deficit of lactase, an enzyme produced by the cells lining the small intestine. This enzyme is necessary to digest lactose, the natural sugar found in milk. When your body does not produce enough lactase enzyme, the lactose sugar is not properly broken down in the intestine and travels through the intestines unchanged. This undigested lactose has a laxative effect and stimulates the growth of bacteria that produce gas in your intestines. Usually within thirty minutes to two hours after ingesting lactose from dairy products, abdominal cramping and diarrhea occur. These symptoms can range from mild to severe.

Most of us have plenty of lactase during infancy and early childhood, when milk is our primary source of nutrition. As we get older, there is a gradual decline in the intestinal lactase activity in our body. Certain groups are much more likely to have lactose intolerance. For example, 90 percent of Asians, 70 percent of African-Americans and Native Americans, and 50 percent of Hispanics are lactose intolerant, compared to only about 15 percent of people of Northern European descent.[2]

Lactose intolerance is not necessarily an all-or-nothing phenomenon. Many individuals have something in between that has been termed lactose "maldigestion." These individuals tend to produce enough lactose to permit the consumption of small portions of dairy products without developing digestive symptoms. Tolerance to lactose can be increased when dairy products are gradually introduced into the diet. Many people find that simply consuming lactose with a meal or solid food minimizes problems.

Certain sources of dairy products may be easier for those with lactase deficiency to digest. Cheese may be better tolerated than milk due to a lower lactose content. For example, ripened cheeses may contain up to 95 percent less lactose than whole milk. Cheese is also well tolerated because during the cheese-making process, most of the whey is removed (and the lactose with it). In mature, ripened cheese, lactose disappears entirely within three to four weeks. Specific kinds of cheese that you may tolerate fairly well include cheddar, Colby, Swiss, Parmesan, and cottage cheese. Like cheese, ice cream has less lactose than milk and may therefore be tolerated better. Yogurt containing active cultures also lessens gastrointestinal symptoms. Yogurt that is labeled "active yogurt culture" or "live and active cultures" is generally well tolerated. Frozen yogurt, as well as yogurt containing fruits, sweeteners, or flavorings, will generally not be digested as well as plain yogurt. Frozen yogurt and ice cream, because of their solids and fat content, are tolerated to about the same degree.

A variety of lactose-reduced dairy products—milk, cottage cheese, and processed-cheese slices—are available. Lactose-reduced milks (low fat, skim, nonfat, and calcium-fortified chocolate) with 70 to 100 percent of their lactose hydrolyzed are widely available today. Lactose-reduced cottage cheese, pasteurized processed cheese, and ice cream are also available in some markets.

If there are foods you love but you can't eat them because of lactose intolerance, taking an oral enzyme replacement tablet at the beginning of a meal improves tolerance to lactose in milk or foods. If you can tolerate the lactose equivalent of a cup of milk per serving, you may find it more convenient and less expensive to just drink a small amount of milk with your meals than to take an enzyme replacement.

Vegetables and Calcium Some dark green leafy vegetables are also a good source of calcium, but the form of calcium contained in these vegetables has varying amounts of absorbable calcium. Kale, bok choy, broccoli, and collard greens are good sources. But the calcium found in spinach and chard is not readily absorbable because these vegetables contain oxalic acid, which combines with the calcium to form calcium oxalate, a chemical salt that makes the calcium less available to the body. Consuming calcium-rich vegetables with foods or drinks rich in vitamin C will enhance your body's absorption of calcium. So combine your broccoli or collards with a bit of tomato or a glass of orange juice, and more of the calcium in these vegetables will make its way into your body.

Calcium Supplements If you find it difficult to meet your daily calcium requirement from your diet, calcium supplements can fill the need. Calcium supplements are sold over the counter and come in many forms. While it can make a difference which type of supplement you choose in order to meet your daily requirement of calcium, the most important thing is that you take it.

Many forms of calcium supplements are available: calcium carbonate, calcium citrate, calcium chloride, calcium acetate, calcium gluconate, and others. The more soluble salts, such as calcium citrate, are better absorbed. However, they are expensive. Calcium carbonate is less expensive, and adequately absorbed, so is often recommended as a compromise. Avoid calcium supplements from unrefined oyster shell, bone meal, or dolomite that do not contain the United States Pharmacopeia symbol (USP). There has been some risk in the past that these may contain higher lead levels or other toxic metals. The USP symbol is a voluntary symbol for which product makers apply. When present, it ensures that the product is purified.

Calcium is absorbed best by the body when it is taken several times a day in amounts of 500 milligrams or less. But taking it all at once is better than not taking it at all. Calcium carbonate is absorbed best when taken with food. Calcium citrate can be taken anytime. Calcium and iron impair each other's absorption, so you should not take your calcium supplement at the same time as an iron supplement. The exception to this is when the iron supplement is taken with vitamin C or calcium citrate.

Maximizing Calcium Absorption from Diet or Supplements
Calcium is best absorbed with meals, because the acid load of the meal provides enhanced absorption. Calcium is better absorbed when the diet is rich in fruits and vegetables. Some substances can hinder the absorption of calcium, including oxalic acid (found in spinach and Swiss chard) and phytic acid (found in tea and the outer layers of whole grains). These substances form insoluble compounds with calcium, binding it in such a way that it cannot be absorbed from the intestine. Therefore, you may not

absorb as much calcium in foods containing these substances. High-phosphate drinks (such as soda—in which phosphate is used as a preservative) also impair the absorption of calcium.

There are several other dietary factors that can affect calcium absorption. Vitamin K, which is found mainly in leafy green vegetables, plays an important role in calcium regulation and bone formation. Thus, you need to ensure that you obtain adequate vitamin K. One or more servings per day of broccoli, Brussels spouts, dark green lettuce, collard greens, or kale should give you all you need. In addition, there is some evidence that drinking large amounts of coffee—four or more cups per day—can promote calcium excretion in urine and increase the risk of fracture. You do not need to eliminate caffeine from your diet, but you should limit caffeine to one to two cups of coffee or tea daily. Finally, eating large amounts of protein, such as you might in some fad diets, can leach calcium from your bones. As your body digests protein, it releases acids into the bloodstream, which the body neutralizes by drawing calcium from the bones. Animal protein seems to cause more of this calcium leaching than does vegetable protein.

1. W. Owusu, W.C. Willett, D. Feskanich, A. Ascherio, D. Spiegelman, and G.A. Colditz, "Calcium Intake and the Incidence of Forearm and Hip Fractures Among Men," *Journal of Nutrition* 127 (1997):1782; D. Feskanich, W.C. Willett, M.J. Stampfer, and G.A. Colditz, "Milk, Dietary Calcium, Bone Fractures in Women: A 12-Year Prospective Study," *American Journal of Public Health* 87 (1997):992–97.
2. National Digestive Diseases Information Clearinghouse–National Institute of Diabetes and Digestive and Kidney Diseases, http://digestive.niddk.nih.gov.

CHAPTER 7

children's health

I t is never too early to teach your children good eating habits, expose them to a variety of foods, and encourage their interest in cooking, food, and health. Setting a good example with healthy eating habits and encouraging them to do the same will reap major rewards for you and your children throughout your lives. Even if they deviate from what you have demonstrated and taught them when they become teenagers, often as adults they will return to these good habits that you set as their foundation. You can start as early as the toddler years. In this chapter, we'll start with the toddler years and continue on until adulthood in the following chapters. You may be surprised to learn that the dietary guidelines for you and your children at these different age groups are quite similar.

Expose Kids to New Foods—and Keep Trying Exposing your children to a variety of foods early in life will increase their acceptance of new foods. A study done on flavor exposure in utero indicates that early exposure to a variety of foods is an effective way to enhance your children's acceptance of new foods. In this study, mothers regularly drank carrot juice while pregnant. After birth, the babies and toddlers of these mothers were given carrot juice, and babies exposed to carrot juice in utero were more likely to accept carrot juice than those whose mothers did not drink carrot juice while pregnant. This study points toward early exposure—as early as in utero exposure—making a difference in your children's acceptance of a vast array of tastes.

Even the most resistant to change and finicky of eaters can be broken down with enough trials and enough choices. It is important to remember that just because your child turned down broccoli last month doesn't mean you can't offer it again this month. The more times you try, the more likely the next time your child may accept it. Studies show that it can take ten or more tries before a child will accept a new food, so keep trying and then try again. We resorted to licking with Leo. We put a new food on his plate as often as we can, and when his screaming fit is over—"What's that green stuff on my plate!" or "You're trying to kill me!"—we usually can convince him to lick the broccoli. The next time broccoli appears we encourage him to take a tiny bit (read microscopic here), which he usually proceeds to wash down with half a glass of water. The more times we do this, the bigger the bite gets. Eventually, the morsel of food is visible to the naked eye. You get the picture.

Joe, on the other hand, will eat plates of tofu grilled with vegetables, spicy salsa, and his personal favorite (which he announced to his kindergarten teacher on the first day of school), "pasta with Swiss chard and pine nuts." We did the same exact thing with both of them by exposing them to cooking and new foods and tastes. While parents play a big role in shaping children's eating habits, children are still individuals. In general, though, when parents eat a variety of foods that are low in fat and sugar and high in fiber, children learn to like these foods as well. Do not give up if your child does not like a new food right away.

From Toddlers to Preteens

THE TODDLER YEARS The toddler years can be a challenge. This is the age when your little angel may turn against you when it comes to eating. You may have easily transitioned from the first year of life, when your little one would eat a variety of foods and was willing to try many new things. Suddenly, the toddler years arrive, and many children suddenly realize their power and make certain to let you know who is in charge (and it is not you!). While some children are open and willing to try anything and everything, others are very picky with new foods and textures.

You Cannot Make Them Eat It When dealing with young children, it is important to keep this basic principle in mind: You are not in charge of making them eat. Your role, instead, is to offer a variety of foods in healthy settings. You cannot make them eat it or determine how much they eat. That is your child's job. If you try to take on this job, you are guaranteed to lose. The harder you try, the more they will resist. Instead, you should spend your time and energy providing healthy and exciting meals and snacks at regular intervals. You should try to make meals a social and engaging environment. It will be a joy for you to watch them learn to relish food and take part in preparation (albeit a bit messy). There is so much to be learned in the kitchen—science, nutrition, the joy of good food. It is a great place to gather the family, and starting early in the toddler years will get you on your way.

Basic Nutrition for Toddlers There is nothing mysterious about a young child's diet, which is quite similar to your own. Your toddler should eat the same basic food types that you do, but there are some differences in quantity. Here are the basics of the food groups and the approximate daily number of servings you should aim for:

Recommended Food Servings for Toddlers

FOOD GROUP	DAILY SERVINGS	SERVING SIZE
Breads and cereals	6	¼–½ slice bread; 4 tablespoons cereal, rice, pasta; 1–2 crackers
Vegetables	2–3	1 tablespoon for each year of age
Fruits	2–3	½ piece; ½ cup cooked or canned; 2–4 ounces juice
Dairy	2–3	½ cup milk; ½ ounce cheese; ⅓ cup yogurt
Protein	2	1 ounce meat, fish, poultry, tofu; ½ egg
Legumes (beans, peas, lentils)	2	2 tablespoons cooked

Toddlers need about one thousand calories a day to meet their needs for growth, energy, and good nutrition. You can divide the foods among three small meals and two snacks a day. It is not necessary to have each food group represented in the exact amount at every meal or even every day. This is a general guide to follow so that on average, after a week of eating, these serving numbers can be followed. It is also important to keep in mind the quality of the foods within each group and to choose a variety of foods within each group to make healthy choices. Choose unrefined breads and cereals; limit red meat; expose them to a variety of beans and legumes. The eating habits of toddlers are erratic and unpredictable from one day to the next—your child may eat everything in sight at breakfast but almost nothing else for the rest of the day. Or he may eat only his favorite food for three days in a row, then reject it entirely the next day.

CHILDREN SIX TO TWELVE YEARS By the age of six, your child is likely to have developed some clear and specific ideas about her likes and dislikes in foods. Try to accommodate your child's tastes as much as possible, as long as the choices are within reason. Boys and girls between the ages of six and ten require about 1,800 to 2,400 calories each day depending on height, growth rate, and physical activity. This number rises considerably as children head into puberty. Girls begin to require about 200 calories per day more between the ages of ten and twelve. Boys start to need about 500 calories per day more after age twelve. These additional calories and nutrients help fuel the incredible growth that occurs during adolescence.

Breads, Cereals, Rice, and Pasta Grains should begin to constitute the majority of a toddler's diet and by age five should constitute 50 to 60 percent of it. Not all breads and cereals are equal in their nutritional value. You will want to avoid highly processed white breads and instead emphasize whole grains. When preparing sandwiches on bread, use whole wheat instead of white. If serving rice as your grain, try brown rice. Mix whole-grain pasta in with regular pasta, or try some spinach, tomato, or other colorful pasta for variety. If you are packing crackers for an easy on-the-

Recommended Food Servings for Children Ages Six Through Twelve

FOOD GROUP	DAILY SERVINGS	SERVING SIZE
Breads, cereals, rice, and pasta	6 servings	1 slice of bread, ½ bagel ¾ cup ready-to-eat cereal ½ cup cooked cereal ½ cup cooked pasta or rice 5–6 whole-grain crackers
Vegetables	2–3 servings	¼–½ cup cooked vegetables ½–1 cup raw vegetables
Fruit	2–3 servings	1 piece of fruit, ½ cup canned fruit ½ cup juice
Dairy products	3 servings	¾–1 cup low-fat or nonfat milk 1–1½ ounces low-fat cheese 1 cup low-fat or nonfat yogurt
Meat, fish, poultry, and legumes	2 servings	2–3 ounces of cooked lean meat, poultry, fish, or tofu, 1 egg, ½ cup cooked dry beans, or 2 tablespoons peanut butter

go snack, choose whole-grain varieties that are not made with hydrogenated oils. If you are serving cereal, emphasize those made from whole grains and avoid the presweetened ones. You can always add a bit of sugar yourself, and in this manner you control the amount of sweetener. You'd be surprised to know how much sugar is in presweetened cereals.

While it is important to expose your children to whole grains and get them used to these flavors and textures, you do not need to be militant in your approach. You are not poisoning your children if you allow them to eat white bread. Having said this, I would not make Wonder bread your first choice—you want them to learn to love good food. Take them to a local bakery—an artisan one if it's nearby—and expose them to the joys of freshly baked French bread. Our children love nothing more than a trip to our favorite local bakery in Brookline, the Clearflour Bakery, where Joe loves the olive rolls and Leo loves the traditional French bread. You can also bake bread with them in the kitchen. There is nothing more wonderful than the aroma of freshly baked bread in the oven.

Vegetables and Fruit There is no one vegetable or fruit that provides all the vitamins and nutrients you and your children need. You should aim for variety—the wider array of fruits and vegetables you consume, the more likely your children are to obtain the nutrients they need to stay healthy and prevent future disease. This can be a challenge with children, who often find one fruit or vegetable they'll eat and then will not eat any other. Remember your job—to present a variety of foods. You can't make them eat it. Just keep trying and eventually you just might succeed.

While fruit juice is fine as one option in this category, you don't want to overemphasize this source of fruit. Try to limit juice to one serving per day. Whole fruits contain fiber and other nutrients that may be missing in juice. Juice contains almost as much sugar as soda, and too much can decrease your child's appetite at mealtimes. It can also cause diarrhea. Water is always a good choice for quenching your child's thirst. And don't forget dried fruit—it is convenient, can be kept in your pantry, and is often appealing to children. The more variety of fruits you offer your children, the better.

Dairy Products and Calcium After age two, you can switch from whole milk to low-fat milk, and then eventually to skim milk. While your children do need calcium from dairy products, you want to minimize the saturated fat in their diets, which dairy products contain. You can retain all the benefits of the nutrients from dairy without the saturated fat by switching to low-fat and skim versions.

Making sure your toddler or preschooler gets enough calcium should be a priority. Sufficient calcium now can mean stronger, healthier bones for your child later. Children ages one to three require 500 milligrams of calcium each day (about 13 ounces of milk, 10 ounces of yogurt, or 3.5 ounces of mozzarella cheese); from age four to age eight, the requirement is 800 milligrams each day (about 21 ounces of milk, 15 ounces of yogurt, or 5 ounces of mozzarella cheese). After age eight, the requirement jumps to 1,300 milligrams per day (about 35 ounces of milk, 25 ounces of yogurt, or 9 ounces of mozzarella cheese). You can meet these guidelines by offering your children good sources of calcium such as:

- low-fat or nonfat milk
- low-fat or nonfat yogurt or frozen yogurt
- low-fat cheese
- tofu
- calcium-fortified fruit juices
- ice cream (occasionally)

Meat, Fish, Poultry, and Legumes Like adults, it is important to limit red meat to about once a week in your child's diet. Introduce your children to fish early in their lives, and they may be more likely to accept it. Serve poultry without the skin. You may find success in introducing beans and legumes into your child's diet if you serve them in the form of a burrito—kids love them. There are several kid-tested burrito dishes found in the recipe section that will give you an idea of how to prepare them simply and quickly. Try the Tofu and Pinto Bean Burritos (see page 228) or the Carnitas and Black Bean Burritos (see page 282). They are nutrition packed. And don't forget nuts as a heart-healthy protein source. Joe loves Rice Noodles with Peanut Sauce and Broccoli (see page 342). Nuts are also terrific packed in school lunches and make great snacks-on-the go.

Fat Recent research has shown that monounsaturated fats, such as olive oil, and polyunsaturated fats, such as fatty acids from fish and nuts, can be a healthy part of the diet, in addition to adding wonderful flavors to foods and a general feeling of satiety. It is healthier to make the majority of fat your children consume come from unsaturated sources, such as canola, corn, safflower, and sunflower oils. Olive oil is monounsaturated, which has been shown to have a cholesterol-lowering effect, and is also a good choice.

Saturated fat in the diet raises blood cholesterol and increases the risk of heart disease later in life. High blood cholesterol causes the buildup of fatty deposits on the inside of arteries (atherosclerosis), which can lead to heart attacks later in life. Researchers have found fatty streaks that can precede such fat deposits in the arteries of children starting as young as age ten, and in many more children after age fifteen. In addition to saturated fat, hydrogenated, or trans fats (which are found in margarine, prepared baked goods, fried foods, and some crackers), also share this undesirable property. So start good health habits early, not only because you want to teach your children well but also because heart disease can begin in youth.

You can limit saturated and hydrogenated fat in your child's diet by:

- switching from whole milk to low-fat or nonfat milk
- serving more fish, poultry, nuts, beans, and legumes, and cutting back on red meat
- removing the skin from poultry and trimming fat from meats
- reducing butter and margarine by using cooking methods such as baking, broiling, grilling, poaching, and steaming
- reading labels and choosing crackers and packaged snacks that are not made with hydrogenated oils

It is important to keep in mind that an ultra-low-fat diet is not necessary or even healthy for children. Fat in the diet enables them to absorb the fat-soluble vitamins A, D, E, and K and plays a role in the ability of blood to clot so that cuts stop bleeding. Fat is necessary for production of hormones that help in development in boys, girls, and pregnancy. Choose fats from vegetable oils and nuts as the primary means of meeting this need.

Taming the Sweet Tooth Almost everyone has a sweet tooth, and the attraction to sweets can make it difficult to keep children from choosing candy, cookies, and cakes over healthier fare. You can't do much to take the sweet tooth out of the kid, but you can keep sweets out of your pantry. Children who feast on sugary foods wind up with little appetite for better food choices, so let sweets be a once-in-a-while snack. This way you'll help your child develop a taste for other foods. Allow your child to enjoy the birthday cake, ice cream, chocolate bars, and other treats that are such a sweet and memorable part of childhood. Simply make sure these foods are eaten in moderation, and balance the treats with more healthful fare at mealtimes. Our children eat dessert after dinner, but we always make certain they have eaten a healthy meal before giving them a few cookies or ice cream.

Adolescents and Food

ADOLESCENT HEALTH Raising adolescents is a challenge in many ways. One area in which you play a big role is in your adolescent's attitude toward diet and nutrition. You are in a unique position to provide your adolescent with the skills necessary to foster lifelong healthy eating behaviors and physical activity. You can teach them to make appealing meals, keep nutritious food readily available, and limit access to junk food. In addition, role modeling from you influences the behavior and attitudes of your adolescent in a major way.

RESPECT AND EMPOWER THEM Treat your adolescent with respect. Educate yourself so that you can give tailored guidance about dietary habits, safe weight management, and the benefits of a healthful diet. Teach them about their body, physical exercise, and nutrition. Teach them to cook for themselves. There is no better way to do this than to set the example yourself through your own diet and exercise routines. In this manner, they can be equal partners in caring for their health. This empowers them while at the same time educating them about important health topics. Connect with your adolescents over meals. Low family connectedness has been associated with inadequate consumption of fruits, vegetables, and dairy foods.

What your adolescent eats outside the home is, to a degree, out of your control. But he will eat the majority of his meals and snacks at home, so you can set an example, provide food in the house, and prepare meals that will not only interest him but be good for him as well. You should, however, read this chapter knowing that despite your best efforts, your adolescent may foil your attempts. This does not mean you should give up. Keep trying—your influence can make long-term differences that you may not see the results of for many years.

PREVENT HEALTH PROBLEMS THROUGH DIET A good diet can prevent many health problems, including iron deficiency, obesity, eating disorders, malnutrition, and dental caries. Additional issues that can involve teen nutrition include diminished school performance, behavioral problems, and use of unsafe weight-loss methods. There are also chronic diseases in adults that are influenced by nutrition at this young age, including osteoporosis, cardiac disease, obesity, hypertension, hypercholesterolemia, stroke, diabetes, and diet-related cancers. Eating well now is an investment in your adolescent's future health.

A TIME OF RAPID GROWTH AND DEVELOPMENT As you are likely witnessing, adolescence is a time of rapid growth and development. During puberty, your child gains 50 percent of her adult weight, 50 percent of her adult skeleton, and 20 percent of her adult height. Good nutrition and regular exercise will maximize healthy gains. Annual surveys by the U.S. Department of Agriculture continue to show that most teens, regardless of ethnicity, income, gender, or education, do not eat diets that meet current nutritional recommendations.

Calories Caloric requirements are based upon age, height, and gender. Peak requirements occur between the ages of eleven to fourteen for girls and fifteen to eighteen for boys, reflecting puberty. So if your children are eating you out of house and home at these ages, know that it won't last forever, and if it does, it is okay to set some limits. We like to say "kitchen is closed!" Teaching your children the principle of restrained eating at this age is an important life skill. Girls require about 2,200 calories daily, and boys need 2,500 to 3,000 each day.

PROTEIN Protein needs are greatest during teens' periods of active growth. Most teens in this country meet or exceed their needs for

Recommended Food Servings for Teens

FOOD GROUP	DAILY SERVINGS	SERVING SIZE
Breads, cereals, rice, and pasta	6–11 servings	1 slice of bread, ½ bagel ¾ cup ready-to-eat cereal ½ cup cooked cereal ½ cup cooked pasta or rice 5–6 whole-grain crackers
Vegetables	3–5 servings	¼–½ cup cooked vegetables ½–1 cup raw vegetables
Fruit	2–4 servings	1 piece of fruit, ½ cup canned fruit ½ cup juice
Dairy products	3 or 4 servings	¾–1 cup low-fat or nonfat milk 1–1½ ounces low-fat cheese 1 cup low-fat or nonfat yogurt
Meat, fish, poultry, and legumes	2 or 3 servings	2–3 ounces of cooked lean meat, poultry, fish, or tofu, 1 egg, ½ cup cooked dry beans, or 2 tablespoons peanut butter

protein, including vegetarians. Two to three servings of protein are recommended daily. One serving of protein consists of 2 to 3 ounces of meat, poultry, or fish; one-half cup of cooked dry beans; one egg; or two tablespoons of peanut butter. These are smaller amounts of protein than the typical adolescent consumes, thus rarely is protein deficiency a problem. Rather, emphasis should be placed on protein choices that are lower in saturated fat. Entice them with beef and tofu in a jazzy taco with our Oven-Baked Tacos (see page 348). Treat them to Smoky Backyard Chicken (see page 259). Whip up a delicious smoothie with silken tofu hidden inside with our Pineapple-Orange Smoothie (see page 366). And don't forget hiding soy milk and silken tofu in our special version of Mashed Potatoes (see page 309) for that meat-and-potatoes kid.

FAT Your adolescent needs some fat in the diet. Fats carry the fat-soluble vitamins A, D, E, and K into the blood. Fat also provides the essential fatty acids omega 3 and omega 6 fatty acids. Without fats, the body cannot get these vitamins and essential fatty acids. Deficiencies of these vitamins is rare, though, because the body can store these vitamins, and because fat in the diet is generally no problem for the average adolescent.

Teach your adolescents to read and interpret food labels and how to avoid foods that are high in saturated and hydrogenated fats. Teach them to limit fried foods, fast foods, and mayonnaise-based salads such as tuna and chicken salad, since all tend to be high in fat content. If they are having that fat craving for a hamburger and French fries, teach them to limit fat in their meals for the remainder of that day. Don't follow this type of lunch with fried chicken for dinner, but rather choose a dinner on the lower end of the fat spectrum, such as a bean-based burrito or a light chicken dish. This give-and-take method for keeping the average fat and calorie content in the healthful range is a good system for lifelong eating.

CALCIUM AND VITAMIN D Calcium intake during adolescence is crucial for achieving peak bone mass. Bone mineralization of the skeleton increases up to about age twenty-five to thirty, after which time, bone mass is lost steadily. Adolescence is a time of peak calcium absorption and retention. Thus osteoporosis and subsequent osteoporotic fractures can develop later in life if adequate calcium is not taken in during this crucial time of growth of the skeleton. Both calcium and vitamin D are needed in the diet to achieve adequate calcium balance in the body.

WEIGHT CONCERNS AND EATING DISORDERS Eating disorders are of special concern as children head into adolescence. Young girls are particularly at risk for developing a poor body image. They see society's obsession with thinness and then starve themselves (anorexia nervosa) or binge and purge (bulimia). Although eating disorders are generally not a problem until after puberty begins, parents should be alert to any danger signs an older school-age child exhibits. Preoccupation with weight and size, a drastic reduction in food intake, or a lack of weight gain despite a large appetite can mean a child may have an eating disorder. Check with your pediatrician for help, since eating disorders can lead to serious health problems and even death. Counseling can successfully guide these children through this difficult time.

Recently, we are seeing a trend growing in some groups of adolescent boys in this area. The development of eating disorders is believed to be related to several factors: personality, self-image, family influences, peer pressures, and sociocultural pressures.

MEDIA AND BODY IMAGE In Western cultures, dissatisfaction with weight and shape is prevalent because the ideal body shape and weight are unattainable for most women. The media is one source believed to encourage girls to form unrealistically thin body ideals. In general, the more frequently girls are exposed to media that depict unrealistically thin models and actresses, the more likely it is that a girl will become concerned with her weight or develop an eating disorder. Some girls who are overweight will be more dissatisfied with their weight because of media images and may then engage in bulimic behaviors. Of course, eating disorders are a complex issue, and multiple causes are involved. With obesity rising in our youth, this increases the population that is at risk for developing weight concerns, bad dieting habits, and bulimic behaviors. The impact of the media on boys is not as well known.

While you cannot entirely control the influence of the media on your children, you can limit the amount of time they are exposed to TV, and limit the types of magazines in your home. The studies on adolescents show more exposure is worse, so limiting the quantity is one way you can control these outside influences on your children, even if you can't control the actual content. In addition, you can explain and emphasize to them that diet and exercise are important for their health, not just for physical beauty.

The media is not the only source of pressure to be thin. Weight-control behaviors among young girls are modeled partially on their mothers' behavior. Several studies have observed that girls whose mothers diet and are concerned with their weight and shape are more likely than their peers to develop unhealthy weight-control practices. Data is lacking on boys, but there is one study that observed that the comments made by mothers had a larger impact than those by fathers, and that daughters were more affected than were sons by the comments. But comments by both parents criticizing a child's weight should be avoided.

Your role is, therefore, to be a role model and health educator. Teach your children about a varied diet, rich in fruits and vegetables. Teach them about moderation and restrained eating. Even if they are of normal weight, they should not be allowed to eat everything and anything they want. When their growth slows down, these habits will be hard to break. Teach them to enjoy and savor their food. Teach them that meals are a family and social affair, and that food preparation is fun to do with family and friends. Your kids may even think you are cool, and certainly their friends will want to eat at your house, where the food is great and the company is even better.

YOUNG ATHLETES While all parents of school-age kids should be stressing the importance of physical activity, it's also important to monitor the eating habits of young athletes. Although everything possible should be done to offer them optimal nutrition to support their efforts, it's also crucial to avoid some risky behavior that can be associated with intense competition. Help your child to understand that his peak athletic performance depends on a balanced and varied diet.

Children should be urged to drink plenty of water when they exercise. For every half hour of strenuous activity, your child should drink an extra 8 to 12 ounces of water—the drink of choice. When drinking sports drinks, avoid those that are high in sugar. Also, make sure your child balances practice and performance with adequate rest and relaxation. These are as necessary to well-being as proper nutrition.

Three Meals a Day for Good Health

BREAKFAST Whether your child eats a full breakfast at home, eats a quick breakfast on the ride to school, or buys a cafeteria breakfast once she gets there, there is no meal that is more important than the first one of the day. Studies show that kids who skip breakfast or eat unhealthy foods, such as doughnuts or pastries, can have a hard time concentrating just a few hours later. To make breakfast a success, find foods your child likes to eat and serve them in the morning, even if they're not traditional breakfast foods. Leo likes to eat leftover pizza at 7 A.M. These options beat sugary cereals and cakes nutritionally, and they will help your child do her best all morning long, whether at school or play. Cold cereal is a simple and healthy solution. If, like most kids, your child loves cereals, buy the lower-sugar or unsweetened varieties and sweeten them up with slices of fruit or raisins. At some point your child may ask you to buy some high-sugar, low-nutrition cereal. We use this sweat cereal as a mix-in with a healthier cereal as the base. On weekends, make breakfast fun by cooking pancakes together and letting everyone help. Choose lower-fat turkey bacon or soy-based breakfast sausages.

LUNCH It can be a challenge to send foods that are healthy and appealing when packing lunches for your child each day. Involve your youngster in the preparation by asking her to help pack her lunch box, encouraging her to pack healthy foods she enjoys as well as the occasional treat. This activity of selecting her own lunch may make your child less likely to trade her food for less nutritious items her friends may have or to throw it away. Teach your child that a bag lunch needs to be well-rounded by packing something from each of the food groups: protein, grains, fruits, vegetables, and dairy. Here are some healthful ideas:

- For protein, try water-packed tuna, sliced ham or turkey, chili, baked beans, peanut butter, nut mixes, or hard-boiled eggs.
- For grains, try whole-grain breads and crackers, low-fat bran muffins, or pretzels.
- For fruits and vegetables, try sliced fresh fruit, dried fruit mixes, carrot and celery sticks, or a thermos of cooked vegetables.
- For dairy, try low-fat milk, a container of low-fat yogurt, low-fat cheese, or a scoop of low-fat cottage cheese.

SNACKS Kids in this age group are often big snackers. Snacking can be a very healthy way to eat if you help them make the right choices. It is very easy to let unwanted saturated and hydrogenated fat and calories creep into a child's diet through snacks, so keep good-tasting alternatives at hand:

- popcorn
- fresh fruit
- celery and carrot sticks

- raisins and other dried fruits
- low-fat or nonfat yogurt
- low-sugar cereals
- unsweetened applesauce
- frozen fruit juice on a stick
- whole-grain crackers (made without hydrogenated oil)
- fresh fruit juice
- pretzels
- trail mix (dried fruit and nuts mixed together)

DINNER You can keep dinner interesting by allowing your child to participate in the planning and purchasing of meals. Encourage your child to design menus, choosing at least one favorite food for each meal, and then take him to the supermarket to buy food for the week. As you shop, explain the choices you make. You and your children can read food labels together and learn how to compare the nutritional content of different foods and different brands. You are giving your children the tools to make healthy food choices for the rest of their lives.

Your child can help out in the kitchen, too: Teach her how to wash and trim vegetables and measure and pour ingredients. Instruct your child on food safety and the safe use of the microwave and stove. By age ten, many kids are comfortable cooking and can be trusted with small heating or baking chores, as long as an adult is close by. Simply being involved in the preparation can make a meal tastier to a child (see chapter 9, "Kids in the Kitchen").

Make dinner the meal for which the family gathers together. Try new and delicious foods from the recipe section, and your family will be certain to keep coming back for more.

family mealtimes— a family that eats together stays healthy and happy

Today's families lead hectic lives. Parents work in and outside the home, coordinate child care, and run complicated households. Children are busy with school, homework, friends, and after-school activities. It can be easy to fall into the trap of spending little or no quality time as a family at the end of the day. Sitting down together to catch up with each other has been shown in study after study to be critically important to your family's well-being.[1] Spending this kind of time with your children is vitally important if you want to help them be successful in school, be informed about their friends and activities, and keep them out of trouble. In addition, research has shown that children who spend more time in the company of adults develop

101

better conversation and decision-making skills. Finally, when parents and children eat together, they are more likely to enjoy a healthy variety of foods.[2] Getting the whole family together at dinnertime can be a great way to interact with your children and to make sure your family makes time for each other. Conversation over the dinner table is something that can make such a difference to your children's health and happiness. When families sit down and eat together, they're more likely to know what's happening with one another.

Value the Evening Meal You can demonstrate that you value the evening meal by making it a daily priority. Organizing this gathering involves a mix of the right attitude, planning, and some cooking skills. It also involves making a commitment to doing it, and sticking with this plan. Your kids should know that dinnertime is not the time to go to a friend's house, watch TV, or do homework.

Getting Started It can seem daunting to plan a meal for the whole family after working a long day away from home, or spending the whole day doing housework, transporting children, and running a household. But with a bit of planning, practice, and a few skills, it can become an easy habit. If you make a commitment, you can make it work. If your children are older, three meals a week may be a more realistic goal. Pick the number of nights you want to eat together as a goal and stick to it. Make it a mandatory event.

There is worry that the family meal is on the decline. Studies show that families with younger children eat together more often than families with older children. Families with teenagers eat together less often because the teens have more evening activities than younger children. Not only do teens have more activities including part-time jobs, sports, boyfriends, and girlfriends, but they can drive or bike to the activities independently. Studies have shown that the varied schedules of family members interfere the most with family meals, especially with adolescents. However, studies show that despite many outside interests, families express a strong commitment to eating together and believe that eating dinner together is important to building a strong family. So your challenge will be in the scheduling. You may need to vary your dinner hour to maximize your number of evenings together. You can lead by example by scheduling your own day so that the dinner hour is reserved for family time. So don't let your family meal decline. Knowing that there is scientific evidence about its benefits may help you to take the time and effort to make it happen in your family.

Make It Age Appropriate Match your expectations to your child's age. Keep in mind that sitting down for a family meal can be difficult for very young children. Some toddlers can sit in their highchairs and enjoy trying different foods for thirty to forty-five minutes. Others can do so for only five minutes. A two-year-old who doesn't want to sit still for more than five minutes can't be expected to sit for half an hour at a dinner table. But by the time they are five, most children can sit at the table and start to learn good table manners, enjoy conversation, and participate in the evening meal.

Communication One of the primary benefits of eating together is strengthening the family by providing opportunities for communication and building relationships.

Not only do parents want to feel attached to their kids, kids want this too. Oprah Winfrey conducted a "Family Dinner Experiment" in 1993. Five families volunteered to accept the challenge to eat dinner together every night for a month, staying at the table for a half hour each time. As part of the experiment, all family members kept journals to record their feelings about the experience. At first, sharing meals was a chore for many families, and the minutes at the table dragged on. But, by the end of the month, the families were happy and planned to continue dining together most evenings, if not every night. When the families appeared on the *Oprah* show at the end of the experiment, the greatest surprise to the parents was how much their children treasured the dependable time with their parents at the table.

Better School Performance Family meals appear to give children an edge in the classroom. Preschoolers have better language skills when the family eats together.[3] It is thought that mealtimes serve as an opportunity for young children to have longer conversations with parents and to hear words they rarely would hear at other times of the day. Researchers believe that extended conversations provide young children with a chance to think, and this enhances their linguistic development. Children who regularly eat dinner with their families four or more times a week score better on standardized tests than those who eat family dinners three or fewer times a week. These results cross racial lines and are not influenced by whether children are in a one- or two-parent family. Researchers have found that children ages seven to eleven who do well on school achievement tests spend a large amount of time eating meals and snacks with their families. Their achievement is not affected by their mother's employment status.

Better Adjustment When researchers evaluated which activities fostered healthy child development—play, story time, events with family members—family dinners won out. According to psychologists, well-adjusted adolescents and frequent family meals are linked.[4] In a survey of teens ages twelve to eighteen, those who were best adjusted ate a meal with an adult in their family an average of 5.4 days a week, compared to 3.3 days for teens who didn't show good adjustment.[5] The well-adjusted teens were less likely to do drugs or be depressed and were more motivated at school and had better personal relationships. Adjustment was correlated more to shared meals than to any other factor including gender, age, or family type.

Better Nutrition Researchers have found that students in grades four to six who eat dinners with their families consume more vegetables, more fruit and juice, and less soda. Researchers from Harvard Medical School assessed the eating habits of more than fifteen thousand boys and girls ages nine to fourteen.[6] When the children ate with their families, they used more low-fat practices such as trimming fat from meat and using low-fat foods at meals. In the Harvard study, children who ate family dinners most days consumed more fruits and vegetables and fewer fried foods, saturated fats, trans fats, and soda than children who ate dinner with family members only a few days a week or less. Children who ate dinners with family members most days had substantially higher intakes of dietary fiber, calcium, iron, folate, and many vitamins.

In addition to these nutritional benefits at your own supper table, research tells us that your children, both younger and older, will eat better when they are not with you. The habits you help instill in them at home lead to better food choices when they are away from home—in the school cafeteria, in restaurants, and at friends' houses. Eating healthy outside the home is the same for children regardless of their body mass index, physical activity level, number of hours they watch television, parenting arrangement, household income, and mother's work status. It appears that the nutritional benefit of a meal together transcends a host of other influences.

Research Shows That Children Eat by Example Research shows that you play a pivotal role in determining how your children perceive food, define a healthful diet, and develop eating habits. It is likely that our feelings about food are passed on to our children. If we as parents do not have a healthy approach to food, our children may lose the ability to properly respond to their feelings of hunger and satiety. For example, children of parents who restrict their own eating, such as on fat diets, or who eat impulsively have greater increases in body fat when compared with those children whose parents are more relaxed in their eating habits and do not eat on impulse. Whether a child is just beginning to eat solid foods or is a teenager with established food preferences, parents can make a difference.

Nutritionists suggest that nutrition-savvy parents keep the

refrigerator and cabinets stocked with a variety of nutritious foods, like fruits, vegetables, low-fat dairy products, whole-grain breads, nuts, and dried fruits. Offer young children new foods more than once—it often takes several encounters for them to learn to like something different. For kids who seem to eat the same foods over and over, mealtime is a good time to exercise some direction over their choices by offering well-balanced dishes and limiting sweets and snacks.

Prepare Together—Relax Together To make the family meal work well and persist over time, you'll need to plan meals that are simple and quick. Assign tasks to the whole family, so that the burden is not all on you. Much of the time, this preparation time can be worthwhile and rewarding to all involved. Young children can set and clear the table. Older children can help with meal preparation—chopping vegetables, pounding chicken breasts, or setting out pots of water to boil. Teaching your children valuable cooking skills will serve them well throughout their lives. Make the mealtime peaceful and uninterrupted by turning off the television and unplugging the phone. Make certain young children speak in "indoor" voices. Then sit down and savor the food and the time together. Be a good role model in conversation by listening without interrupting. Relax, interact, and have fun together.

1. T.M. Videon and C.K. Manning, "Influences on Adolescent Eating Patterns: The Importance of the Family Meal." *Journal of Adolescent Health* 32 (2003):365–73; M.W. Gillman, S.L. Rifas-Shiman, A.L. Frazier, et al., "Family Dinner and Diet Quality among Older Children and Adolescents," *Archives of Family Medicine* 9 (2000):235–40.
2. K.N. Boutell, A.S. Birnbaum, L.A. Lytle, D.M. Murray, and M. Story, "Associations Between Perceived Family Meal Environment and Parent Intake of Fruit, Vegetables and Fat," *Journal of Nutrition, Education, and Behavior* 35 (2003):24–29.
3. L. Lynn, "Language-Rich Home and School Environments Are Key to Reading Success," http://www.edletter.org/past/issues/1997-ja/language.shtml, 1997; E. Reese "Predicting Children's Literacy from Mother-Child Conversations," *Cognitive Development* 10 (1995):381–405.

4. Dwight B. Heath, "Being an Effective Parent Requires Making the Time to Do So," *Brown University Child and Adolescent Behavior Letter* 14 (1998):8.

5. S. Carpenter, "Teens' Risky Behavior Is about More than Race and Family Resources," *Monitor on Psychology* 32 (2001):22–23.

6. M.W. Gillman, S.L. Rifas-Shiman, A.L. Frazier, H.R. Rockett, C.A. Camargo, Jr, A.E. Field, C.S. Berkey, and G.A. Colditz, "Family Dinner and Diet Quality among Older Children and Adolescents," *Archives of Family Medicine* 9 (2000):235–40.

CHAPTER 9

kids in the kitchen

Children bring great enthusiasm, boundless energy, and an innate desire to help into the kitchen. They love cooking and being a part of the hustle and bustle that is inherent in preparing meals. Children learn by touching, tasting, feeling, smelling, and listening. They love to help prepare food and cook because they can use all their senses. Cooking takes advantage of the natural receptivity in children, especially since they love to eat the foods they make. Cooking can even be a fun education experience. For example, a particular meal can involve learning about foods cooked by a foreign culture, their farming history, geography, folklore, literature, music, dance, crafts, and other artistic traditions. The natural sciences can be taught through cooking and the use of the scientific method by observing the properties of ingredients and their combinations. Mathematical concepts can be reinforced through measuring and weighing foods.

Because of children's natural interest in food and cooking, it has become popular to offer formal cooking classes for kids. While this is a fine extracurricular activity, you can also accomplish this by teaching your children in your own kitchen. Why not buy groceries with the money you would have used for the class fee and instead teach your children to cook and learn about nutrition and health?

From the time our kids could stand, they have been part of meal preparations in our home. At first they weren't doing any real cooking, but they were sticking their hands into the flour bin, turning the mixer on and off (almost always at the wrong times), and cracking or, rather, smashing eggs. We have fond memories of them dragging over a stool to watch us whenever we used the mixer so they could help. They knew that flour, one of their favorite ingredients, was going to be involved and they didn't want to miss any of the action. As time has passed, they have gained some basic skills and have learned some interesting facts along the way.

Using Their Senses While cooking with your children, explain to them the role their senses play in the preparation of a meal. Slowly cook thinly sliced garlic in olive oil and let them savor the delightful aroma. Toast nuts in a skillet and they will become aware of the connection between the changing aroma and the color of the nuts. To illustrate how important their eyes are in cooking, prepare pancakes with them. Have them flip the pancakes when bubbles appear on the surface. Show them how to use their sense of touch while cooking. Sear a steak in a pan and have them press on it to feel its firmness. Tell them that the firmer it is, the more well done the meat will be. While making bread, allow them to poke the risen dough. Tell them if it fails to spring back, the dough is ready for another rising or shaping. Teach them to season and taste their creations at various intervals and they will quickly realize how food changes flavor during cooking.

More of a Hindrance than a Help Since cooking with children combines fun with learning, it's a great activity. But in the beginning they are definitely more of a hindrance than a help. It certainly is less complicated to cook without having to maneuver around a pair of tiny hands. And things are definitely messier when kids are involved. Of course, there have been plenty of times when we were in a rush to get dinner on the table and purposely got our kids involved in another activity so we could work quickly. But most of the time, when they want to help in the kitchen, they are warmly welcomed. Their presence brings a warmth and laughter that is more precious than efficiency in the kitchen. Eventually, when you see them learning some skills and gaining some proficiency, you will be rewarded.

Kitchen Safety Your children's first lesson should be kitchen safety. Too many accidents occur in the kitchen because of carelessness or lack of attention to the task at hand. These safety lessons are invaluable and will enhance your children's confidence in every kitchen project they tackle. Teach them important safety techniques:

- Show them how to turn pot handles toward the stove so they don't protrude into the walking area.
- Demonstrate the sharpness of your knives and explain to them why they are carefully stored on a wall magnet or in a block and not in a drawer with other utensils. This way when you reach into a cluttered and dark drawer you will not get cut.
- Help older children to hold a knife correctly and show them how to chop with the fingers of their other hand curled under to prevent accidents. Allow your youngsters to use an oyster or butter knife to practice this technique while cutting a potato.
- Let them turn the mixer on and off while you explain to them the dangers involved in touching the attachment while it is still spinning. Do the same with the food processor and make it clear how all the safety features need to be engaged in order for the machine to operate.
- Show them how to stand away from a pot of simmering liquid while removing the lid and allowing the steam to dissipate before putting your face or hands near the pot.

- Demonstrate how to safely open the oven door while the oven is on so you aren't in the direct line of the escaping heat.

Cleanliness Cleanliness is also an aspect of safety. You can start with some very basic microbiology. Teach them to wash their hands to remove any germs before starting to prepare food, and again after touching any raw meat or poultry. Show them how to wash fruit and vegetables to remove any dirt and germs. When working with meat and poultry, emphasize the importance of using separate plates for raw and cooked food. Teach them to wash the cutting board and knives used in preparing the raw meat and poultry with hot, soapy water prior to using them again to avoid cross contamination in the kitchen.

Education in the Kitchen Cooking with your children exposes them to organized thinking. They will realize that there is a clearly defined process to cooking meals. Involve them in all the stages of preparation from planning and shopping to stowing the groceries. Ask them what they would like to eat. Discuss and list the ingredients that are needed to create the meal. Kids are more apt to eat something they had a hand in planning and making. When it is time to cook, pull out the recipe and emphasize that great cooking is a simple process of following several steps in a particular order. If you have forgotten a particular ingredient, improvise; this will highlight the creative aspect of cooking.

When your children are helping in the kitchen, it is a wonderful teaching opportunity. It is important, though, not to alienate them by making it too much like school. It has to be fun or it won't be successful. The mere mashing of a potato or peeling of a banana enhances a young child's sensory awareness, develops his early motor skills, and allows him to interact with you by exploring a part of the adult world. Two-year-olds can scrub vegetables and fruits, tear lettuce for salad, and snap the tips off green beans. Three-year-olds can pour liquids into a batter and help mix it, and knead bread dough. Four- and five-year-olds can mash soft fruits and vegetables, measure dry and liquid ingredients, and crack and beat eggs. Older children can be taught math concepts, science, language, and cultures. In addition, older children will see that they are helping you by doing something adult.

Working with recipes is a great way to allow children of varying ages to grasp a variety of math skills. Young children can learn how to measure and begin simple addition. Show them a one-cup measure. Tell them that there are eight ounces in a cup and ask them how many ounces are in two cups. Introduce older children to fractions by using a pizza as an example. Slice one of your delicious homemade pizzas in half and then in half again and they will quickly understand the concept.

Nutrition Since children start to study nutrition in kindergarten, it is never too early to begin teaching them about the importance of fueling their growing bodies with healthy meals and snacks. Show them a picture of the new Healthy Eating Pyramid, and while you are cooking, discuss with your kids where the foods you are using fit into the pyramid and what their roles are in the body. It is likely that they will still be using the Food Guide Pyramid at school, so show them the differences and then they can teach their teachers a thing or two! Teach them that a variety of fruits and vegetables is important in supplying the many vitamins and nutrients their bodies need to stay healthy. They will quickly learn that whole-grain breads, cereals, and pastas supply their muscles with carbohydrates, and it is the carbohydrates that provide them with the energy to run around on the playground all afternoon. They will easily grasp that fish, meat, beans, and nuts are different protein sources that make their muscles strong.

Kitchen Science Kids can become knowledgeable about simple kitchen science. Most of us don't think of cooking as chemistry, but when batter turns into pancakes or cookies, it is definitely chemistry. One of our kids' favorite activities is making pizza and bread. They love watching the yeast foam and grow when it is dissolved in warm water and sugar. Teach them that yeast, when mixed with a liquid, produces carbon dioxide gas, which causes the batter or dough to rise and produces the wonderful "bread baking" aroma. Discuss the similar role baking soda and baking powder play in quick breads and cookies.

Do a simple experiment with apple slices. Let them help cut up apple slices and put a slice in a plastic bag. Then put another slice in a different bag and sprinkle some lemon juice on it. Later in the day, take a look at the two bags. The section of the apple with no lemon juice is now brown, while the one with the lemon juice, which contains vitamin C, is still nice and white. Tell them the brown color is caused by enzymes that react with oxygen in the air to digest the cells of the fruit—a process called oxidation. The vitamin C prevents this chemical reaction. Vitamin C (an antioxidant) does a similar thing in your body to prevent diseases like cancer and heart disease. For more simple science experiments, try reading *365 Simple Science Experiments with Everyday Materials* (authors E. Richard Churchill, Anthony D. Fredericks, and Louis V. Loesching, Black Dog & Leventhal Publishers, Inc.).

Where Does Food Come From? One of the most interesting and valuable kitchen lessons you can teach your children is where their food comes from. Take a walk in the woods during a period of cool and wet weather. Search around rocks and fallen trees for mushrooms. Explain to your children that mushrooms are fungi and that they love damp weather. And of course, clarify the importance of never eating wild mushrooms unless they are with someone who is absolutely certain that they are not poisonous. Something wild and quite possibly dangerous growing in an area they explored will delight and intrigue children. Take them to a dairy farm and watch the cows being milked and observe the great vats of milk. See if you can coax the farmer into giving you a bit of cream in a small container. Vigorously shake the container and watch the butter and buttermilk form.

Two of our favorite family activities are going to a farm and picking seasonal fruit and exploring the Maine woods during the summer months in search of wild blueberries. Teach your children about seasonal fruit and vegetables and what is grown locally in your community: snap peas in the early spring, strawberries and tomatoes in summer, and apples and pears in fall. Take them berry picking and bake a pie or muffins together. Nothing can be more pleasurable than apple picking on a crisp fall day. We love to bring our bounty home and together prepare quick breads, smoothies, and jams. One summer in Maine we happened upon some delicious high-bush wild blueberries. We picked (and ate) a large amount and went home to bake muffins. We found we didn't have any muffin tins but had an old cast-iron frying pan. Thus was created Blueberry Black Pan Bread (see page 367). Experiences such as these will help your children begin to understand the connection between the earth, animals, and the food on your table.

Gardening Grow a small kitchen garden and let your children help with the planting, weeding, and harvesting of vegetables. A home garden is a wonderful place to teach your children about the environment, soil composition, plant care, and nutrition. Grow some vegetables from seeds and some from starter plants. They can learn about the basic needs and life cycles of plants. Teach them that during the day plants use sunlight and the green in their leaves to make sugars from carbon dioxide, which the plants breathe in through their leaves. This sugar is then used to give the plant energy so that it can grow in a process called photosynthesis. During the night, plants breathe in oxygen in a process called respiration. The plant also needs minerals to grow, which it takes from the soil where the minerals are dissolved in water. They can learn about fertilizing, weeding, and watering. Show them the birds and worms that are so important to garden health.

Teach them about composting, a natural way of recycling. Basically, plant waste plus moisture plus warmth plus air plus microorganisms plus time equal compost. All dead plants will rot down and decompose if you leave them alone and turn into a soil-like material called compost. Compost and soil are are living things. Compost can be made in a number of ways, from simply piling up old plant material to using more complicated bins. Worms are excellent at making compost. Show your children how you add compost to the garden to nurture the soil. The best gardeners know that gardening is not the art of cultivating good plants, but of cultivating good soil.

Being Green Children can also begin to grasp the impact that takeout and fast food have on the environment. Cooking at home, especially with raw ingredients rather than processed foods, has a less profound impact on the environment than eating out. Next time you purchase takeout or eat in a fast-food restaurant, make a mental note about the quantity of packaging in which your food is wrapped. These establishments use an inordinate amount of plastic, paper, and foam. All that trash needs to go somewhere. Homemade meals, prepared from "scratch," produce much less waste from packaging. Try this mental exercise. Compare nonrecyclable packaging from Spaghetti with Broccoli, Garlic, and Pine Nuts (see page 206) with takeout. Purchasing whole foods such as a head of broccoli or a bulb of garlic, especially if you forgo or recycle the plastic bag, will make no nonrecyclable waste. A pound of pasta comes in a narrow box, which in many communities can be recycled. Contrast this with everyone going out to a fast-food restaurant, ordering a separate meal with each item individually wrapped, including straws, cups, and covers. Compare the amount of nonrecyclable waste, and they'll get the idea.

What's Cooking? You may now be asking yourself: "So, what types of food should I make with my children?" A good rule of thumb is that kids generally like to cook what they like to eat. This includes all the usual favorites, such as chicken fingers, pizza, breads, cookies, and muffins. Anything that rises is particularly appealing to youngsters, especially if you have an oven that they can peer into and watch the process. Our kids love going to a pizza shop, watching the cook twirl a piece of dough into a circle, and coming home and trying it themselves. They also enjoy making cinnamon swirls. The entire process from mixing and kneading the dough to shaping and cutting the swirls is great fun. Kids like to help with quickly prepared meals, such as pastas, rather than long-cooking stews and roasts. They also love to make anything frozen such as ice cream and ice cream pies as well as anything that uses a blender, mixer, or food processor. They are intrigued by whole fish and live shellfish such as mussels, clams, and lobsters. On a recent field trip to a fish market with kindergarteners, the fishmonger showed us an anglerfish and the stomach contents of a bluefish. Every child in the shop was mesmerized. Unfortunately, this enthusiasm doesn't guarantee that your children will eat fish. Our kids still don't like it unless it is in fish stick form. We still kid our son Leo about all the fish sticks swimming around in the ocean.

CHAPTER 10

vitamins and supplements

One of the most common questions we are asked is "Should I be taking a vitamin supplement?" In general, we advise getting the majority of the nutrients you need through your diet, since there are likely to be as yet unrecognized co-factors that are necessary for the maximum health-promoting properties you obtain from vitamins and minerals in whole foods. However, the reality is that almost 80 percent of Americans do not eat the recommended amounts of fruits and vegetables that would provide sufficient amounts of key vitamins and minerals needed for good health. Recent evidence has shown that a lack of these vitamins and minerals can be risk factors for chronic diseases such as cardiovascular disease, cancer, and osteoporosis. We therefore currently recommend taking a multivitamin as insurance to make certain you have included the vitamins and nutrients you need in your diet. Think of a multivitamin not as an *alternative* therapy, but rather as a *complementary* therapy. No multivitamin will make up for a poor diet. By eating a healthy diet and taking a supplement, you will achieve the best of both worlds. There is some recent well-done data that supports this stance.

Vitamin Supplements and Disease Prevention Scientific information has evolved in recent years so that we now think of vitamins and supplements as part of an overall scheme of disease prevention. This differs from our past uses of vitamins and supplements, when they were largely taken to prevent diseases related to deficiencies, such as scurvy and rickets. Today, low folic acid levels, along with lower levels of vitamins B_6 and B_{12}, are risk factors for cardiovascular disease, neural tube defects, and colon and breast cancer. Low levels of vitamin D contribute to osteopenia (low bone mass) and fractures. And low levels of the antioxidant vitamins (A, E, and C) may increase the risk for several chronic diseases. Since most people do not consume an optimal amount of all vitamins by diet alone, it is prudent for all adults to take a multivitamin supplement. Your choice of a multivitamin should be tailored to your specific health needs so that you achieve the appropriate nutrient levels for your particular situation and phase of your life cycle.

The Medical Community Recommends a Daily Multivitamin Until recently, the medical community did not recommend that healthy adults take a daily multivitamin. This stance changed due to a landmark article from Harvard Medical School that appeared in 2002 in the *Journal of the American Medical Association* which showed that vitamins can be a key part of disease prevention. The authors reviewed studies published between 1966 and 2002 that investigated the links between vitamin intake and diseases such as cancer and coronary heart disease. From this pooled data they concluded that all adults, regardless of age or health status, should take a daily multivitamin. This new health recommendation makes choosing a multivitamin an important part of a healthy lifestyle.[1] You also may need other supplements to achieve the minimum daily requirement of certain vitamins and minerals (calcium, for example) beyond the amount contained in any multivitamin depending on your age, gender, health issues, and risk factors for disease. Your health-care provider can help you decide which is right for you.

Proper Dosing Is Needed in Taking Vitamins and Supplements
One basic principle to keep in mind with vitamin supplements is that more is not better. It is important to avoid "megadosing" on vitamin supplements. In some cases, too much of a good thing can be toxic, so you should take only the recommended dosages. For example, higher-than-recommended vitamin A intake during pregnancy is linked to certain birth defects. In addition, one size does not fit all with supplements. To prevent the possibility of excessive intake, you should take into account the fact that your current diet already contains some vitamins and minerals.

Check with Your Health-Care Provider about Drug Interactions Multivitamins can interact with other medications and disease conditions. The way your body utilizes a vitamin and mineral supplement can vary depending on many factors such as your dietary habits, genetic factors, physical condition, disease status, and medications. Sometimes it is necessary to take your multivitamin at a separate time from your other medications. When taken together, it is possible that they can adversely affect one another or impair your absorption of the active metabolites. That's why education on what is right for you and what time of day you should take your multivitamin can be so important. For example, taking a multivitamin at the same time as thyroid medication can impair your body's absorption of the thyroid medication. This can often be alleviated by taking them at different times of day. Sometimes, though, you actually need to raise the dosage of your thyroid medication to ensure adequate levels in your body when you are also taking a multivitamin.

Choosing a Multivitamin Choosing the right multivitamin requires some knowledge about your life-cycle stage. For example, if you are a menopausal women and you choose a supplement that is high in iron, this may not be optimal for your current situation. When you are no longer menstruating, often you don't need extra iron. And that extra iron may impair your absorption of calcium, which you do need in higher amounts in this phase of your life cycle. Ask your health-care provider to help you choose what is optimal for you.

Choosing a multivitamin can be very confusing, especially since much of the information in stores is based on advertising and marketing rather than science and research. The following is a list of tips to use when choosing a multivitamin. Choose one that:

- contains minerals as well as vitamins.
- comes as close as possible to the Recommended Daily Allowances, which are the minimum daily requirements of each vitamin and mineral your body needs.
- is made specifically for your age group and life stage. There are multivitamins designed for children, for adults, for seniors, and for pregnant women.
- is a brand name you trust. Select a supplement that is labeled GMP (Good Manufacturing Practices). Supplements are considered food and are not regulated during production. Good Manufacturing Practices facilities use the highest standards in production. The testing required to receive this label assures the highest levels of purity, potency, and stability.
- has an expiration date on the bottle. Reliable companies all list them.

Fish-Oil Supplements The American Heart Association does not recommend routine supplementation with fish oil for all adults. Instead, they recommend eating fish, particularly fatty fish, at least two times a week, because fish are a rich source of omega-three fatty acids. Omega-three fatty acids are heart-healthy fats that are excellent for cardiovascular disease prevention. Fatty fish include mackerel, trout, herring, sardines, albacore tuna, and salmon. For those individuals who have high triglycerides (blood fats) or coronary heart disease, the American Heart Association states that you may benefit from taking a fish-oil supplement. These individuals should talk to their doctors about taking supplements to reduce heart disease risk. But caution is needed in taking fish-oil supplements, since high intakes can cause excessive bleeding. If you find it difficult to eat the beneficial amount of fish, speak to your doctor about whether you should take a fish-oil supplement.

Pregnant women need to use caution in consuming both fish and fish-oil supplements. Some fish-oil supplements, such as cod-liver oil, may contain high levels of retinol (the animal form of vitamin A), which can cause birth defects if taken in large amounts during early pregnancy. So it is best for pregnant women to avoid fish-oil supplements. In addition, children and pregnant and nursing women are at higher risk of exposure to excessive mercury from fish, and should avoid those fish that contain high levels of mercury: swordfish, tuna steak, shark, tilefish, and king mackerel.

Does Your Child Need a Multivitamin? Most children do not need supplemental vitamins or minerals. According to the American Academy of Pediatrics, a diet based on the Food Guide Pyramid provides adequate amounts of all the vitamins a child needs. As much as possible, try to maximize the vitamins your child receives in regular meals and snacks. Children whose nutrition may be improved with multivitamins include those who are very picky eaters, have poor appetites, or have a highly selective diet. Examples of children who may need a multivitamin supplement include those who do not eat meat or dairy, or who do not eat many vegetables. In addition, some children with certain medical conditions may need vitamins to supplement their diet. You and your pediatrician should discuss if a multivitamin is right for your child. Chewable tablets are available for children who have difficulty swallowing pills.

As in adults, beware of megavitamin therapy in your children. This has no proven scientific value and may pose risks to your child's health. For example, consuming megadoses of vitamin C in hopes of minimizing or preventing a cold can cause headaches, diarrhea, nausea, and cramps. Finally, keep multivitamins securely closed and in the medicine cabinet, so that your child does not accidentally take too many.

Iron Supplements and Children Children and adolescents need the mineral iron to prevent anemia. Those most at risk for iron deficiency are infants who are not given extra iron after six months of age and babies who drink low-iron formula, cow's milk, or goat's milk. Extra iron is usually given in the form of an iron-fortified infant cereal. Good sources of iron include meat, fish, legumes, and fortified foods such as breads and cereals. Adolescent girls are also at risk of anemia once they begin having their periods. Speak to your pediatrician if you think your child might benefit from an iron supplement.

Calcium and Children Calcium is necessary for healthy bones and teeth. Children who drink milk and eat dairy products such as yogurt, ice cream, and cheese usually get enough calcium from their diet. Children with milk allergies or who don't like milk can still meet calcium requirements, but it takes a bit of effort to ensure adequate amounts from nondairy sources. Vitamins, even those with extra calcium, generally only have about 200 milligrams, or 20 percent of daily requirements, so speak to your pediatrician about whether a calcium supplement is necessary.

Fluoride Supplements and Children Most children get enough fluoride to build healthy teeth if they are drinking fluoridated water, either from tap water in a city that adds fluoride to the water or bottled water that also has added fluoride. Since too much fluoride can cause staining of your child's teeth, talk with your pediatrician or dentist before giving your child fluoride supplements.

1. K. Fairfield and R.H. Fletcher, "Vitamins for Chronic Disease Prevention: Scientific Review and Clinical Applications," *Journal of the American Medical Association* 23 (2002):127–29.

CHAPTER 11

exercise—
a family affair

Getting fit and staying active is an essential part of your and your family's health. While getting started on any exercise routine is difficult, the rewards are rich. Your important position in role-modeling an active lifestyle for your children is just as essential as your role in demonstrating healthy eating habits. Your children will see you expending the extra effort to stay fit, and will recognize that you value this activity. Numerous studies support that active parents have active children.

In 1995, the U.S. surgeon general recommended that everyone get at least thirty minutes of exercise a day. There are multiple studies that show that regular aerobic physical activity is associated with lower morbidity and mortality rates from cardiovascular disease, cancer, and overall death rates from all causes. A number of studies in the past ten years conclude that physical activity reduces the risk of developing heart disease, diabetes, colon cancer, and

125

breast cancer. Evidence exists that it may also improve cognitive functioning and resistance to disease. Inactivity is now considered an independent risk factor for a shorter life, along with smoking, high blood pressure, and high cholesterol. You need to get at least thirty minutes daily of moderate physical activity that involves moving your whole body.

Exercise—Beginners Can Start with an Hour a Week and Still Benefit Light to moderate physical activity, such as walking, lowers heart attack rates in women. Heart disease is the leading cause of death among U.S. women, and physical activity has been shown to lower the risk substantially. A study in the *Journal of the American Medical Association* found that women who walked for up to one hour over the course of a week lowered their heart disease risk by 14 percent compared with women who did not exercise. Those who walked one to one and a half hours a week at a pace of at least three miles per hour reduced their heart disease risk by 51 percent. This reduced heart attack risk holds true for both normal-weight and overweight women, smokers and ex-smokers, and those with high cholesterol.[1] This suggests real benefits for women from light activities like walking—even from only one hour of walking per week—and offers encouragement for those who undertake no regular exercise. One hour a week is attainable by almost everyone. In addition, it is information that may come as good news to many women who don't like to sweat or don't have time to change clothing after a workout, since this level of exercise can even be done in work clothing and other nonexercise clothing. It is true, however, that vigorous exercise is associated with a lower risk of heart disease than light exercise. Nonetheless, this gives beginners a reachable goal—walking one hour a week. Once you accomplish that, you can gradually increase to two to two and a half hours a week. In addition to lowering the risk of heart disease, women who exercise the most have the lowest rates of high blood pressure, high cholesterol, and diabetes. Exercisers are also less likely to smoke and consume more fruit, vegetables, and fiber than sedentary individuals do.

Exercise—You Benefit Even If You Are Overweight According to new research published in the *Journal of the American Medical Association*, even if you are overweight, regular, moderate exercise can lower the risk of heart disease among older women by boosting fitness and trimming tummy fat.[2] Intra-abdominal fat is considered a major risk factor for heart disease and is also associated with type II diabetes, high blood pressure, and high cholesterol. Researchers found that postmenopausal women who began an exercise program of brisk walking or cycling five days a week lowered their levels of abdominal fat by about 6 percent, regardless of body weight or age. These findings suggest a strategy for lowering the risk of heart disease, a leading cause of death among women—forty-five minutes of aerobic exercise (walking or stationary cycling), five days per week. According to the researchers, women should be aware that even if they don't see much weight loss with regular exercise, they are doing good things for heart health. This means that even if you are overweight, you should continue to exercise, since you will reap health rewards even if you don't lose weight from it. It suggests that the health benefits from exercise are not limited to those benefits derived through weight loss.

Men and Exercise—Harvard Study In 1960, a group of investigators from the Harvard School of Public Health began tracking thousands of past graduates from Harvard College as well as alumni from the University of Pennsylvania. The Harvard part of the study includes men only. Some women participate in the University of Pennsylvania group, but they are relatively few in number. They found that men who exercised regularly had less risk of death from heart disease and stroke whether they were obese or not. Researchers have found regular exercise can add almost four years to your life, even if you are overweight. And the quality of those years is also enhanced. They found that you don't have to do intensive jogging, calisthenics, and weight lifting to obtain the benefits. Brisk walking, golf, tennis, gardening, and swimming also give you the benefit of extra years. They found that a brisk, hourlong walk five days a week cuts the risk of having a stroke almost in half. Even walking thirty minutes a day, five days a week drops the risk by 24 percent. The benefits are present regardless of the age at which you begin exercising.[3] It is never too early or too late to start exercising.

The surgeon general's recommendation of moderate-intensity activity for thirty minutes a day most days of the week generates an energy expenditure of about one thousand calories a week. Men sixty and older who smoke, have high blood pressure, and diabetes can still cut their risk of heart disease about 20 percent by burning one thousand calories a week, according to the Harvard study.

Women and Exercise—Harvard Study Many studies, including the Harvard study, prove that women get the same benefits from physical activity as men. Postmenopausal women who exercise for about thirty minutes each day cut their risk of breast cancer in half compared with those who stay sedentary. You can obtain the same benefit by breaking up a thirty-minute session into two fifteen-minute parts. It's the total amount of energy expended that's important. Physical activity also helps women who smoke, are overweight, or have high cholesterol to avoid heart disease. The more exercise the better, but even walking an hour a week is associated with some reduction of risk. It's best to walk three or four miles an hour, that is, a pace that works up a sweat, but even a more leisurely pace helps women forty-five years and older.

Former Athletes—You Can't Rest on Your Laurels You cannot rely on your past exercise achievements to help you in the future. The protective effect of strenuous exercise tends to disappear if it is not maintained. To hold on to any health advantage achieved in their competitive years, athletes must continue to keep physically active in their middle and older years. Sedentary individuals who take up an active lifestyle are at lower heart-attack risk than former varsity players who gave up or reduced their physical activity in middle age. Thus, those who were formerly physically fit need to continue to be active for the health benefits to continue as they age.

Inactivity—as Bad as Smoking Being physically inactive is as damaging to your health as smoking cigarettes. While many of us shun smoking because of the health implications and negative role modeling of this behavior for our children, we are often much more comfortable with our inactivity. As busy parents, it is all too easy to fall into the inactivity routine.

Use Self-Management Skills to Fit Exercise into Busy Lives

For so many of us, exercise is viewed as an impractical burden that complicates rather than complements a busy life. As a parent, it is hard to find time in a busy day to get to a gym, change, work out, shower, change again, and drive home. In order to fit exercise into a busy day, you need to use self-management skills such as goal setting, monitoring, and barrier minimization to maintain active lifestyles. Many of us are so good at using these self-management skills in the workplace. They work equally well in setting exercise goals, as we'll show below.

There are many options that can work in your life. Moderate physical activities like brisk walking can promote health nearly as much as vigorous workouts. Those physical activities that are less demanding—walking from the train or parking lot to your office, parking at a greater distance from your destination and walking the remainder of the way, taking the stairs instead of the elevator, using your coffee break for a walk—can be incorporated into your daily routines without adding more complexity to your life. Don't focus on exercises you find unpleasant or uncomfortable. Choose activities you enjoy so that you stick with your program. You owe it to yourself and your family to be as healthy as you can be.

Getting Started The first step is to commit yourself to a routine. A good way to start is by breaking it up into smaller pieces. As a busy person, you can get the same benefits when you exercise in bits and pieces throughout the day as when you work out in one block of time. This helps you to avoid the all-or-nothing trap. If you don't have a full free hour in a day, then find a half hour. If you don't have a free half hour, then use fifteen minutes. Hopefully, you can then find another fifteen-minute slot in your day, and you'll have achieved the recommended amount of activity. If circumstances prevent you from doing everything you planned for the day, do what you can and don't worry about it. Tomorrow is a new day with new opportunities to exercise. If you fall off your routine for a time because of injury or illness, just get restarted as best you can. If you have only ten minutes today, try to add fifteen to twenty minutes extra in tomorrow or the next day.

Set realistic short-term and long-term goals so that you do not get discouraged. A short-term goal could be starting from scratch and adding a minute a day to your exercise regimen. A long-term goal may be to lose weight or to lower your blood pressure.

Plan Ahead and Squeeze It In Look ahead at your daily schedule and plan when you'll fit in your exercise. If you don't plan ahead, you are not as likely to make the arrangements necessary to be able to exercise. With planning, you will almost certainly be able to find fifteen minutes even on your busiest days. So pencil in an exercise appointment, and consider it mandatory. Spontaneous exercise may depend on having walking shoes or a change of clothes available. Stock a gym bag with exercise clothing and toiletries so that you are always prepared and keep it with you.

Here are some ideas of ways to squeeze in a few minutes of exercise here and there without making your day any longer:

- Use stairs instead of the elevator or escalator. When at home, climb to the second floor as often as possible. For variety, take the stairs two at a time, or step up the pace.
- Walk when you can. Park an extra block from your destination or at the rear of the parking lot. Look for the longest, rather than the shortest, walking route.
- Limit TV and computer viewing times for all of you.
- Start an active hobby like gardening—your children will enjoy helping out.
- View chores like lawn mowing, dusting, and vacuuming as opportunities to exercise.
- Turn off the TV and play with your children.

- Turn on the radio or CD and dance.
- Learn a new sport. Take golf, tennis, or racquetball lessons.
- Take your children for a walk, hike, or bike ride often, even if for only a short while.
- Go for a walk on the beach together to beachcomb instead of sitting in your chair.
- Instead of watching your kids play with their friends in the park, join in and play tag, catch, or other active games.

Home Gym We are firm believers in having some exercise equipment in your home. This way, your exercise schedule is not totally dependent on your ability to find baby-sitters or enough time to go to the gym. It gives you a way to squeeze in fifteen to twenty minutes when you have a packed schedule, or to wake up just a half hour earlier for a thirty-minute workout. Buy a piece of exercise equipment, place it in a convenient location at home, and jump on it when you have a few minutes to spare. Even if you have a gym membership or prefer outdoor physical activity, your home gym equipment—treadmill, stationary bike, Nordic Track, etc.—gives you an alternative that varies your routine and allows an indoor venue in your home when there is inclement weather. Then, on weekends or other days off, take your time and go to the gym or outdoors and exercise a bit longer. This takes the pressure off your busier days during the week.

Balance Your Workouts New guidelines suggest three to five days of aerobic workouts, two to three strength-training sessions, and two to three flexibility workouts per week. You may need to work up to that level, but try to incorporate all three types of exercise into your week. As a starting point try three days of aerobic workouts (start with twenty minutes and try to increase a minute every workout) of activities such as running, biking, elliptical training, Nordic Track, or brisk walking.

In addition to cardiorespiratory exercise, perform two days of strength training and then do some stretching just after you finish with the weights. Strength and flexibility are two aspects of fitness that decline with aging. Both men and women benefit from being stronger and more flexible. In addition to giving you strength, weight training increases your muscle mass, and muscles burn calories. The more muscle mass your body contains, the more calories you burn for any given weight. You'll also look better and feel stronger.

Strength training (weight training) should involve one set each of eight to ten exercises that work all major muscle groups. Flexibility exercises should stretch the major muscles throughout the body. You can do these two types of exercises together in one session, starting with the weights and ending with the stretching.

Remember, there is no one exercise program that is best for all. The best program is one that you enjoy so that you continue it on a regular basis.

Aerobic Exercise Intensity Goals for Health Aerobic exercise means that you are exercising at about 75 percent of your maximum heart rate for your age. Your maximal heart rate (in beats per minute) is the highest number of times your heart can beat (contract) in one minute. Genetics and age determine maximal heart rate. The formula for calculating maximal heart rate is:

Maximal heart rate = 220 − age (in years)

Your maximal heart rate does not tend to rise or fall with your level of fitness as much as do your resting and submaximal heart rates. Once you have calculated this number, you can then figure what your target heart rates should be in order to exercise in the aerobic zone.

Target heart rate = 75% × (220 − age)

An optimal aerobic program has three phases:

1. warmup (five to ten minutes)
2. 75 percent maximal heart rate intensity (fifteen to thirty minutes)
3. cooldown (five to ten minutes)

Following this program will result in exercise routines totaling twenty-five to fifty minutes. For cardiorespiratory fitness, exercise sessions should be twenty to thirty minutes at the beginning, gradually increasing to forty to fifty minutes.

Always check with your health-care provider to ensure that any exercise program is right for you. Certain medical problems, such as heart disease, may preclude your being able to exercise at these heart rates.

Warm Up We recommend a five-minute warmup, during which you are gradually working harder so that by the end of the first five minutes you are at your target heart rate. Then, for a minimum of twenty minutes, you want to maintain this heart rate. Finally, you should do a five-minute cooldown, during which you gradually ease off until you are walking for the last minute, allowing your heartrate to decrease to below 100 beats per minute. This allows you to recover more fully, so that you feel energized and relaxed after your workout.

The "Afterburn" The reason you need to exercise with some intensity during the workout is that this effort increases your metabolism. This increased metabolism continues even after the workout is over. This is referred to as the "afterburn." Your metabolic rate is increased, so that you continue to burn calories at a faster rate for some time after the workout, even when you are at rest.

Avoid Energy Foods for Athletes The energy food market is booming. Sports drinks, energy bars, and energy gels can be found at the checkout counter of every supermarket and health-food store. These foods, drinks, and gels are high in sugar and carbohydrate enhanced and can contribute unwanted calories to your diet. Yet they are low in satisfaction, and often expensive. You can easily eat more calories in one energy bar than you burned in your workout, which from a weight standpoint totally negates the effect of the workout. When you are thirsty after a workout, it is all too easy to chug down five hundred calories in a sports drink, when water would have done the trick for zero calories. Unless you are an endurance athlete, exercising two hours a day intensively, you are better off drinking water and eating a banana to replete your fluids and nutrients. This is a far more economical and more natural approach to diet. Save the calories for a nice meal that will leave you feeling more satisfied and less deprived.

Not Many of Us Adults Are Setting a Good Example A recent Gallup Poll found that the number of American adults who reported regular (three or more times per week), vigorous exercise—at least twenty minutes of activity that produces a surge in heart or breathing rates—declined to 45 percent in 2002 (from 52 percent in 2001). The majority of Americans—54 percent—are now considered sedentary or low activity, compared with 48 percent the previous year. And just 25 percent of adults said they follow recent recommendations to participate in weight-training activities at least once a week. If we don't want our children to follow this example, it is time for us adults to get moving.

Children and Exercise We are much better at making certain our children exercise their minds than their equally important bodies. Taking care of your child's physical health involves so much more than trips to the pediatrician and providing healthy diets. Exercise is equally important in a healthy lifestyle. As children spend more time watching TV and playing computer and electronic games, they spend less time being active. Parents play a big role in helping children learn to love being active and making physical exercise a part of their everyday lives. Children are naturally and spontaneously active, but they need to be given the proper opportunities to be physically active. Like adults, children should be physically active most, if not all, days of the week. Experts suggest thirty to sixty minutes of moderate physical activity daily for most children. The American Heart Association recommends a daily combination of moderate and vigorous physical activity for both children and adults. Specifically, they recommend a total of thirty minutes of moderate-intensity activities on most days of the week, and a minimum of thirty minutes of vigorous physical activity at least three to four days each week, to achieve cardiovascular fitness. Walking fast, bicycling, jumping rope, dancing, playing tag, and playing sports of all kinds are all good ways for your child to be active.

Most children are naturally active, and just need to be in an environment where they can expend their energy through active play. As a parent, your role is to allow this to occur, to provide more structured physical activity when appropriate, and to a be a role model in the area of exercise and physical fitness by being active yourself.

Some Worrisome Trends in Childhood Physical Activity Fewer than half of U.S. children engage in activity that is sufficient for cardiovascular benefit and long-term health promotion. According to the surgeon general's report on physical activity and health, activity levels decline as grade levels advance. This decline is particularly dramatic as children enter adolescence. Nearly half of young people ages twelve to twenty-one are not regularly vigorously active. One-fourth engage in no vigorous activity, and 14 percent report no recent activity at even the light-to-moderate level. Girls are at greater risk of inactivity than boys, particularly during and after puberty.

Physical Activity Can Start in the Toddler Years Keeping your toddler active should be based upon unstructured play such as running, swinging, climbing, playing in a sandbox, and carefully supervised water play. Your toddler gets exercise from jumping, skipping, and running. Although there are a number of programs to introduce toddlers to water activities and gymnastics or even to get them started in peewee leagues, you should carefully investigate these programs to make sure they are safe as well as developmentally appropriate for your child. At this age, your job is to make certain your toddler has enough room to get exercise through these natural and unstructured ways. Walking, playing, and running in the backyard or using playground equipment at a local park can be fun for the entire family.

Health Benefits of Exercise in Childhood As with adults, children and adolescents can prevent or delay the development of hypertension, and those young people who already have hypertension can reduce blood pressure through physical activity. Children and adults who already engage in regular activity may benefit from even more vigorous activity than the current recommendations of a thirty-minute minimum per day, but the specific amount of energy expenditure needed by children to decrease their risk of cardiovascular disease is not known.

Children need to learn fundamental motor skills and develop health through cardiovascular endurance, muscular strength and endurance, flexibility, and body composition. Physical activity produces overall physical, psychological and social benefits. Regular physical activity at any age can help your child learn to play and meet challenges. Part of helping your child commit to fitness includes becoming a positive role model by exercising regularly on your own or with your child. Active children are likely to become active adults. And physical activity helps with:

- reduction of anxiety
- improvement in body image and mood
- gaining more self-confidence and higher self-esteem
- development of physical fitness
- promotion of weight control through caloric expenditure. This benefit is of particular importance to children, who are experiencing the same epidemic of being overweight as adults
- raising HDL ("good") cholesterol
- reducing the risk of diabetes and some kinds of cancer

Exercise and Weight Control in Children More children today are overweight or obese than ever before. Being overweight means that the child weighs more than is recommended for a given height (see chapter 1). When this excess weight is in the form of fat, health problems may develop. Obesity is a more extreme form of being overweight, and in children has been variously defined as:

- ≥20% over the recommended weight for height

- ≥85th percentile for Body Mass Index, which is calculated by dividing weight in kilograms by height in meters squared
- ≥25% of weight as fat for boys and ≥30% of weight as fat for girls

According to the CDC, when the percent fat definition is used, data indicates that 11 percent of six to eleven-year-olds and 14 percent of twelve to seventeen-year-olds are obese. This is double the prevalence of obesity thirty years ago. There is particular concern about this data because body weight and too much body fat in children are significant cardiovascular disease risk factors. This risk tracks into adolescence and young adulthood if it is not checked in childhood. Particularly detrimental to health is abdominal body fat, which is linked to cardiovascular disease and diabetes. Studies examining the relationship between physical activity and abdominal fat suggest that those who are more active are less likely to deposit fat in the abdominal area. Physical activity is thus a key element in the prevention and treatment of both chronic disease and obesity.

Exercise helps to prevent children from being overweight or obese. Overweight children are at increased risk of many health problems, including hypertension, hyperlipidemia (elevation of fats in the bloodstream), type II diabetes, growth hormone deregulation, and respiratory and orthopedic problems. In addition, overweight children frequently suffer from difficulties with self-esteem and socialization. Obesity follows children into adulthood—40 percent of overweight children and 70 percent of overweight adolescents become obese adults.

Exercise Should Be Fun No single sport or exercise regimen is uniquely beneficial for the physical or emotional well-being of children. It is far more important to help your children find activities that are interesting and enjoyable and which are appropriate for their age and physical abilities. Here are some tips to keep your children active and help them learn to love exercise:

- Make walking a part of any activity. You can walk for miles without realizing it at a zoo, park, or miniature-golf course.

- Include your children in household activities such as gardening, dog walking, car washing, or lawn mowing.
- Encourage your children to be physically active every day. Help them by taking them to the local gym to shoot baskets or swim; take them to the park to run and climb; put up a swing set, soccer goal, or basketball hoop (or all three) in your backyard; buy them bicycles (and helmets).
- Be a role model for your children. If they see you being physically active and having fun, they are more likely to be active and stay active throughout their lives.
- Plan active weekends and vacations. Go hiking, biking, sledding, snowboarding, skiing, dancing, or roller-skating as a family.
- Limit your children's TV and computer time. Offer them active options, like joining a local recreation center or after-school program, or taking lessons in a sport they enjoy.

Exercise in Childhood and Bone Building Physical activity in childhood may have lasting effects on bone development. Exercise may lower osteoporosis risk by increasing bone mineral density. Though most attention has focused on exercise in later years to reduce or restore bone loss, the skeleton appears to be most responsive to the effects of activity during a child's growth period. Evidence of a positive effect of childhood activity on bone density, either immediately or later in life, is mixed, but a number of studies have made this implication. One followed forty prepubertal boys (mean age, 10.4 years), half of whom participated in thirty minutes of weight-bearing exercise three times a week for thirty-two weeks. The increase in lumbar spine, leg, and total body bone mineral density was twice as great in the exercise group as in the control group. Another study that involved forty-five prepubertal female gymnasts (mean age, 10.4 years), thirty-six retired gymnasts (mean age, 25 years), and fifty matched controls found significantly greater bone mineral density in the young and retired gymnasts. The researchers observed that bone density did not diminish during retirement, despite the lower frequency and intensity of exercise. They concluded that exercise before puberty may reduce fracture risk after menopause. As the evidence builds, it is likely to point toward exercise in youth as the best prevention for osteoporosis-related fractures as we age.

Exercise in Childhood and Heart Disease Prevention While cardiovascular disease is primarily evident in adulthood, risk factors appear much earlier in life and often persist. Evidence links lipid and lipoprotein profiles in childhood and adolescence with the development of the beginnings of atherosclerosis (hardening of the arteries) and high-normal blood pressure in young people. These conditions significantly increase the risk of high blood pressure in adulthood. Several well-designed studies in children suggest that aerobic exercise is beneficial in this age group in the reduction of heart disease risk. One trial compared twenty-eight prepubertal children who took part in a twelve-week exercise program (stationary cycling for thirty minutes, three times per week) with twenty in a control group who did not. The exercise group had significant improvement in low-density lipoprotein (LDL) cholesterol, high-density lipoprotein (HDL) cholesterol, and the total cholesterol/HDL and LDL/HDL ratios. These are beneficial lipid changes that may decrease a lifetime risk of developing heart disease. Another study found positive effects on blood pressure. Ninety-nine ninth-grade girls whose systolic (top number) or diastolic (bottom number) blood pressure was in the top third for their grade were randomized to a semester of aerobic exercise or standard physical education (PE) classes. Among the eighty-eight who completed the study, systolic blood pressure dropped significantly in the aerobic exercise group compared with the standard PE group (6 mm mercury versus 3.7 mm mercury). Though decreases were modest, the blood pressure reduction was notable, considering that the girls did not start out with high blood pressure. The authors concluded that changes of this magnitude, if widely achieved, could have important public health benefits and observed that similar reductions have been seen in other trials of physical training in adolescents.

Exercise in Childhood and Mental Health Benefits There is evidence that exercise has a beneficial effect on mental health for children (as well as adults). For example, one review of adults and exercise showed improvements in depressive and anxiety symptoms. Some studies in children suggest that the positive effect of exercise is in an improved physical self-image (but not academic or general self-worth). Exercise may improve the ability of young people to cope with stress. A study of 220 adolescent girls during a high-stress period found that those who adhered to a rigorous exercise program reported less physical and emotional distress than those who exercised less. Sports participation has some mixed reviews in this area. It appears that the positive mental health benefits of exercise in children depend upon the specific context and conditions such as role models and leadership. Always be careful in this area, as poor role modeling and treatment of our youth in organized sports can have terribly negative effects and undermine all your other efforts in this area. One study suggested that childhood exercise, if promoted unwisely, can impede adult physical activity. An analysis of the preteen and teenage experience of 105 middle-age men found that coercion to exercise in youth had a weak but statistically significant negative effect on physical activity in adulthood. The authors noted that the results seem to emphasize the need to give children a voice in their physical activity and sports participation.

Schools and Physical Activity for Your Child According to studies conducted by the Centers for Disease Control (CDC), only 47 percent of middle/junior high schools and 26 percent of high schools require at least three years of physical education. Only 19 percent of high-school students are active for at least twenty minutes a day during physical education class. Since very little physical activity is currently happening during school hours, this responsibility lies largely with you as a parent. You can work with your child's school to create ways to increase the amount of physical activity that occurs there:

• Help coordinate extracurricular physical activity programs in your child's school through clubs and activities such as walking/ hiking clubs, in-line skating, jumping rope, or other noncompetitive activities.

- Schools might allow use of school facilities by community agencies that sponsor physical activity programs, such as after-school yoga, dance, karate, gymnastics, fitness classes, or organized sports. Easy access to these classes just after school and right in the school building makes busy lives less complicated.
- Be an involved parent. Parental leadership is very important in promoting activity among children. You don't have to be a professional athlete to coach youth sports—you just have to love working with children and have patience.
- Lobby for access to your school gymnasium which enables physical activity (especially important in winter). For example, schools might allow access to facilities before and after school hours and during vacation periods.
- Promote physical activity in your child's classroom. For example, classroom teachers may use "fitness breaks" where five-minute aerobic activities could be used to break up the school day.

Exercise and Your Family Your general goal as a family should be to make physical activity an enjoyable part of your everyday lives and generally be less sedentary. For adults, some of this should be in a formal exercise program. As a family, physical actives should be part of your everyday lives together through chores, family outings, play, and school-related activities. This will set the stage for a lifetime of fitness together. Remember that exercising your children's bodies is equally important as exercising their minds.

1. I.M. Lee, "Physical Activity and Coronary Heart Disease in Women: Is "No Pain, No Gain" Passé?" *Journal of the American Medical Association* 285 (2001):1447–54.

2. M.L. Irwin, "Effect of Exercise on Total and Intra-Abdominal Body Fat in Postmenopausal Women: A Randomized Controlled Trial," *Journal of the American Medical Association* 289 (2003):323–30.

3. I.M. Lee, "Physical Activity and Coronary Heart Disease Risk in Men: Does the Duration of Exercise Episodes Predict Risk?" *Circulation* 102 (2000):981–86.

CHAPTER 12

home-cooking basics

Two questions we are frequently asked are "How do you find the time to cook?" and "Do your kids eat everything you prepare for them?" The answers may surprise you. We find the time to cook because we *want* to and, no, our children *don't* eat everything we serve them. Unfortunately, with today's busy lifestyles and hectic pace, few of us have time to prepare healthful meals at home and instead settle for picking up takeout, having dinner delivered, or eating in a restaurant. We love to eat and we love to eat well, but we rarely eat out. When we do, it is often an ethnic meal, where we can enjoy food that we don't regularly prepare (and never as well) at home. Restaurant and takeout meals are always more expensive, often don't taste as good, and are not as healthful as a homemade meal. Kids who eat homemade meals develop discriminating palettes. Joe, our eight-year-old, thinks everything we make for him, including pizza, chicken fingers, and French fries, tastes far better than the fast-food versions.

Many parents arrive home in the early evening and have no dinner plans in mind. They aren't even certain what foods are in their kitchen cabinets and refrigerators and may not even know what they can make that their children will enjoy. They do know, though, that their kids would love a pizza or a fast-food hamburger and French fries. It is always going to seem less stressful to stop on the way home for dinner than it is to prepare something in your kitchen. We'll show you how to keep out of this trap. When you cook at home, you are setting a positive example for your children and saving money. By observing and helping you with all the aspects of food preparation, your children will become knowledgeable about ingredients and basic cooking techniques and, most important, will acquire lifelong kitchen skills.

Although we are in the cookbook business, it is a misconception that we are constantly being creative in the kitchen. Certainly, when we are in the midst of a book, we need to think and cook creatively in order to develop interesting recipes. But the majority of the time our cooking routine is similar to that of most other families. We have seven or eight meals that we enjoy and prepare regularly. When we make a new dish that our kids love, we add it to our repertoire. You can learn to do the same.

Our goal is to guide you through the details about cooking great meals at home from setting up your kitchen and planning meals, to shopping and cooking and finally to cleaning up. You can follow our recipes as they are written or alter them to suit your tastes. They won't leave you spending hours in the kitchen and will hopefully inspire you to create your own delectable meals. You will find cooking at home to be a quick, easy, and wonderfully rewarding experience for the entire family.

Planning Your Meals The initial step and arguably the most important one in cooking healthful and delicious meals at home is meticulous planning. We sit down on Saturdays with a pencil and paper and plan an entire week of dinners. On the bottom portion of the paper, we list all the ingredients that are needed to prepare the meals. At this time, we also note if we need to make a larger quantity than usual and plan accordingly. Often, we prepare a double or triple batch of meatballs and divide the extra into bags containing four portions each and freeze them. During the week, we effortlessly prepare a quick tomato sauce, drop in the meatballs, and enjoy a great meal in less than forty-five minutes.

Once all the ingredients have been listed, we cross off the items that we are certain we have on hand. They usually include non-perishable foods such as dried beans, canned tomatoes, pastas, and vegetables with a long shelf life such as onions, garlic, potatoes, shallots, and winter squashes. By taking the time to do this, you will eliminate buying duplicates of items and can almost be certain that food won't spoil. Our breakfasts are usually prepared from staples such as bagels, whole-grain breads and cereals, peanut butter, fruit, and milk. Lunches are almost always leftovers from the previous night's dinner.

Efficient Planning To be more efficient during this planning stage, we note any meals that contain the same ingredients. For example, if we are planning to make Tofu Provolone Lasagna and Baked Tofu Parmesan in the same week, we will press all the tofu to remove its moisture at one time. And since both recipes use similar tomato-based sauces, we will prepare a double batch of a basic red sauce. We will use the sauce in both recipes, adding a bit of cream and tomato paste to one-half of it. We also note if portions of the recipes can be prepared in advance and try to work the time into our preparation schedule. By painstakingly planning your meals in this manner, you will take all the guesswork out of what to have for dinner and will be more efficient in the kitchen and at the market.

Shop Once a Week With your meal plans and shopping list in hand, it is now time to journey to the market. Our strategy is to shop once a week. Multiple stops at the market are inefficient and a sure ticket to an unnecessarily high grocery bill. We are fortunate to be in an area where we can do "one-stop-shopping." These stores have gorgeous produce, sparkling seafood, fresh meats, cheeses from around the world, artisan breads, and a variety of bulk goods. If you live in an area without these types of markets or simply prefer to go to specialty stores for all your food, then you will obviously spend more time shopping. With your children in tow, "making the rounds" can be fun and often educational. Not only do you receive personal service, you may even get a tour of a walk-in freezer, peek into a bread oven, or watch whole fish being filleted.

To cook the best meals, it is important to choose the freshest and highest-quality ingredients available. Many of our recipes emphasize simple preparations and fresh ingredients so the natural flavors and textures of the food you are cooking are highlighted. Squeeze the garlic and onions to be certain they are firm and not bruised or moldy. Choose broccoli with straight deep green florets and firm stalks. Purchase fish and shellfish that smell of the sea. Examine refrigerated meat and poultry to be certain they are not crystallized. Ice on the package is a possible indication that the product has been repeatedly frozen and thawed.

Shopping Economics In addition to purchasing top-quality food, take note of special buys that will save you money. If seasonal fruit is in prime condition, purchase more than you immediately need. Freeze the extra in individual portions for use in smoothies, muffins, and ice cream. If chicken thighs are on sale, purchase twice the amount you need. You can either double the recipe and serve the meal again later in the week or rinse, dry, wrap, and freeze the extra for a future meal. If top-quality canned Italian plum tomatoes are "buy one, get one free," purchase enough for a month. If a gallon container of olive oil is half price, buy one. To keep it fresh, store it in a cool and dark place.

Whether you shop in one store or several, with a detailed list and attention to the quality and price of food, you will have everything you need to prepare delicious meals. Just don't leave your list in the lettuce bins at the store, as we often do, because it's never there when you return for it!

Stocking Your Kitchen Your grandmother surely had one and perhaps even your mother. Your kitchen, however, probably does not.

A pantry, that is, a small room beside the kitchen used for storing food. In a physical sense, although many contemporary kitchens lack them, a well-stocked pantry containing a variety of staples—ingredients with a shelf life of at least a week—is critical to cooking healthful and creative meals.

An organized and well-stocked kitchen will allow you to come directly home from work and prepare healthful meals in a reasonable amount of time. It will also rescue you on those evenings toward the end of the week when you believe you are out of food and just don't know what to make. With your stocked kitchen, you will be pleasantly surprised when you are able to make "something out of nothing." A kitchen doesn't need to be stocked in one fell swoop. It will require several weeks to determine the foods and quantities you will need to prepare all your family's favorite dishes. If you are patient, organized, and thorough, in no time you will have a pantry that even the most organized cook will envy.

Equipping Your Kitchen Family and friends are always surprised when they see how little kitchen equipment we have and just how worn most of it is. We are definitely minimalists when it comes to equipping a serious home cook's kitchen. We don't believe you need to spend hundreds of dollars on knives, pots, pans, small appliances, and the latest gadgets. Often, you pay top dollar for a pot simply for its style and brand, not its practicality. In fact, the most useful pot you can own is a mundane cast-iron Dutch oven. A Dutch oven is a deep, high-sided pot. If it has ovenproof handles, it can go directly from the stovetop to the oven, making it ideal for many recipes. For ten years, in addition to a stockpot in which to cook pasta and a skillet, our only other pot was a five-quart cast-iron Dutch oven. We used it to prepare everything, from stir-fries to soups. Although, as our family has grown, we have purchased two other similar pots, the first is still our workhorse. It is so well seasoned, you can sear tofu or chicken breasts in it in as little as one tablespoon of olive oil and the food will still take on a gorgeous golden color, the sign of perfectly seared food.

When shopping for kitchen equipment, it is best to consider ahead of time your cooking style so you have a clear idea of exactly what you are looking for. Then you will purchase only the versatile equipment that will allow you to successfully execute your recipes. The colorful displays and sales tags in kitchen stores make it too easy to become overwhelmed and confused.

POTS AND PANS Pots and pans are your most important purchase. The best advice we can offer is to not buy packaged sets of cookware. They often contain only one or two pieces that you actually regularly use; the remaining ones will end up in your broom closet. Instead, purchase open-stock cookware. In this manner, you will be able to choose the pieces that are most practical for your cooking style. Pots and pans need to be of good quality, functional, and durable. Thin ones are tricky and difficult to cook with. Although they heat quickly, if they are not closely monitored, food tends to burn in them, and then they are difficult to clean.

Our top choice is enameled cast iron because it is versatile, stylish, and easy to maintain. Although it takes some time to heat, once it is hot, it has the ability to hold a steady temperature. It is also very durable. An excellent alternative to enameled cast iron is the cookware your grandmother likely cooked in—cast iron. It hasn't outlived its usefulness and can be had for rock-bottom prices.

Although many would choose copper for its function and beauty, it takes effort to keep it looking good, and it is extremely expensive. A cast-iron skillet or Dutch oven costs significantly less than the identical piece in aluminum or copper yet is just as functional. With cast iron you can cook as they do in restaurants. You can sear a piece of meat, poultry, or fish on the stove top in a skillet and then transfer the pan directly to the oven to finish cooking. If you are fond of nonstick cookware, you may be concerned that food will stick to cast iron. However, a well-seasoned piece of cast-iron cookware is as good a nonstick surface as you are going to get. Cast-iron cookware is also easy to clean and practically indestructible.

KNIVES In addition to pots and pans, good knives are essential to a well-equipped kitchen. Invest in top-quality ones. With proper maintenance, they will last a lifetime. Just as with pots and pans, don't buy sets of knives. Start with purchasing one good ten-inch chef's knife. Ours is fifteen years old and still in great condition. A few strokes on a sharpening steel are all that is needed to keep it razor sharp. In addition to a chef's knife, an ideal knife collection includes a paring knife, a bread knife, and a ten-inch-long slicing knife. When buying knives, keep in mind that they should feel comfortable in your hand, be well-balanced, and have the ability to hold an edge. High-carbon, stainless-steel knives are an excellent choice. Keep them sharp and properly stored. Knives lurking among spoons and forks in a silverware drawer are dangerous. Store cutlery on a knife magnet attached to a wall out of the reach of children.

UTENSILS AND SMALL APPLIANCES Most of us probably have too many utensils and small appliances. All that a kitchen truly needs are the most basic equipment and utensils. An assortment of long-handled spoons and forks, a whisk, box grater, potato masher, cutting board, and a blender are all that are needed to do some serious home cooking. Certainly, a standing mixer, food processor, and specialty utensils are useful to have and make certain tasks easier and quicker, but they are not necessary. The current trendy kitchen gadgets usually find a home in the back of your tallest cabinet alongside the previous year's impulse purchase.

WHERE TO SHOP FOR KITCHENWARE The most obvious question you may now have is: "Where is the best place to purchase kitchenware?" Specialty kitchen stores and the houseware sections of large department stores are the most obvious answers. If you shop in these places, though, you are likely to pay top dollar. Mail-order companies often carry the same items at lower prices. Discount department stores are another viable option. If you hit it right, you may be able to find first-quality or cosmetically flawed kitchenware at steep discounts. Or you could be like us and frequent yard sales and secondhand shops. You will be pleasantly surprised at what you can find at these places. Beautiful copper pots, butcher-quality knives, and steel skillets are just some of the items we have found, and at give-away prices to boot. Also, you would be amazed at what people toss away. We have inherited several great woks and a restaurant-quality stockpot that friends no longer needed.

As a serious home cook, you don't need to spend a fortune to out-fit your kitchen. With a few good pieces of cookware, a cutting board, a sharp knife, and a wooden spoon, you have all the equipment you need to tackle even the most ambitious recipes.

Efficiency in the Kitchen By now it is clear that efficiency is vital to successful home cooking. As we have mentioned, this efficiency begins with planning your meals and having all the ingredients on hand that are necessary to cook them. Efficiency also includes organizing your staples and equipment so they are within easy reach, knowing how to read a recipe, adjusting the recipe to meet your quantity needs, and doing a good job at the most dreaded task of all: cleaning.

ORGANIZING YOUR KITCHEN The next important step is to be certain that both your food and equipment are readily accessible. If your kitchen has deep cabinets, refrain from putting foods too far back. You may forget they are there. Our two largest cabinets are reserved for our most frequently used dry goods. The bottom shelf of one cabinet holds canned tomatoes, whole-grain pasta, brown rice, and dried legumes. The next shelf contains breakfast cereals and healthy snacks (cookies, too) for the kids. The top shelf is reserved for foods we don't use daily such as canned beans, tuna, anchovies, bread crumbs, and cornmeal. We also store backups of kosher salt, mustards, peanut butter, and jam on this shelf.

In the other cabinet we stock oils, vinegars, and a jar each of white sugar and brown sugar. The shelf directly above it holds dried herbs and spices as well as specialty baking items like extracts and cocoa powder. Since we bake a lot of bread and pizza, we keep our flour in a large container in a separate cabinet. We keep vegetables with a long shelf life such as potatoes, squashes, onions, and garlic stored in a large drawer by the sink. A bottle of olive oil, a bowl (our older son, Joe, made it for us) of kosher salt, and a pepper mill sit on a windowsill adjacent to the stove.

We store our most frequently used cooking vessels in a large cabinet directly below the counter where we perform most of our prep work. We don't keep them piled inside one another since that makes it difficult to get the pan you need quickly. Our cutting board is on the counter leaning against the wall. Kitchen spoons, a whisk, meat pounder, metal spatula, and corkscrew are stored in a single layer in a drawer next to the stove. Sheet pans are directly below the oven.

THE NEARLY EMPTY REFRIGERATOR You would chuckle if you saw our nearly empty refrigerator. It contains only a week's supply of milk, tofu, fruit juice, unsalted butter, mozzarella and Parmesan cheeses, vegetables, seasonal fruit, and of course, light cream for our beloved coffee. We keep enough beef or chicken for one meal, and we buy fish the day we plan to serve it. To avoid waste, rotate the foods in your refrigerator so you know what is in there and make sure you use them before they spoil. Our freezer holds frozen fruit for smoothies, ice cream, homemade baguettes and sliced bread, and portioned packages of meat and poultry.

Organizing your food and equipment will keep you from spending needless time searching for that one elusive ingredient or special pot to cook your favorite meal. You will be able to open a cabinet and find exactly what you need where you expected it to be.

Cooking Lean Although the new food guidelines emphasize that healthy fats may be used more liberally, the basic tenet of keeping calories in a reasonable range still holds true. Therefore, it is important that you arm yourself with a few cooking techniques to keep calories lower when preparing meals. While you do not need to eat fat-free, you want to eat healthy fats and prepare meals in as "light" a fashion as possible while maximizing taste. By "light," we mean keeping calories and saturated fats low.

We have all heard it plenty of times—when it comes to food and cooking, fat means flavor. Whether it is a well-marbled steak or a silky-smooth cream sauce, a meal containing an abundance of fat is almost always going to be delicious. It is, however, easy to prepare terrific-tasting meals using a minimal amount of butter, cream, and other saturated-fat-laden and calorie-dense ingredients.

After years of cooking, we have formulated new ideas and adapted classic techniques to ones that are lower in saturated fat and calories. These methods of lean cooking are a way of life for us. By using a few of our techniques, all your cooking can become leaner and healthier, yet you'll never miss the saturated fat or calories. Once you start cooking this way, you'll wonder why everyone doesn't do it, since the end result is just as delicious and flavorful.

BUTTER AND CREAM AS SEASONINGS We view butter and cream as seasonings rather than major components of a meal. For example, if you are preparing a broth-based sauce for a quick pasta or chicken dish, a tablespoon of cold, unsalted butter added to the sauce during the last several minutes of cooking will emulsify it and give it a delightful texture and consistency. Olive oil and cream can be used in similar ways. Drizzling a fruity olive oil or cream into a soup or pasta just prior to serving will give the food a burst of flavor without breaking the fat and calorie bank. While olive oil is a heart-healthy ingredient, it is high in calories, so you want to us it in moderation. The end result will taste as if you used a great deal more butter, oil, or cream than you really did.

SUBSTITUTE LOW-FAT VERSIONS While low-fat does not mean calorie-free, you can still make your meals lower in saturated fat and calories if you substitute low-fat versions of classic ingredients. This does not–repeat, *does not*–mean you can eat as much of these recipes as you want. It simply means that these low-fat versions have fewer calories than the full-fat versions.

Our lean-cooking suggestion is to attempt to rework your favorite dessert recipes and make them healthful without sacrificing flavor. Rich-tasting and nutritious "ice creams" can be prepared with a base of firm tofu (see Frozen Chocolate-Marshmallow Soy Cream Pie, page 380). Real Chocolate Pudding (see page 379) is made with low-fat milk. Experiment with ground flaxseed and pureed fruits as replacements for the butter and oil in quick breads and cookies (see Raspberry-Oat Squares, page 377). The flavor and moistness these ingredients deliver will pleasantly surprise you.

SUBSTITUTE SILKEN TOFU FOR CREAM Another great way to reduce the saturated-fat content of your meals is to substitute leaner and more healthful ingredients in your recipes. Pureed silken tofu can replace the cream in all your favorite sauce recipes and the oil in your salad dressings and pestos. When the tofu is combined with bold-flavored ingredients such as vinegars, tamari, herbs, and olives, you will be able to create great sauces and will never miss the cream and oil. Silken tofu is a versatile ingredient that is a terrific source of protein and antioxidants. Many people claim not to like tofu yet are stupefied when they learn that their "Creamy" Caesar Salad (see page 326) is actually a salad dressing based upon tofu, or that their mashed potatoes are made with silken tofu instead of cream. It is a perfect substitute. This substitution is used throughout this cookbook.

COOKING WITH FLAVORFUL LIQUIDS Cooking with flavorful liquids such as broths, pasta cooking water, and water in which dried vegetables have soaked or beans and vegetables have been cooked is another simple technique to create flavor in your cooking with no fat. A cup of pasta-cooking water added to a pasta sauce will enhance its flavor and ability to cling to the noodles. The soaking liquid from dried mushrooms and tomatoes is so flavorful it can practically be a sauce on its own. Potato-cooking water and broccoli-steaming water not only taste good but are nutritious as well. The possibilities are endless for other sources of flavorful liquids.

SEARING Searing is a low-fat and basic cooking technique that you should add to your repertoire on a daily basis. Although searing is most often associated with meat and fish, vegetables and tofu can be seared as well. The crust that searing develops gives the food eye appeal and great flavor. In a well-seasoned pan, it is possible to sear enough food to serve four people with as little as one tablespoon of oil. In addition to giving your food great color, texture, and flavor, searing also leaves behind caramelized particles. These bits can be deglazed in the pan to create a delectable and no-fuss sauce. Many of the recipes in this cookbook utilize this technique.

To successfully sear, you need to adhere to several principles.

First, the appropriate pan material and size need to be chosen. Since they get very hot and hold their heat so well, a well-seasoned cast-iron skillet or Dutch oven are the top choices. The food that is going to be seared needs to fit comfortably in the pan. If it is crowded, it won't sear properly. Also, the food, whether in one large piece or sliced, needs to be thoroughly dried. Moisture will prevent a good crust from forming. After the food is dried, it is sprinkled on all sides with kosher salt and black pepper. This step will enhance the color of the crust and draw out the natural juices of the food.

Before the food hits the pan, a tablespoon or so of oil is heated over medium-high heat. Once the oil is very hot, you place the food into the pan. Once in the pan, it should not be moved until the bottom is deeply colored and crisp. Then turn it and crust it on the opposite side.

Once the food is seared, remove it from the pan. Then reduce the heat and begin the deglazing. To deglaze, first gently cook aromatics such as garlic or shallots in the pan. Then raise the heat and add broth, wine, or water and scrape the bottom of the pan with a spoon to dissolve any caramelized particles. This liquid will add a great flavor to your dish. The food is then returned to the pot and cooked over low heat until it is fork tender.

SWEATING Sweating involves cooking lightly salted vegetables, most often onions, leeks, garlic, potatoes, squashes, bell peppers, or carrots in a covered pot over low heat. The combination of heat and salt causes the vegetables to release their natural juices, thus creating a delicious layer of flavor for a soup, stew, or sauce.

BRAISING Braising involves cooking tougher cuts of meat in a liquid over low heat for an extended time period—on average three hours. Tougher cuts of meat are used because they contain an abundance of connective tissue, and the long, slow cooking process breaks this down. The braising liquid is usually wine, tomatoes, or stock. After the meat is cooked, the fat is skimmed from the liquid. This extended and gentle cooking method results in very tender meat. Examples of these cuts of meat include beef brisket, rump roast, pork shoulder, chicken thighs, and short ribs of beef. These cuts tend to be inexpensive, thus braising is very economical.

Just because you have committed to cooking healthful and low-fat food does not mean that you are destined to eat bland and unexciting meals. With a few new ideas and cooking skills, you will be creating lean and tasty food in no time. If you keep in mind that the best meals are the simplest—meals that combine fresh ingredients with straightforward techniques that allow the true flavors of the ingredients to fully develop and stand out—you will discover that to cook great food, you don't need fancy equipment or esoteric ingredients, just a bit of practice and a great imagination.

PART TWO

recipes

CHAPTER 13

egg dishes

Nutritional knowledge is continually improving, and it is common for new research findings to contradict older information. Eggs are a perfect example of this scenario. Eggs were once thought to be an unhealthful, cholesterol-raising food; however, recent findings have indicated that it is saturated fat, not cholesterol, in the diet that has the most profound effect on blood cholesterol. The dietary, cholesterol, and egg restrictions that were once part of American dietary folklore were easily justified by our fat-phobic and cholesterol-phobic lifestyles; however, consuming an average of one egg per day is acceptable for many people, but not everyone. Although there are no longer specific recommendations for strict egg limitations, the American Heart Association continues to recommend that the intake of dietary cholesterol be limited to an average of 300 milligrams per day. If an individual's overall diet is low in cholesterol, an egg a day falls within that limitation.

Eggs are one of nature's perfect foods. They are an excellent source of high-quality protein, essential vitamins A, D, and E, and the minerals iron and zinc. They are relatively low in saturated fat and calories, making them an ideal healthy fast food for all the family. Some egg producers are now able to modify certain aspects of the nutritional composition of their eggs by feeding their hens special diets. These "designer" eggs contain greater amounts of omega-three fatty acids and vitamin E.

Eggs need to be chosen, handled, and prepared with care to ensure safety. Unfortunately, there is no way to determine if an egg is fresh without cracking it. If spoiled, an egg's yolk will be discolored and have a very unpleasant odor. Eggs should always be stored in the refrigerator and cooked thoroughly. Although there have been great efforts to remove salmonella from eggs, people should continue to refrain from eating raw or undercooked eggs. In addition, wash all implements and work surfaces thoroughly after handling raw eggs. Also, avoid tasting anything that contains raw eggs, such as cookie dough and cake batter.

Eggs play a vital role in a variety of recipes, sweet and savory. Egg whites provide lightness to soufflés and meringues and richness to cheesecakes. Eggs bind stuffings and ground-meat dishes and are used to thicken soups and sauces. In our home, eggs are the ultimate fast food. For a quick lunch, try our Any Pasta Frittata (see page 164). It is a great way to transform the previous evening's pasta leftovers into a simple, fast, and creative meal. Or, rather than stuffing your midday pita with vegetables and hummus, fill it with our Potato, Turkey Bacon, and Egg Roll Ups (see page 167). One of our favorite Sunday night dinners is a Spanish Tortilla with Spinach and Garlic (see page 165). One taste will have you reminiscing about your favorite tapas restaurant. Next time you crave an egg salad sandwich, don't reach for the mayonnaise jar. Prepare our intensely flavored Egg Salad (see page 169) studded with finely chopped scallions and seasoned with olive oil and parsley. You will never make the traditional fat-laden version again. Whether they are scrambled or used in an elegant omelet or peasant-style frittata, the combination of convenience, versatility, and nutrition that eggs provide is difficult to match.

Broccoli and Cheddar Frittata

PREPARATION:
10 MINUTES

COOKING:
10 MINUTES

YIELD:
4 MAIN-COURSE
SERVINGS

With abundant amounts of folate, calcium, and fiber, broccoli is a superfood. Children either love or loathe broccoli. If your kids are in the former group, this quickly prepared dish is a great way to get plenty of this nutritious vegetable into their diets. **TIP:** Don't toss the broccoli-blanching water down the drain. Freeze it and use it to enhance a future soup, sauce, or pasta dish.

1½ cups water
1 pound broccoli, trimmed, florets separated and stems peeled and sliced into discs
4 eggs
4 egg whites
½ teaspoon kosher salt
2 teaspoons unsalted butter
3 ounces cheddar cheese, sliced or grated

1. Preheat the broiler and prepare an ice bath.
2. Bring the water to a boil in a medium-sized saucepan and add the broccoli. Cover the pot and steam the broccoli for 3 minutes. Drain it and shock it in the ice bath.
3. Whisk the eggs and egg whites in a medium bowl for 2 minutes. Add the salt. Stir in the broccoli.
4. Heat an ovenproof skillet over medium heat. Add the butter. Once it stops foaming, add the egg mixture. After approximately 1 minute, as the eggs begin to set, push and lift the edges of the frittata with a spatula and tilt the pan to allow the egg to run underneath. Continue cooking the frittata in this manner until the surface is no longer runny but still wet, approximately 3 minutes.
5. Scatter the cheese onto the frittata. Transfer the skillet to the oven. Finish cooking the frittata until the cheese melts and the surface is dry, approximately 3 minutes.
6. Slide the frittata onto a plate and slice it into 4 wedges. Serve it hot or at room temperature with whole-grain bread and a green salad.

Frittata

An Italian frittata has more in common with a traditional Spanish tortilla than a French omelet. In a frittata, the filling is combined with the eggs and the mixture is cooked in a skillet until it is set. The frittata is then finished under the broiler until it is golden. This technique creates a finished product that is a bit firmer and drier than an omelet.

A frittata is versatile. It can be served hot or at room temperature. It is wonderful for breakfast or lunch and when accompanied by roasted potatoes or a green salad, makes a simple and satisfying dinner.

PREPARATION:
10 MINUTES

COOKING:
10 MINUTES

YIELD:
4 MAIN-COURSE
SERVINGS

Zucchini, Tomato, Onion, and Provolone Frittata

Gently cooking zucchini and onions in olive oil enhances their natural sweetness. A tomato provides just the right amount of acidic contrast. Prepare this frittata often during the summer when great zucchini and tomatoes are abundant.

1 tablespoon olive oil
1 medium onion, peeled and thinly sliced
   Kosher salt
1 medium zucchini, trimmed, cut in half lengthwise and thinly sliced
1 plum tomato, diced
1 teaspoon unsalted butter
4 eggs
4 egg whites
3 ounces provolone cheese, sliced or grated

1. Preheat the broiler.
2. Heat the olive oil in an ovenproof skillet over medium heat. When the oil is hot, add the onion. Sprinkle it with kosher salt. Cook the

onion until it begins to soften, stirring often, approximately 2 minutes.

3. Add the zucchini. Cook the zucchini until it is tender, stirring often, approximately 5 minutes. Add the tomato and cook for 30 seconds. Transfer the vegetables to a plate. Wipe out the skillet.

4. Heat the butter in the skillet over medium heat. Whisk the eggs and egg whites in a medium bowl for 2 minutes.

5. Once the butter stops foaming, add the eggs. Quickly stir in the vegetables. After approximately 1 minute, as the eggs begin to set, lift the edges of the frittata with a spatula and tilt the pan to allow the egg to run underneath. Continue cooking the frittata in this manner until the surface is no longer runny but still wet, approximately 3 minutes.

6. Scatter the cheese onto the frittata. Transfer the skillet to the oven. Finish cooking the frittata until the cheese melts and the surface is dry, approximately 3 minutes.

7. Slide the frittata onto a plate and slice it into 4 wedges. Serve it hot or at room temperature with whole-grain bread and a green salad.

PREPARATION:
10 MINUTES

COOKING:
10 MINUTES

YIELD:
4 MAIN-COURSE
SERVINGS

The Any Pasta Frittata

We take pride in our goal of not wasting food and our innovative use of leftovers. You can always simply reheat leftovers and that is something we often do, but occasionally we turn a mundane bowl of the previous evening's supper into something completely different and almost always tasty. This is one of those recipes. Any leftover pasta will suffice, but we are particularly fond of Spaghetti with Broccoli, Garlic, and Pine Nuts (see page 208). **TIP:** Allow your children to help you prepare this meal. When they observe you combining eggs and pasta, their innate curiosity alone will lead them to sample the final product.

2 tablespoons olive oil plus extra for drizzling
2 cups cooked pasta
4 eggs
4 egg whites
   Kosher salt
   Black pepper
2 ounces fresh mozzarella cheese, sliced

1. Preheat the broiler.
2. Heat the olive oil in an ovenproof skillet over medium-high heat. When the oil is hot, add the pasta and cook for 4 minutes, stirring occasionally.
3. While the pasta is cooking, whisk the eggs and egg whites for 2 minutes. Season them with kosher salt and black pepper.
4. Add the eggs to the skillet. After approximately 1 minute, as the eggs begin to set, lift the edges of the frittata with a spatula and tilt the pan to allow the egg to run underneath. Continue cooking the frittata in this manner until the surface is no longer runny but still wet, approximately 3 minutes.
5. Scatter the cheese onto the frittata. Transfer the skillet to the oven. Finish cooking the frittata until the cheese melts and the surface is dry, approximately 3 minutes.
6. Slide the frittata onto a plate and slice it into 4 wedges. Serve it hot or at room temperature with whole-grain bread and a green salad.

Spanish Tortilla with Spinach and Garlic

A traditional Spanish tortilla is prepared in a similar manner to a frittata but is cooked entirely on the stove. In Spain, tortillas are often prepared with fried onions and potatoes or simply scallions and served at room temperature in bars as tapas (little snacks). You may not find our version, starring garlicky spinach, in Spain, but it is delicious and one that we make often. Spinach is an excellent source of iron and fiber.

PREPARATION:
5 MINUTES

COOKING:
10 MINUTES

YIELD:
4 MAIN-COURSE
SERVINGS

4   eggs
4   egg whites
    Kosher salt
    Black pepper
1   tablespoon olive oil
3   cloves garlic, peeled and thinly sliced
1   10-ounce package frozen chopped spinach, thawed and
        thoroughly squeezed

1. Whisk together the eggs and egg whites. Season them with kosher salt and black pepper. Set them aside for a moment.
2. Heat the olive oil in a nonstick skillet over medium heat. When the oil is hot, add the garlic. Cook it for 30 seconds. Add the spinach and cook it for 2 minutes, stirring often.
3. Add the eggs to the skillet. After approximately 1 minute, as the eggs begin to set, lift the edges of the tortilla with a spatula and tilt the pan to allow the egg to run underneath. Continue cooking the tortilla in this manner until the surface is no longer runny but still wet, approximately 3 minutes.
4. Loosen the sides and the bottom of the tortilla with a spatula. Place a large plate over the tortilla and invert the pan onto the plate. Remove the pan and slide the tortilla, which is now on the plate, back into the pan, runny-side down. Cook for an additional 2 minutes.
5. Transfer the tortilla to a plate and slice it into 4 wedges. Serve it hot or at room temperature.

PREPARATION:

5 MINUTES

COOKING:

5 MINUTES

YIELD:

4 MAIN-COURSE
SERVINGS

Breakfast Burrito

Tofu, cooked beans, bell peppers, salsa, and leftover meat are just a few suggestions that can be combined with eggs and rolled into flour tortillas to create quick and wholesome breakfast burritos. **TIPS:** Try not to stir scrambled eggs too often. Frequent stirring will break them into small, dry, and crumbly pieces. Also, we suggest microwaving the tortillas to warm them and melt the cheese. If you don't have a microwave, preheat the oven to 300°F, divide the cheese among the tortillas, roll them and wrap them in foil, and heat them for 5 minutes.

- 4 eggs
- 4 egg whites
  - Kosher salt
  - Black pepper
- 1 tablespoon unsalted butter
- 4 scallions, trimmed and thinly sliced
- 1 large tomato, cored and diced
- 1 ripe avocado, peeled, pitted, and diced
- ¼ cup cilantro, chopped
- 2 ounces cheddar cheese, grated or sliced
- 4 whole-grain flour tortillas

1. Whisk the eggs and egg whites in a large bowl. Season them with kosher salt and black pepper. Set the mixture aside for a moment
2. Heat the butter in a large, nonstick skillet over medium heat. When it stops foaming, add the scallions and cook them for 30 seconds. Add the tomato, avocado, and cilantro and cook the ingredients for another minute, stirring often.
3. Add the eggs. When soft curds form, lift them away from the sides with a large spoon and tilt the pan so that the undercooked eggs can flow to the bottom. Continue cooking the eggs in this manner until they are firm but the top is still moist. Remove the pan from the heat.
4. Divide the cheese among the tortillas. Microwave each until the cheese melts and the tortillas are warm, approximately 30 seconds.
5. Divide the tortillas among 4 plates. Divide the eggs among the tortillas. Fold in the sides and then roll each tortilla up from the bottom to enclose the filling completely.

Potato, Turkey Bacon, and Egg Roll Ups

One afternoon while writing the introduction to this chapter, we had an intense craving for eggs. We were also in need of several quick and creative egg dishes to complete this section. This simple dish satisfied our hankering and was a welcome addition to our book. We now prepare it regularly, and it has proven to be a winner with our children as well. **TIP:** Traditional bacon or pancetta (uncured Italian bacon) can be substituted for the turkey bacon. Also, the meal can be served on toast or tucked into a whole-grain pita or crusty roll.

PREPARATION:
10 MINUTES

COOKING:
20 MINUTES

YIELD:
4 MAIN-COURSE
SERVINGS

1 tablespoon canola oil
4 slices turkey bacon, chopped
1 russet potato, peeled and sliced into ¼-inch cubes
  Kosher salt
2 ounces Monterey Jack cheese, sliced or grated
4 whole-grain flour tortillas
4 eggs
4 egg whites
2 tablespoons milk
  Black pepper

1. Preheat the oven to 300°F.
2. Heat the canola oil in a large skillet over medium heat. When the oil is hot, add the bacon. Render the bacon until crisp, approximately 5 minutes, stirring occasionally. With a slotted spoon, transfer the bacon to a plate lined with paper towels. Set the bacon aside for a moment.
3. Pour off all but a tablespoon of the accumulated fat in the pan. Place the pan over medium-high heat. Add the potatoes and sprinkle them with kosher salt. Cook them until they are golden and tender, approximately 10 minutes, tossing occasionally.
4. While the potatoes are cooking, divide the cheese among the tortillas. Place the tortillas in the oven. Heat them until the cheese melts, approximately 5 minutes.
5. Remove them from the oven. Divide them among 4 plates.
6. In a large bowl whisk the eggs, egg whites, and milk. Season the mixture with kosher salt and black pepper.

7. Add the mixture to the pan containing the potatoes. When soft curds form, lift them away from the sides with a large spoon and tilt the pan so that the undercooked eggs can flow to the bottom. Continue cooking the eggs in this manner until they are firm but the top is still moist.

8. Divide the egg-and-potato mixture among the tortillas. Garnish each with the bacon. Fold in the sides and then roll the tortilla up from the bottom to enclose the filling completely.

Vanilla-Apple French Toast

French toast, like pancakes, is a breakfast that is loved by parents and kids alike. A custard of eggs and milk makes a fine base, but the addition of apple-juice concentrate and vanilla gives the meal a delightful and interesting flavor. Eggs are a great source of protein and iron, and the bread is rich in fiber and complex carbohydrates. **TIPS:** If you have a large griddle, it can be used instead of two skillets. Also, the best bread for this recipe is a bakery-style loaf that you can slice yourself. If only sliced bread is available, plan on two slices per person.

3 eggs
4 egg whites
2 tablespoons apple-juice concentrate
2 teaspoons vanilla
½ cup milk
4 1-inch-thick slices whole-grain bread
4 teaspoons unsalted butter, divided
Powdered sugar for sprinkling
Maple syrup for serving, warmed

1. In a large bowl whisk the eggs, egg whites, apple-juice concentrate, vanilla, and milk.

2. Divide the mixture between 2 pie plates. Place 2 slices of bread into each plate. Soak the bread for 5 minutes on each side, turning once.

3. Heat two skillets over medium-low heat. Add 2 teaspoons of butter to each skillet. When the butter stops foaming, place 2 slices of bread into each skillet.
4. Cook the bread until golden and slightly crisp on each side, approximately 5 minutes per side, turning once.
5. Divide the bread among 4 plates, sprinkle with powdered sugar, and accompany with the maple syrup.

Egg Salad

We read about this healthful and unique version of egg salad in a food article and decided to re-create it at home. With scallions, parsley, and olive oil it has a fresher and richer taste and is more nutritious than a traditional mayonnaise-laden version. Serve it between slices of whole-grain country bread garnished with slices of garden tomatoes or use it as a topping for your favorite salad greens.

PREPARATION:
5 MINUTES

COOKING:
10 MINUTES

YIELD:
4 SANDWICH OR SALAD SERVINGS

8 eggs
2 scallions, trimmed and thinly sliced
2 tablespoons flat-leaf (Italian) parsley, finely chopped
3 tablespoons olive oil
Kosher salt
Black pepper

1. Prepare an ice bath.
2. Bring a pot of water to a boil. With a large spoon, carefully drop the eggs into the water. Return the water to a boil. Reduce the heat to a simmer and cook the eggs for 10 minutes.
3. Drain the eggs. Transfer them to the ice bath. When they are cool enough to handle, peel them, removing and discarding 4 yolks.
4. Place the remaining eggs and egg whites in a bowl. Coarsely mash them with a fork. Stir in the scallions, parsley, and olive oil. Season the egg salad with kosher salt and black pepper.

CHAPTER 14

soups

There are few meals more satisfying and nutritious on a cool evening than a steaming bowl of soul-warming soup. And from a cook's perspective, nothing is more enjoyable than preparing a homemade soup—except, of course, eating it. You don't need expensive or hard-to-find ingredients to make a great soup. A soup can be prepared with ingredients you probably already have in your kitchen. An imaginative cook can create a tasty and healthful soup with nothing more than onions, garlic, a few root vegetables, a handful of dried peas, and a can of tomatoes.

Since we like to serve soup as a main course, ours are hearty and sustaining. A soup that contains beans, meat or tofu, grains, and a variety of vegetables is an ideal one-pot dish. A hunk of crusty bread and one of our green salads are all that are needed to round out a soup meal. Several of our soups can be on the table in less than thirty minutes while others require an hour or two of slow cooking. For the majority of the time, though, these long-simmering creations need little attention, just a stir now and then. You can go about your work and enjoy the wonderful aromas wafting from your kitchen.

If you favor a filling, bean-based soup, you are certain to enjoy our White Bean, Tomato, and Fennel Soup (see page 175). During a busy week, you may want to try our Chicken Noodle Soup (see page 173). It contains nothing more than chicken broth, noodles, spinach, and chicken. If you have the ingredients prepared, it can be ready in fifteen minutes. For a gusty-tasting soup in no time, our simple Meatball and Broccoli Rabe Soup (see page 174) fits the bill. We always keep several portions of meatballs in our freezer so we can enjoy this soup regularly. With an abundance of protein, fiber, carbohydrates, and vitamins our Lentil and Barley Soup (see page 177) is as nutritious as any meal.

Soup making is an excellent way to introduce cooking to your children. As we already mentioned, since preparing delectable soups requires nothing more than first-rate ingredients and an imagination, children will learn the importance of fresh food and creativity while simultaneously being taught basic kitchen skills. Beginning at three years of age, youngsters can assist in preparing a cutting board bursting with raw ingredients and then lend a hand in adding them to the pot at various intervals to create a delicious soup. These experiences will help them to begin to identify a variety of vegetables, meats, grains, and legumes. They will also gain knowledge of nutrition and learn the importance of safety, organization, and cleanliness in the kitchen. Most important, though, they will be likely to eat their creations and be more open-minded in the future when trying new foods.

Chicken Stock

The aroma of a pot of chicken stock simmering on the stove gives us a feeling of comfort and warmth. While preparing a homemade stock is not difficult, it does take quite a while to make a deeply flavored one. The anticipation of a delicious bowl of soup is well worth the wait. This stock can be used in any recipe calling for some and is a must in our Chicken Noodle Soup (see below) and Meatball and Broccoli Rabe Soup (see page 174). **TIP:** To produce a clear and flavorful stock, keep the heat low enough so the bubbles just reach the surface and skim the stock frequently.

PREPARATION:
10 MINUTES

COOKING:
4 HOURS

YIELD:
1 GALLON

3½–4-pound chicken (including neck)
3 medium carrots, sliced into 1-inch pieces
3 ribs celery, cut into 1-inch pieces
1 large onion, peeled and chopped
6 sprigs flat-leaf (Italian) parsley
1 gallon plus 2 cups cold water
1 tablespoon kosher salt

1. Place all the ingredients in a large stockpot. Bring the liquid to a boil. Reduce the heat to low. The bubbles should just be breaking the surface. Simmer the stock for 4 hours, skimming it frequently.
2. Remove the chicken from the pot. Allow it to cool. When it is cool, remove the meat from the bones.
3. Strain the stock into a large bowl. Refrigerate the stock overnight. The following day, remove the fat from the stock. Use the stock and meat in your favorite recipes.

Chicken Noodle Soup

Whether you use a homemade stock or a low-sodium commercially produced one, you are sure to enjoy this soup for its great taste and ease of preparation. If you use a store-bought stock and have no chicken to add to the soup, don't fret; the soup is excel-

PREPARATION:
5 MINUTES

COOKING:
15 MINUTES

YIELD:
4 MAIN-COURSE
SERVINGS

lent without it. If you want to enhance the soup's texture and flavor, though, you can add diced boneless and skinless chicken
breast or cubed firm tofu during step two.

1 recipe Chicken Stock (see page 173) or 2 quarts low-sodium
   canned chicken broth
   Meat from 1 chicken (if using homemade stock)
12 ounces broad egg noodles
12 ounces spinach, trimmed, washed, drained, and chopped
   Kosher salt
   Black pepper

1. Place the stock in a large pot and bring to a boil.
2. Add the noodles and cook according to the package instructions.
3. Remove the pot from the heat and stir in the spinach. Stir the
   soup until the spinach wilts, approximately 2 minutes.
4. Season the soup with kosher salt and black pepper. Divide the
   soup among 4 large bowls and serve at once.

Meatball and Broccoli Rabe Soup

PREPARATION:
5 MINUTES

COOKING:
15 MINUTES

YIELD:
4 MAIN-COURSE
SERVINGS

This simple soup uses a portion of meatballs from Spaghetti
and Meatballs (see page 336). A garnish of peppery broccoli rabe
provides a delightful flavor contrast to the rich meatballs and
stock. Children may find the rabe too pungent tasting. Since it
is prepared separately from the soup, their portions can be made
easily without it. The meatballs provide protein and iron and
the rabe is rich in calcium, fiber, and folate.

10 cups homemade chicken stock (see page 173) or low-sodium
   canned broth
8 meatballs (see page 336), quartered
   Kosher salt
   Black pepper
1 tablespoon olive oil
3 cloves garlic, peeled and thinly sliced
1 pound broccoli rabe, rinsed, trimmed, and chopped

1. Bring the stock to a boil in a Dutch oven. Add the meatballs. Reduce the heat to low, and simmer the soup for 15 minutes. Season it with kosher salt and black pepper.
2. While the soup is simmering, heat the olive oil in another Dutch oven over medium heat. When it is hot, add the garlic and cook for 1 minute. Add the rabe, sprinkle with kosher salt, and stir until it begins to wilt. Cover the pot and steam the rabe until tender, stirring occasionally, approximately 3 minutes.
3. Divide the rabe among 4 large bowls, ladle the soup into bowls, and serve at once.

White Bean, Tomato, and Fennel Soup

We often slow-cook our bean soups in the oven. Although this technique is more time-consuming, it requires no additional effort. The slow cooking allows all the flavors to develop and meld, creating a rich and hearty soup. The sweetness of the tomatoes and fennel and the earthy-tasting white beans are sure to please children and adults alike. Bean soups are wonderfully nutritious. This one contains plenty of protein, fiber, calcium, and iron. **TIP:** Consider preparing this soup in advance. As with many soups and stews, this one tastes even better after it has been refrigerated for a day or two. When reheating the soup, add a bit of water to reach your desired consistency.

PREPARATION:
10 MINUTES

BEAN SOAKING:
OVERNIGHT

COOKING:
2 HOURS

YIELD:
4 MAIN-COURSE SERVINGS PLUS LEFTOVERS (SEE PAGE 189 FOR A RECIPE)

- 2 tablespoons olive oil
- 4 cloves garlic, peeled and thinly sliced
- 2 medium yellow onions, peeled and diced
  Kosher salt
- 1 medium head fennel, trimmed, cored, and diced
- 3 heaping tablespoons tomato paste
- 2½ cups small white or navy beans, sorted, rinsed, and soaked overnight
- 10 cups water
- ½ cup half and half
- ½ cup flat-leaf (Italian) parsley, chopped
  Black pepper

1. Preheat the oven to 350°F.
2. Heat the olive oil in a large Dutch oven over low heat. Add the garlic and cook until soft, approximately 3 minutes.
3. Add the onions and sprinkle them with kosher salt. Raise the heat to medium. Cook the onions until they begin to soften, stirring occasionally, approximately 7 minutes. Add the fennel and cook until soft, approximately 7 minutes.
4. Add the tomato paste and cook for 1 minute, stirring constantly.
5. Raise the heat to high and add the beans and water. Bring the soup to a boil. Transfer the soup to the oven. Cook the soup for 2 hours.
6. Remove the pot from the oven. If necessary, add 1 to 2 cups of water to thin the soup. Puree 4 cups of the soup in a blender or food processor. Return the puree to the pot.
7. Stir in the half and half and parsley. Season the soup with kosher salt and black pepper.
8. Divide the soup among 4 bowls and serve at once.

Fennel

Sweet, crisp, and refreshing, fennel is a delicious and versatile vegetable that is rapidly becoming a staple in American kitchens. In Italy, they often begin a meal with raw fennel that is thinly sliced and sprinkled with salt and drizzled with olive oil. Or they may end a meal with fennel to cleanse their palates. When cooked, fennel is prized for the sweet and earthy flavor it adds to soups, stews, and sauces. It is also a wonderful accompaniment when braised in chicken stock or roasted in the oven. Brushed with olive oil, it can also be a unique addition to your grilling repertoire. Purchase fennel with firm stalks and bright white bulbs with no hint of discoloration. To prepare fennel for a recipe, first remove its stalks (don't discard them as they are a wonderful addition to chicken and vegetable stocks), then cut the bulb in half, core it, and slice it into thin strips. The fernlike leaves can be used as a garnish or added at the end of cooking for a burst of flavor.

Lentil and Barley Soup

With its earthy and sweet flavors, this hearty and healthful soup is certain to be a family favorite. Lentils are the Cadillac of dried legumes. They are an excellent source of iron, folate, fiber, and calcium. **TIP:** This soup tastes even better on the second day after all the flavors have had a chance to intensify. When reheating it, be sure to thin it with water and correct the seasoning.

1½ cup lentils, sorted and rinsed
¾ cup barley, rinsed
7 cups plus 2 cups of water
   Kosher salt
1 tablespoon olive oil
3 cloves garlic, peeled and thinly sliced
1 medium onion, peeled and diced
1 fennel bulb, trimmed, cored, and diced
2 heaping tablespoons tomato paste
   Black pepper

1. Combine the lentils, barley, and 7 cups of the water in a Dutch oven. Season the mixture with kosher salt. Cover the pot and bring the water to a boil. Reduce the heat and simmer the lentils until tender, approximately 35 minutes.

2. While the lentils are simmering, heat the olive oil in another Dutch oven or large skillet over medium heat. When the oil is hot, add the garlic and cook for 1 minute. Add the onion, sprinkle it with kosher salt, and cook for 2 minutes, stirring constantly. Add the fennel and cook for 5 minutes, stirring often.

3. Stir in the tomato paste and cook for 1 minute. Raise the heat to high and add the remaining 2 cups of water. Bring the liquid to a boil. Reduce the heat, and simmer the ingredients for 4 minutes. Set the mixture aside for a moment.

4. After the lentils have cooked for 35 minutes, stir in the fennel mixture. Simmer the soup for 10 more minutes.

5. Season the soup with kosher salt and black pepper. Ladle the soup into 4 bowls and serve at once.

PREPARATION:
10 MINUTES

COOKING:
45 MINUTES

YIELD:
4 MAIN-DISH SERVINGS
PLUS LEFTOVERS
(FOR A RECIPE,
SEE PAGE 190)

Salt and Great Food

There is a very direct relationship between delicious food and salt. Meals prepared without salt never have a chance to develop any depth of flavor and simply taste flat. We are not advocating a heavy hand with the saltshaker but rather suggesting salting your food carefully and at the appropriate times. There are three critical intervals when you should salt: just prior to cooking, whenever a new ingredient is added during the cooking, and when the cooking is complete.

Meat, poultry, and fish benefit greatly from a sprinkling of salt prior to cooking, as do vegetables that are going to be roasted or grilled. This initial salting improves the texture of the food and enhances its moisture and natural flavors. Along similar lines, brining, the process of soaking meat or poultry in a solution of water, salt, and a bit of sugar for an extended period of time (generally twenty-four hours), transforms an ordinary piece of meat or poultry into a succulent, tender, and deeply flavored meal.

Salting as you go along can best be illustrated by soup cookery. The first step in preparing a soup is to sauté a few cloves of sliced garlic in a tablespoon or two of olive oil. After a minute or so, a diced onion is added. The onion is sprinkled with salt and cooked for several minutes. The salt causes the onion to release its moisture and thus flavor the soup. Celery and carrots are then added and sprinkled with salt. Again, the salt causes the vegetables to sweat (covering the pan enhances this process), adding yet another layer of flavor to the final product. The same salting technique is used in the preparation of stews and sauces, and when sautéing or braising vegetables for a side dish.

The final salting occurs just prior to serving the meal. It is critical to dip a spoon into the sauce or taste a noodle or vegetable and determine if the food has a well-rounded flavor or tastes flat. If it tastes flat, add a sprinkle of salt, gently stir, and taste again. Continue adding small amounts of salt, stirring, and tasting until the food tastes perfect. It is difficult to state exactly how much salt is needed. But what can be noted is that after cooking for several months, experimenting, and taking notes, you will discover by taste and repeated successes exactly how much salt is needed for your food to taste bright and full of flavor. Your goal, as a cook, should be to serve food that requires no added seasoning at the table.

With the wide variety of salts available today, it can be confusing which type to choose. In our kitchen, we use either kosher salt or sea salt. Sea salt is wonderful if you can locate a brand with a slightly coarse texture. Often, the only type available is the "fine" variety, which has a texture similar to superfine sugar, making it difficult to sprinkle onto food with your fingers. Kosher salt is widely available and an excellent choice for all your cooking needs. It is coarse textured and has a clean and fresh flavor. Be certain to purchase kosher salt that contains no additives. Some kosher salts now contain anticaking agents that will add an unpleasant flavor to your food. If you are accustomed to using "table salt," you will find that because of its larger and irregularly shaped crystals, you will need more kosher salt than regular salt to achieve the same level of flavor.

Split Pea and Sausage Soup

With plenty of fiber, carbohydrates, and protein, dried-legume-based soups are comforting and nutritious cold-weather meals. Traditionally a ham bone is simmered with the peas in this type of soup. But since we don't often have a ham bone, we usually add chicken or turkey sausage to enhance the soup's flavor and texture. **TIP:** We have also made this soup with leftover barbequed pork butt. The pork adds a wonderful richness and smoky flavor.

PREPARATION:
20 MINUTES

COOKING:
1¼ HOURS

YIELD:
4 MAIN-COURSE
SERVINGS

 1 tablespoon canola oil
12 ounces (4 links) sweet Italian turkey or chicken sausage
 2 cloves garlic, peeled and thinly sliced
 1 onion, peeled and diced
 3 carrots, scraped and diced
    Kosher salt
1½ cups green split peas, sorted and rinsed
 6 cups homemade or low-sodium chicken broth
    Black pepper

1. Heat the canola oil in a Dutch oven over medium-high heat. When the oil is hot, add the sausages. Sear the sausages, rolling them occasionally, until golden, approximately 5 minutes. Remove the sausages from the pot and set them aside for a moment.

2. Reduce the heat to low. Add the garlic and cook for 30 seconds. Stir in the onion and carrots and sprinkle them with kosher salt. Cook them until they begin to soften, stirring occasionally, approximately 5 minutes.
3. Raise the heat to high and add the split peas. Cook them for 3 minutes, stirring often. Add the chicken broth and bring the soup to a boil.
4. Reduce the heat and simmer the soup for 45 minutes, stirring occasionally.
5. Slice the sausage into ½-inch pieces and add it to the soup. Simmer the soup for 15 more minutes or until thick, stirring occasionally.
6. Season the soup with kosher salt and black pepper. Ladle the soup into 4 large bowls and serve at once.

Soup Rice

PREPARATION:
10 MINUTES

COOKING:
50 MINUTES

YIELD:
4 MAIN-COURSE
SERVINGS

While at Vince's parents' home one weekend and enjoying a delicious salt cod paella, the conversation around the table was about Vince's grandmother's cooking. She had a kitchen in the basement of their house where she would prepare wonderful Spanish meals. Soup rice was one of everyone's favorites. We couldn't agree on the exact ingredients but we all decided that rice, chicken stock, and saffron were the basics. Although our version isn't exactly like the original, it's still pretty tasty.

1 tablespoon olive oil
3 cloves garlic, peeled and thinly sliced
1 onion, peeled and diced
    Kosher salt
    A pinch of saffron threads
⅔ cup brown rice
10 cups homemade or low-sodium canned chicken broth
2 Yukon Gold or other yellow-fleshed potatoes, scrubbed and sliced
    into ½-inch pieces
12 ounces spinach, trimmed, washed, drained, and chopped
    Black pepper

1. Heat the olive oil in a Dutch oven over medium heat. When the oil is hot, add the garlic and cook for 30 seconds. Add the onion and sprinkle it with kosher salt. Cook the onion for 3 minutes, stirring often.
2. Stir in the saffron and cook for 2 minutes. Stir in the brown rice.
3. Raise the heat to high. Add the chicken broth. Bring the soup to a boil. Reduce the heat and simmer the soup for 30 minutes.
4. Add the potatoes and simmer the soup for 15 more minutes.
5. Stir in the spinach, a couple of handfuls at a time, and cook until wilted.
6. Remove the pot from the heat. Season the soup with kosher salt and black pepper. Ladle into 4 large bowls and serve at once.

Potato and Pesto Soup

When the weather turns cool, we instinctively prepare soups for dinner several times a week. Potato soups are among our favorites. They are delicious, healthful, and versatile. Broccoli, carrots, peeled and cubed winter squash, and even cooking greens can be simmered and pureed with the potatoes to create wonderful meals. Be imaginative and use tasty combinations of familiar vegetables that your children enjoy.

PREPARATION:
15 MINUTES

COOKING:
40 MINUTES

YIELD:
4 SIDE-DISH SERVINGS

1 tablespoon unsalted butter
1 onion, peeled and diced
  Kosher salt
2 russet potatoes, peeled and cubed
3 cups water
2 cups milk
⅓ cup light cream
  Black pepper
4 tablespoons basil pesto (see page 231)

1. Melt the butter in a Dutch oven over medium heat. When it stops foaming, add the onion. Sprinkle it with kosher salt and cook for 3 minutes, stirring often.
2. Stir in the potatoes. Sprinkle them with kosher salt. Reduce the

heat. Cover the pot and sweat the vegetables for 5 minutes, stirring occasionally.

3. Raise the heat to high and add the water. Bring the soup to a boil. Reduce the heat and simmer until the potatoes are tender, approximately 25 minutes.

4. Carefully transfer the soup to a blender or the work bowl of a food processor fitted with a metal blade. If using a blender, it will be necessary to perform this step in 2 batches. Puree the soup and return it to the pot over low heat.

5. Stir in the milk and cream. Season the soup with kosher salt and black pepper.

6. Divide the soup among 4 bowls. Garnish each portion with a tablespoon of pesto and serve at once.

Chicken and Cheese Soup

PREPARATION:
15 MINUTES

COOKING:
30 MINUTES

YIELD:
4 MAIN-COURSE
SERVINGS

With two varieties of cheese and whole milk, this decadent soup is not one that we prepare regularly. It's so tasty, though, that when we do serve it, it's difficult not to have a small second portion. The soup contains plenty of protein and calcium. So, if you can afford the calories, go ahead and indulge.

2 tablespoons unsalted butter
1 onion, peeled and diced
  Kosher salt
2 carrots, scraped and diced
1 red bell pepper, cored, seeded, and diced
12 ounces boneless and skinless chicken breast, trimmed and diced into ½-inch pieces
1 tablespoon all-purpose flour
2 cups homemade or low-sodium canned chicken broth
4 ounces Monterey Jack cheese, sliced or grated
4 ounces cheddar cheese, sliced or grated
1 cup whole milk
  Black pepper

1. Melt the butter in a Dutch oven over medium heat. When it stops foaming, add the onion and sprinkle it with kosher salt. Cook the onion for 3 minutes, stirring often.
2. Add the carrots and bell pepper. Cover the pot and sweat the vegetables for 5 minutes, stirring occasionally.
3. Stir in chicken. Cook ingredients for 3 minutes, stirring often.
4. Add the flour to make a roux. Cook the roux for 2 minutes, stirring often.
5. Raise the heat to high and whisk in the chicken broth. Bring the soup to a boil. Reduce the heat and simmer for 5 minutes.
6. Add the cheeses, 2 ounces at a time, and stir continually until all of them have been incorporated.
7. Add the milk. Gently heat the soup to serving temperature.
8. Season the soup with kosher salt and black pepper. Ladle the soup into 4 large bowls and serve at once.

Mushroom Stock

We use this stock as the base for our mushroom soups but it can also enhance a sauce for pasta, chicken, or beef. Four ounces of dried shiitake mushrooms is quite a large amount. We are fortunate to have a market that sells them in bulk at a reasonable price. If you can't find them in bulk, it is a worthwhile endeavor to seek out a mail-order company and purchase a large amount so you will always have some on hand. Besides making a rich and deeply flavored stock, they can be used in stir-fries, stews, and pasta dishes.

PREPARATION:
30 MINUTES

COOKING:
45 MINUTES

YIELD:
1 GALLON

4 ounces dried shiitake mushrooms
4 cups boiling water
1 tablespoon canola oil
2 cloves garlic, peeled and sliced
1 1-inch piece gingerroot, peeled and sliced
1 onion, peeled and chopped
 Kosher salt
2 ribs celery, chopped
2 carrots, chopped
1 gallon cold water

1. Place the mushrooms in a medium bowl. Pour the boiling water over them. Allow them to soak until they are soft, approximately 30 minutes.
2. While the mushrooms are soaking, heat the canola oil in a large Dutch oven over medium heat. When the oil is hot, add the garlic and gingerroot. Cook them for 1 minute, stirring often.
3. Add the onion and sprinkle it with kosher salt. Cook the onion for 5 minutes, stirring often. Add the celery and carrots and sprinkle them with kosher salt. Cover the pot and sweat the vegetables for 10 minutes, stirring occasionally.
4. Raise the heat to high. Add the softened mushrooms along with their soaking water. Add the cold water. Bring the stock to a boil. Reduce the heat and simmer the stock for 30 minutes.
5. Remove the pot from the heat. Strain the stock through a colander into a large bowl. Press down on the vegetables with the back of a spoon to extract as much liquid as possible. Discard the solids. Use the stock in your favorite recipe. If you don't use it immediately, store it in the refrigerator for 5 days or in several small containers in your freezer for up to 4 months.

Mushroom and Barley Soup

PREPARATION:
20 MINUTES

COOKING:
45 MINUTES

YIELD:
4 MAIN-COURSE
SERVINGS

If your children are mushroom eaters, the aroma of this meal simmering on the stove will lead them to exclaim: "What is that delicious smell?" After they devour this wholesome and hearty soup, you will have a new meal to add to your weekly repertoire.

1 tablespoon olive oil
2 cloves garlic, peeled and thinly sliced
1 onion, peeled and diced
  Kosher salt
3 carrots, scraped and chopped
1 pound white button or crimini mushrooms, sliced
½ cup barley
8 cups mushroom stock (see page 183)
  Black pepper

1. Heat the olive oil in a Dutch oven over medium heat. When the oil is hot, add the garlic. Cook the garlic for 1 minute, stirring often.
2. Add the onion and sprinkle it with kosher salt. Cook the onion for 5 minutes, stirring often. Add the carrots and mushrooms. Sprinkle them with kosher salt. Cook them for 3 minutes, stirring often.
3. Cover the pot and sweat the vegetables for 7 minutes, stirring occasionally.
4. Raise the heat to high. Stir in the barley. Add the mushroom stock.
5. Bring the soup to a boil. Reduce the heat and simmer the soup until the barley is tender, stirring occasionally, approximately 40 minutes.
6. Season the soup with kosher salt and black pepper. Divide the soup among 4 large bowls and serve at once.

Vietnamese Tofu, Mushroom, and Noodle Soup

Our favorite restaurant meals are nutritious and soothing Vietnamese noodle soups. These soups feature a light and deeply flavored broth garnished with meat, tofu, chicken, or seafood. Crisp vegetables and a generous amount of noodles make these soups the ultimate one-dish meals. We have created a vegetarian version starring our mushroom stock and healthful soba noodles. Calcium- and fiber-rich broccoli, bok choy, and tofu add body and texture to the broth. While this soup isn't exactly like a restaurant's, it is nonetheless wonderfully satisfying.

PREPARATION:
20 MINUTES

COOKING:
30 MINUTES

YIELD:
4 MAIN-COURSE
SERVINGS

Kosher salt
8 ounces soba noodles
1 tablespoon canola oil
1 1-inch piece gingerroot, peeled and minced
2 carrots, scraped and chopped
6 ounces button mushrooms, sliced
3 large stalks bok choy, leaves separated and reserved, stems
  chopped
8 cups mushroom stock (see page 183)
8 ounces soft tofu, cubed
½ pound broccoli florets
½ cup cilantro, chopped

1. Bring a large pot of water to a boil. Add kosher salt to the water
   followed by the noodles. Cook the noodles according to the package instructions. Drain them and set them aside for a moment.
2. Heat the canola oil in a Dutch oven over medium heat. When the
   oil is hot, add the gingerroot. Cook it for 30 seconds, stirring
   often.
3. Add the carrots, mushrooms, and bok choy stems. Sprinkle the
   vegetables with kosher salt. Cook them for 3 minutes, stirring
   often.
4. Cover the pot and sweat the vegetables for 7 minutes, stirring
   occasionally.
5. Raise the heat to high. Add the mushroom stock. Bring the soup
   to a boil. Reduce the heat and simmer the soup for 10 minutes.
6. Add the tofu and broccoli. Simmer the soup for 3 more minutes.
   Season the soup with kosher salt.
7. Divide the noodles among 4 large bowls. Divide the soup among
   the bowls. Garnish each portion with cilantro and serve at once.

pasta dishes

We would have no problem eating a whole-grain pasta meal night after night, and often we do. In fact, in each of our books, the pasta chapter is always the first to be completed. Pasta dishes are an opportunity for an imaginative cook to use a variety of ingredients to create wonderful and nutritious meals that the entire family will enjoy. A package of dried pasta is one of the world's most versatile foods. There is an endless combination of vegetables, shellfish, cheeses, meats, and nuts that can be used to craft quick and easy meals. Unfortunately, many of the pasta dishes we crave are overwhelmed by oil or cream sauces, making them fat-and-calorie-laden affairs. We have reworked these pasta meals, making them more nutritious without sacrificing taste and texture. We have also made the transition from traditional white pasta to the more healthful whole-grain variety. In most recipes whole-grain noodles complement the other ingredients in the dish well. However, certain pasta dishes, especially those containing seafood in an olive-oil-based sauce, taste far better with traditional pasta and that is how we continue to enjoy them. Families who are in shape can afford to eat a bit more white pasta, and everyone can enjoy it on occasion.

Several recipes in this section, such as Baked Penne With White Beans, Fennel, Tomatoes, and Provolone (see page 189), transform leftover soup into an easy and tasty pasta meal. Others, such as Spaghetti with Broccoli, Garlic, and Pine Nuts (see page 208) and Orecchiette with Roasted Cherry Tomatoes, Arugula, and Goat Cheese (see page 197) focus on combining a few first-rate ingredients with simple and quick cooking techniques. In these recipes, after you have added the pasta to the boiling water, you can begin the sauce, and the two will be ready simultaneously. For those times when you feel like something a bit more special but still want it on the table in a reasonable period of time and without much fuss, try our Linguine with Smoky Scallops and Garlicky Tomatoes (see page 205) or Linguine with Flank Steak, Fennel, and Sweet Peppers (see page 201).

Children love pasta. It is our experience that younger children are partial to tubular-shaped noodles such as penne and ziti and interestingly shaped ones like farfalle (bow ties) and orrechiette (little ears). Older kids enjoy the challenge of twirling long strands of spaghetti, linguine, and tagliatelle. Feel free to substitute your family's favorite pasta varieties in all the recipes. Many children enjoy tomato-based sauces but don't like pungent or overly seasoned sauces. Strong-tasting cheeses, such as blue and goat's milk, also seem to be an acquired taste. Many kids (ours included) don't like all the elements of a pasta dish tossed together. There is no need to make them anything different as this problem is easily solved. Before combining the noodles and sauce in the final step of a pasta recipe, plate your children's meals, creating separate sections of pasta, vegetables, and protein. Drizzle their pasta with extra-virgin olive oil and sprinkle it with kosher salt and Romano or Parmesan cheese. Over time, they will begin to enjoy their pasta meals served in the traditional manner.

Baked Penne with White Beans, Fennel, Tomatoes, and Provolone

PREPARATION:
5 MINUTES

COOKING:
30 MINUTES

YIELD:
4 MAIN-COURSE
SERVINGS

This recipe uses leftover White Bean, Tomato, and Fennel Soup (see page 175) as a sauce in a hearty, baked pasta dish. Provolone cheese and a sprinkling of parsley are the only additional ingredients that are needed to create a great meal. Whole-grain penne works well with beans. **TIPS:** The dish can be assembled a day in advance and popped into the oven thirty minutes prior to serving. Also, a pound of spinach cooked in a tablespoon of olive oil and a few cloves of chopped garlic is an excellent addition to the pasta.

Kosher salt
1 pound whole-grain penne
3 cups leftover White Bean, Fennel, and Tomato Soup (see page 175)
½ cup flat-leaf (Italian) parsley, chopped
6 ounces provolone cheese, grated or sliced

1. Preheat the oven to 400°F.
2. Bring a large pot of water to a boil. Add kosher salt to the water followed by the pasta.
3. Cook the pasta 2 minutes less than indicated on the package. Drain it, reserving 1 cup of its cooking water. Transfer it to a large ovenproof casserole.
4. Stir in the soup, pasta cooking water, and parsley. Sprinkle on the cheese.
5. Transfer the casserole to the oven. Bake the pasta until the cheese is golden, approximately 20 minutes.
6. Divide the pasta among 4 shallow bowls and serve at once.

PREPARATION:
5 MINUTES

COOKING:
30 MINUTES

YIELD:
4 MAIN-COURSE
SERVINGS

Baked Penne with Lentils, Barley, and Feta

Leftover Lentil and Barley Soup (see page 177) is the sauce in this hearty and healthful meal. A sprinkling of slightly salty feta cheese provides a pleasant contrast to the earthy and sweet flavor of the lentils. Lentils are a great source of iron, fiber, folate, and calcium. The texture and flavor of the whole-grain penne go great with the lentils in this dish.

> Kosher salt
> 1 pound whole-grain penne
> 3 cups leftover Lentil and Barley Soup (see page 177)
> ½ cup flat-leaf (Italian) parsley, chopped
> 6 ounces feta cheese, crumbled

1. Preheat the oven to 400°F.
2. Bring a large pot of water to a boil. Add kosher salt to the water followed by the pasta.
3. Cook the pasta 2 minutes less than indicated on the package. Drain it, reserving 1 cup of its cooking water. Transfer it to a large ovenproof casserole.
4. Stir in the soup, pasta cooking water, and parsley. Sprinkle on the cheese.
5. Transfer the casserole to the oven. Bake the pasta until the cheese is melted and the noodles are hot, approximately 20 minutes.
6. Divide the pasta among 4 shallow bowls and serve at once.

Penne with Tomato Sauce

Few meals are as simple and delicious as pasta with a quick tomato sauce. The whole-grain pasta is a great source of unrefined carbohydrates that will provide you with sustained energy. We think the whole-grain pasta adds an earthy flavor to this classic dish.

1 tablespoon olive oil
4 cloves garlic, peeled and thinly sliced
1 onion, peeled and diced
  Sea salt to taste
1 35-ounce can whole tomatoes, chopped
  Black pepper to taste
1 pound whole-grain penne
½ cup fresh basil, snipped
4 tablespoons grated Parmesan cheese

PREPARATION:
5 MINUTES

COOKING:
30 MINUTES

YIELD:
4 MAIN-COURSE
SERVINGS

1. Heat the olive oil in a Dutch oven over medium heat. Add the garlic and sauté it, stirring constantly, until it is soft and fragrant, approximately 1 minute. Add the onion and a pinch of sea salt. Sauté the onion, stirring it often, until it is soft, approximately 4 minutes.
2. Raise the heat. Add the tomatoes and bring the sauce to a boil. Reduce the heat and simmer the sauce, stirring it often, for 20 minutes. Season the sauce with sea salt and black pepper.
3. Cook the pasta in lightly salted water, according to the package instructions. Drain the pasta, and divide it among 4 shallow bowls. Add the basil to the sauce. Ladle the sauce over each serving of pasta. Sprinkle each portion with 1 tablespoon of the Parmesan cheese and serve at once.

Canned Tomatoes

Several recipes in this book call for canned tomatoes. Top-quality canned tomatoes are a staple in our kitchen. Unfortunately, significant differences in quality are found in the large selection of tomatoes available. The best are those from the San Marzano region in Italy. San Marzano plum tomatoes are grown specifically for cooking, but beware: some producers claim their tomatoes are "San Marzano Type" or "San Marzano Quality." If San Marzano tomatoes are not available, we suggest trying several brands to find one that you enjoy. Search for a can that contains deep-red tomatoes that are neither too soft nor too firm, with little or no added salt and a clean tomato flavor.

PREPARATION:
10 MINUTES

COOKING:
1 HOUR

YIELD:
4 MAIN-COURSE
SERVINGS PLUS
LEFTOVERS

Penne with Bolognese Sauce and Provolone

In Italy, a traditional Bolognese sauce is a long-simmered affair. Our version has the same hearty texture, rich meat taste, and intense tomato flavor but cooks in only an hour. Since the sauce can be prepared several days in advance and yields enough for two meals, it is ideal for busy times. This type of rich sauce is complemented perfectly by whole-grain pasta. **TIP:** The leftovers are wonderful tucked into crusty baguettes, topped with mozzarella, and baked until bubbly and hot.

1½ pounds chuck steak
1 tablespoon olive oil
12 ounces ground pork
Kosher salt
Black pepper
1 tablespoon unsalted butter
4 cloves garlic, peeled and thinly sliced
1 medium onion, peeled and diced
2 medium carrots, scraped and diced
1 cup milk
1 cup red wine
1 35-ounce can whole tomatoes in juice, chopped
12 ounces whole-grain penne
6 ounces provolone cheese, sliced or grated

1. Place the steak in a food processor fitted with a metal blade. Turn the machine on and process the meat until it is thoroughly ground, approximately 15 seconds. Set it aside for a moment.
2. Heat the olive oil in large and ovenproof Dutch oven over high heat. When it is hot, add the beef and pork. Season the meat with kosher salt and black pepper. Cook the meat until it is well browned, stirring occasionally, approximately 7 minutes. Transfer the meat to a bowl. Set it aside for a moment.
3. Bring a large pot of water to a boil. Preheat the broiler.

4. Melt the butter in the Dutch oven over medium heat. When it stops foaming, add the garlic and cook for 1 minute. Add the onions and carrots and sprinkle them with kosher salt. Cook them for 2 minutes, stirring often.

5. Raise the heat to high. Add the milk and simmer for 2 minutes. Return the meat to the pot. Add the wine and simmer for 2 minutes.

6. Add the tomatoes to the Dutch oven. Bring the sauce to a boil. Reduce the heat and simmer the sauce for 35 minutes, stirring occasionally.

7. While the sauce is simmering, add kosher salt to the boiling water followed by the penne. Cook the pasta for 2 minutes less than the package indicates.

8. Place the oven rack on its lowest level. Set the oven to the broiler setting.

9. Season the sauce with kosher salt and black pepper. Transfer one-half of the sauce to a container for another recipe. Add the pasta to the Dutch oven and combine well with the sauce.

10. Top the pasta with the provolone. Transfer the pot to the oven. Broil the pasta until the cheese melts, approximately 5 minutes.

11. Remove the pot from the oven. Divide the pasta among 4 shallow bowls and serve at once.

PREPARATION:
15 MINUTES

COOKING:
20 MINUTES

YIELD:
4 MAIN-COURSE
SERVINGS

Penne with Chicken
and Summer Vegetables

During the peak of the growing season, we prepare this meal often. We vary the vegetables regularly, using the best from our garden or the local farmer's market. Serving chicken without the skin will decrease the saturated-fat content. This is a very heart-healthy meal, since it is made with olive oil and canola oil—both healthy fats. Cubed tofu or sliced flank steak can be substituted for the chicken.

1 cup all-purpose flour
1 pound boneless and skinless chicken breast, trimmed and sliced into thin strips
Kosher salt
Black pepper
1 tablespoon plus 1 tablespoon canola oil
1 pound whole-grain penne
1 tablespoon olive oil
4 cloves garlic, peeled and thinly sliced
1 onion, peeled and thinly sliced
1 red bell pepper, cored and diced
2 medium zucchini, trimmed and sliced into 1-inch pieces
8 ounces cherry tomatoes, halved
½ cup fresh basil, snipped
4 tablespoons grated Romano cheese

1. Bring a large pot of water to a boil.
2. Place the flour in a bowl. Sprinkle the chicken with kosher salt and black pepper. Dredge the chicken in the flour, tossing well. Remove the chicken, shaking off the excess flour, and transfer it to a plate.
3. Heat 1 tablespoon of the canola oil in a Dutch oven over medium-high heat. When the oil is hot, add one-half of the chicken strips. Sear them for 2 minutes on each side, turning once. Transfer the cooked chicken to a clean plate. Repeat the procedure with the remaining oil and chicken. Reduce the heat to low under the Dutch oven.

4. Add kosher salt to the boiling water followed by the pasta. Cook the pasta according to the package instructions.

5. Add the olive oil to the Dutch oven. When it is hot, add the garlic and cook for 1 minute. Raise the heat to medium. Add the onion and sprinkle it with kosher salt. Cook the onion for 2 minutes, stirring often. Add the bell pepper and cook for 2 minutes, stirring often. Add the zucchini and cook for 2 minutes, stirring often.

6. Raise the heat to high, carefully remove 1 cup of the pasta-cooking water from the pot, and add it to the Dutch oven. Simmer the sauce for 2 minutes.

7. Remove the pot from the heat and stir in the tomatoes and basil.

8. Drain the pasta and transfer it to the Dutch oven. Cook the pasta and sauce for 2 minutes, stirring occasionally. Season the pasta with kosher salt and black pepper. Divide the pasta among 4 shallow bowls. Garnish each portion with the Romano cheese and serve at once.

Ziti with Chicken, Spinach, and Pine Nuts

We love the gutsy combination of olive oil, garlic, and spinach. Sometimes we serve it as an accompaniment to fish or beef, but most often we toss it with pasta to create a simple and quick weekday supper. In this recipe, we have rounded out the dish with protein-rich chicken, and for a pleasant crunch, toasted pine nuts. Nuts are part of a heart-healthy diet, and pine nuts make a great addition to this dish. Spinach is an excellent source of folic acid and iron. Children may prefer to eat their noodles and spinach separately. Plate their meals prior to starting step eight, making separate sections of pasta, spinach, chicken, and nuts.

PREPARATION:
10 MINUTES

COOKING:
20 MINUTES

YIELD:
4 MAIN-COURSE
SERVINGS

¼ cup pine nuts

   Kosher salt

¼ cup all-purpose flour

1½ pounds boneless and skinless chicken breasts, trimmed and
      thinly sliced

1 tablespoon plus 1 tablespoon plus 1 tablespoon olive oil

1 tablespoon plus 1 tablespoon balsamic vinegar

1 pound whole-grain ziti or penne

6 cloves garlic, peeled and thinly sliced

1½ pounds spinach, trimmed, chopped, washed, and drained

1½ cups homemade or low-sodium canned chicken broth

   Black pepper

4 tablespoons grated Romano cheese

1. Bring a large pot of water to a boil.
2. Place the pine nuts in a small skillet over low heat. Sprinkle with
   kosher salt. Toast them until they are golden and fragrant, shaking the pan occasionally, approximately 8 minutes. Remove the
   pan from the heat.
3. Place the flour on a large plate. Place the chicken slices on the
   plate and sprinkle them with kosher salt. Toss the chicken with
   the flour and shake each slice to remove any excess flour. Transfer the chicken to a clean plate.
4. Heat 1 tablespoon of the olive oil in a Dutch oven over medium-
   high heat. Add one-half of the chicken and sear for 1½ minutes on
   each side, turning once. Add 1 tablespoon of vinegar to the
   chicken and cook 15 seconds more. Transfer the chicken to a
   plate. Repeat the procedure with another tablespoon of olive oil
   and the remaining chicken and vinegar. Set the chicken aside for
   a moment.
5. Add kosher salt to the boiling water followed by the pasta. Cook
   the pasta according to the package instructions.
6. Reduce the heat to low under the Dutch oven. Add the remaining
   tablespoon of olive oil. Add the garlic and cook for 30 seconds.
   Raise the heat to high and add 3 handfuls of spinach. Stir the
   spinach until it begins to wilt. Continue adding spinach and stirring until it has all wilted.

7. Pour in the chicken broth. Bring the sauce to a boil. Add the cooked chicken. Reduce the heat and simmer the sauce for 2 minutes. Season the sauce with kosher salt and black pepper.
8. Drain the pasta and add it to the Dutch oven. Cook the pasta and sauce for 2 minutes, stirring occasionally.
9. Divide the pasta among 4 shallow bowls. Garnish each portion with the Romano cheese and serve at once.

Orecchiette with Roasted Cherry Tomatoes, Arugula, and Goat Cheese

PREPARATION:
10 MINUTES

COOKING:
20 MINUTES

YIELD:
4 MAIN-COURSE
SERVINGS

One year, following a few warm days in early spring, we were pleasantly surprised to discover that the arugula in our garden survived the mild winter and was actually thriving. It was even more peppery-tasting than usual, so we decided to cook it to tame its sharp edge. This quick recipe stars this delightful green as well as roasted cherry tomatoes (which have a far superior flavor than slicing tomatoes during nonsummer months). Creamy goat cheese ties the flavors and textures together. Arugula is an excellent source of calcium, and tomatoes are rich in vitamin C. We chose to serve this dish with traditional white pasta, as the lighter taste seemed called for in this early-spring dish. **TIP:** The arugula and tomatoes with the goat cheese may be too bold tasting for young children. Plate their meals prior to combining the pasta and greens and mixing the goat cheese with the roasted tomatoes. They may enjoy the tomatoes and arugula as side dishes.

    Kosher salt
1 pound traditional orecchiette or penne
1 tablespoon olive oil
4 cloves garlic, peeled and thinly sliced
1 pound cherry tomatoes
⅓ cup water
1 pound arugula, washed, drained, and chopped
2 ounces plus 2 ounces goat cheese, room temperature

1. Preheat the oven to 450°F.
2. Bring a large pot of water to a boil. Add kosher salt to the water followed by the pasta. Cook the pasta according to the package instructions.
3. While the pasta is cooking, heat the olive oil in a large and oven-proof skillet over medium heat. When the oil is hot, add the garlic and cook for 45 seconds. Add the tomatoes and cook for 1 minute. Sprinkle them with kosher salt and transfer the pan to the oven. Roast the tomatoes for 10 minutes.
4. While the pasta is cooking and the tomatoes are roasting, bring the ⅓ cup of water to a boil in a Dutch oven. Add the arugula. Cover the pot and steam it for 2 minutes. Remove the pot from the heat. Drain the pasta. Add it to the Dutch oven and stir well.
5. Remove the tomatoes from the oven. Add one-half of the cheese to the tomatoes and stir until it melts. Stir the tomatoes into the pasta.
6. Divide the pasta among 4 bowls. Garnish each portion with the remaining cheese and serve at once.

Chilled Bow Tie Pasta with Asparagus and Spinach

Chilled pasta salads are great picnic fare and are also ideal to have in your refrigerator for a snack or light lunch. With plenty of asparagus and spinach, this salad provides the body with calcium, folate, and iron. **TIP:** Be certain to cook the bow ties until their centers are tender. Often their edges are cooked but the middles are still too firm.

PREPARATION:
15 MINUTES

COOKING:
15 MINUTES

CHILLING:
1 HOUR

YIELD:
6 SIDE-DISH SERVINGS

     Kosher salt
12 ounces traditional bow tie (farfalle) pasta or elbow macaroni
 1 pound asparagus, trimmed and sliced into 2-inch pieces
 8 ounces baby spinach, washed and spun dry
 1 red bell pepper, cored, seeded, and chopped
 ½ cup fresh basil, snipped
     Juice from 1½ lemons
 3 tablespoons olive oil
 1 teaspoon sugar
 ½ cup grated Romano cheese
     Black pepper

1. Bring a large pot of water to a boil. Add kosher salt to the water followed by the pasta. Cook the pasta for 8 minutes.
2. Add the asparagus pieces to the pot. Cook the ingredients until the pasta is tender, approximately 4 minutes longer.
3. Drain the ingredients and run cold water on them to cool. Transfer them to a large serving bowl.
4. Add the spinach, bell pepper, and basil. Toss the salad thoroughly. Set it aside for a moment.
5. In a small bowl whisk together the lemon juice, olive oil, and sugar. Pour the dressing onto the salad and toss well. Stir in the Romano cheese.
6. Season the salad with kosher salt and black pepper. Cover the salad and refrigerate for an hour prior to serving.

PREPARATION:
10 MINUTES

COOKING:
25 MINUTES

YIELD:
4 MAIN-COURSE
SERVINGS

Linguine with Peppers, Onions, and Mushrooms

Great recipes are often created serendipitously; this is one of those recipes. One evening with nothing more than a handful of mushrooms, a few bell peppers, and our usual staples, we made this meal. The whole-grain pasta in this dish works well with the white sauce. We enjoyed it so much that it has become part of our weekly repertoire.

1 tablespoon unsalted butter
2 cloves garlic, peeled and thinly sliced
2 medium onions, peeled and thinly sliced
　Kosher salt
1 pound whole-grain linguine or spaghetti
2 red bell peppers, cored, seeded, and thinly sliced
1 yellow or orange bell pepper, cored, seeded, and thinly sliced
12 ounces white button mushrooms, sliced
1 cup homemade or low-sodium canned chicken broth
⅓ cup light cream
⅓ cup flat-leaf (Italian) parsley, chopped
　Black pepper
4 tablespoons grated Romano cheese

1. Bring a large pot of water to a boil.
2. Heat the butter in a large Dutch oven over medium heat. When it stops foaming, add the garlic and cook for 1 minute.
3. Raise the heat slightly. Add the onions and sprinkle them with kosher salt. Cook them until they begin to soften, approximately 4 minutes, stirring often.
4. Add kosher salt to the boiling water followed by the pasta. Cook the pasta according to the package instructions.
5. Add the bell peppers to the pot containing the onions. Cover the pot and sweat the peppers until they begin to soften, approximately 4 minutes, stirring often.
6. Add the mushrooms to the pot containing the vegetables. Raise the heat to high. Cover the pot and sweat the vegetables for 6 minutes, stirring often.

7. Add the chicken broth and simmer for 2 minutes. Add the cream and parsley. Reduce the heat to low.
8. Drain the pasta and add to the vegetables. Season the pasta with kosher salt and black pepper.
9. Divide the pasta among 4 bowls. Garnish each with a tablespoon of Romano cheese and serve at once.

Linguine with Flank Steak, Fennel, and Sweet Peppers

PREPARATION:
10 MINUTES

COOKING:
20 MINUTES

YIELD:
4 MAIN-COURSE
SERVINGS

Through trial and error we have discovered the pasta meals that feature sauces our kids enjoy and those that are too boldly flavored for their evolving palates. This meal is one they love. With a sauce of braised fennel, red bell peppers, and a touch of cream, it tastes richer than it actually is. Quickly seared balsamic-glazed flank steak is the ideal garnish. Flank steak is a lean choice for red meat, which can be a once-a-week choice in a heart-healthy diet. It is a good source of iron, and with plenty of vitamin C from the peppers, the iron is well absorbed by your body.

1 tablespoon plus 1 tablespoon olive oil
12 ounces flank steak, thinly sliced across the grain
Kosher salt
Black pepper
2 tablespoons balsamic vinegar
3 cloves garlic, peeled and thinly sliced
1 medium onion, peeled and thinly sliced
1 pound whole-grain linguine
1 bulb fennel, trimmed, cored, and thinly sliced
2 red bell peppers, cored, seeded, and thinly sliced
1⅓ cup homemade or low-sodium canned chicken broth
¼ cup light cream
4 tablespoons Romano cheese, grated

1. Bring a large pot of water to a boil.
2. Heat 1 tablespoon of the olive oil in a Dutch oven over medium-high heat. Sprinkle the beef with kosher salt and black pepper.

When the oil is hot, carefully place the beef in the pot. Sear it until a crust forms, turning each slice once, approximately 1½ minutes per side. Add the vinegar and cook for 30 seconds more. Transfer the beef to a plate and set it aside for a moment.

3. Reduce the heat to low under the Dutch oven. Add the remaining tablespoon of oil to the pot. Add the garlic and cook for 30 seconds. Add the onion. Sprinkle it with kosher salt, and cook for 1 minute, stirring often.

4. Add kosher salt to the boiling water followed by the pasta. Cook the pasta according to the package instructions.

5. Raise the heat to medium under the Dutch oven. Add the fennel and bell peppers, and cook for 2 minutes, stirring often. Cover the pot and sweat the vegetables for 2 minutes, stirring occasionally.

6. Raise the heat to high. Add the chicken broth, and cook for 2 minutes.

7. Reduce the heat to low. Add the cream and simmer for 2 minutes. Season the sauce with kosher salt and black pepper.

8. Drain the pasta. Transfer it to the Dutch oven. Cook the pasta and sauce together for 2 minutes, stirring often.

9. Divide the pasta among 4 shallow bowls. Garnish each portion with the flank steak and a tablespoon of Romano cheese and serve at once.

PREPARATION:
15 MINUTES

COOKING:
10 MINUTES

YIELD:
4 MAIN-DISH SERVINGS

Linguine with Tofu, Flank Steak, Bok Choy, and Asparagus

Like much of Asian cookery, the beef in this recipe is used more as a garnish than as the main component of the dish. The tofu absorbs the wonderful flavors of the beef, but allows you to keep your intake of red meat to one-half what it would be if you made this dish with just beef. This way you can keep beef as a part of your diet but minimize your amount of saturated fat and cholesterol. Both bok choy and asparagus are rich sources of antioxidants and folic acid, a B-vitamin important in heart disease prevention.

4 tablespoons oyster sauce

4 tablespoons shoyu sauce or tamari

4 tablespoons orange juice

1½ cups low-sodium chicken broth

1 teaspoon sugar

2 teaspoons sesame oil

1½ cups water

Kosher salt

1 pound asparagus, trimmed, each stalk sliced into 3 diagonal pieces

1 pound whole-grain linguine

2 tablespoons canola oil, divided

8 ounces flank steak, thinly sliced on the bias

8 ounces firm tofu, cut into small cubes

4 cloves garlic, peeled and sliced

1 1-inch piece gingerroot, peeled and minced

8 ounces white mushrooms, sliced

1 red bell pepper, cored and sliced

½ pound bok choy, trimmed, stems sliced diagonally into ¾-inch-thick pieces and leaves coarsely chopped

1. In a bowl, whisk together the oyster sauce, shoyu, orange juice, chicken broth, sugar, and sesame oil. Set the sauce aside.
2. Bring the 1½ cups of water to a boil. Add a dash of kosher salt to the water. Place the asparagus in the water and cover the pot. Steam the asparagus until it is bright green and tender. Drain it and cool it under running water. Set it aside.
3. Bring a large pot of water to a boil. Add kosher salt to the water followed by the pasta. Cook the pasta according to the package instructions.
4. Heat 1 tablespoon of the canola oil in a wok over high heat. When the oil is hot, scatter the flank steak and tofu around the pan. Cook the ingredients until they are golden, turning them 2 or 3 times. Whisk the sauce and add ½ cup of it to the wok. Cook the ingredients for 30 seconds more. Transfer them to a plate and set it aside.
5. Heat the remaining tablespoon of canola oil in the wok and add the garlic and ginger to the pan. Cook them for 30 seconds. Add the mushrooms, bell pepper, and bok choy to the pan. Cook the vegetables for 4 minutes, stirring them often.

6. Add the remaining sauce to the wok. Bring the sauce to a boil, reduce the heat, and simmer it for 2 minutes. Add the flank steak, tofu, and asparagus to the sauce.

7. Drain the pasta and add it to the wok. Cook the pasta and sauce together for 2 minutes. Divide the pasta among 4 plates.

Linguine with Prosciutto and Roasted Asparagus

PREPARATION:
10 MINUTES

COOKING:
20 MINUTES

YIELD:
4 MAIN-COURSE
SERVINGS

One beautiful early spring afternoon, we were in the park basking in the first warmth of the year. The kids became thirsty, but the fountains had yet to be turned on for the season. We walked across the street to a tiny takeout Italian shop to get them something cold. While at the counter, the cook walked by with a bowl of pasta studded with prosciutto and tiny green peas; it smelled and looked wonderful. We knew then what we were having for supper that evening. Fortunately, the first asparagus of the season were ready in our garden, so we substituted them for the peas. It was a simple and memorable meal and one that we now enjoy regularly. This is one of the meals we serve with traditional white pasta. **TIP:** Rather than steaming asparagus, we roast them in the oven with a sprinkle of kosher salt and a drizzle of olive oil. The high heat enhances their naturally sweet flavor and gives them a delightfully smoky taste.

1 pound asparagus, trimmed
1 tablespoon olive oil
  Kosher salt
1 pound traditional linguine
1 tablespoon unsalted butter
1 onion, peeled and thinly sliced
1 cup homemade or low-sodium canned chicken broth
⅓ cup light cream
4 ounces prosciutto, coarsely chopped
  Black pepper
4 tablespoons grated Romano cheese

1. Preheat the oven to 450°F. Bring a large pot of water to a boil.
2. Place the asparagus on a sheet pan. Toss it with the olive oil and sprinkle with kosher salt. Place the tray in the oven and roast the asparagus for 10 minutes.
3. While the asparagus is roasting, add kosher salt to the boiling water followed by the pasta. Cook the pasta according to the package instructions.
4. While the asparagus is roasting and the pasta cooking, heat the butter in a Dutch oven over medium heat. When it stops foaming, add the onion and cook for 4 minutes, stirring occasionally.
5. Raise the heat to high. Add the chicken broth and simmer for 2 minutes. Add the light cream and simmer for 1 minute. Reduce the heat to low. Add the prosciutto and simmer for 30 seconds. Season the sauce with kosher salt and black pepper.
6. Drain the pasta and add it to the Dutch oven. Cook the pasta and sauce for 2 minutes, stirring occasionally.
7. Divide the pasta among 4 shallow bowls. Garnish each portion with the Romano cheese and roasted asparagus and serve at once.

Linguine with Smoky Scallops and Garlicky Tomatoes

This delightful pasta dish uses the same sauce as Cod Baked with Tomatoes and Breadcrumbs (see page 292). We often prepare a double batch of sauce and use one-half in this recipe and the remaining in the fish dish later in the week. Their sweet and briny taste, firm texture, and quick cooking time make sea scallops one of the true treasures of the sea and very versatile in the kitchen. They can be baked, broiled, grilled, or pan-fried. Children may find the smoky flavor of the scallops in this recipe too strong tasting, but they will love the sauce and pasta. We prefer this seafood dish with traditional white pasta.

PREPARATION:
10 MINUTES

COOKING:
20 MINUTES

YIELD:
4 MAIN-COURSE
SERVINGS

1 tablespoon olive oil
6 cloves garlic, peeled and thinly sliced
1 cup dry white wine
1 28-ounce can whole tomatoes in juice, drained (juice reserved for another use) and chopped
⅓ cup flat-leaf (Italian) parsley, chopped
   Kosher salt
   Black pepper
1 pound traditional linguine
1 tablespoon canola oil
1½ pounds sea scallops, attached muscle removed and discarded, scallops thoroughly dried

1. Bring a large pot of water to a boil.
2. Heat the olive oil in a Dutch oven over medium heat. When the oil is hot, add the garlic and cook for 1 minute.
3. Raise the heat to high. Add the wine, and simmer for 2 minutes. Add the tomatoes and bring the sauce to a boil. Reduce the heat, and simmer for 10 minutes, stirring occasionally. Add the parsley to the sauce. Season the sauce with kosher salt and black pepper. Remove the pot from the heat.
4. Add kosher salt to the water followed by the pasta. Cook the pasta according to the package instructions.
5. While the pasta is cooking, heat the canola oil in a cast-iron skillet over high heat. Sprinkle the scallops with kosher salt. When the oil begins to smoke, carefully place the scallops into the pan. Sear the scallops for 1½ minutes or until they are deep brown. Turn them over and sear for another minute. Remove the pan from the heat.
6. Drain the pasta. Add it to the Dutch oven containing the tomatoes and toss well. Divide the pasta among 4 shallow bowls. Garnish each portion with the scallops. Spoon any juices from the skillet onto each portion and serve at once.

Linguine with Roasted Striped Bass and Tomatoes

PREPARATION:
10 MINUTES

COOKING:
15 MINUTES

YIELD:
4 MAIN-COURSE
SERVINGS

In our refrigerator one evening, we had a large piece of striped bass that our son Joe had caught in Maine (with the help of a local expert named Roger) two days prior. We had eaten more than our share of striper that weekend and frankly had had enough. But there was no way we were going to waste this pristine specimen. At first, we were going to simply roast it and enjoy it with bread and a salad. But while it was in the oven, we decided to use it as the star ingredient in a simple pasta dish. Borrowing an idea from Asian cooking, where their noodle dishes often contain bits of roasted meat, we came up with this recipe. Now, whenever we are fortunate to catch a striper, this is one of our favorite ways to prepare it.

FISH

1¼ pounds boneless, skin-on striped bass fillet
2 tablespoons olive oil
   Kosher salt
   Black pepper

PASTA AND SAUCE

   Kosher salt
1 pound traditional linguine
1 tablespoon olive oil
6 cloves garlic, peeled and thinly sliced
1 cup dry white wine
1½ cups homemade or low-sodium canned chicken broth
6 tomatoes from a can, chopped
1 tablespoon unsalted butter
½ cup flat-leaf (Italian) parsley, chopped
   Black pepper

1. Preheat the oven to 450°F. Bring a large pot of water to a boil.
2. Place the fish on a heavy sheet pan. Drizzle it with olive oil and sprinkle it with kosher salt and black pepper.
3. Transfer the fish to the oven and roast it until it is just cooked through, approximately 13 minutes. Remove the pan from the oven and set aside for a moment.
4. While the fish is roasting, add kosher salt to the boiling water followed by the pasta. Cook the pasta according to the package instructions.
5. While the fish and pasta are cooking, heat the olive oil in a Dutch oven over medium heat. When the oil is hot, add the garlic and cook for 1 minute. Raise the heat to high. Add the wine and simmer for 2 minutes. Add the chicken broth and simmer for 3 minutes.
6. Reduce the heat to medium. Add the tomatoes and butter and simmer for 2 minutes. Reduce the heat to low and stir in the parsley. Season the sauce with kosher salt and black pepper.
7. Drain the pasta, add it to the sauce, and toss well. Slide a spatula between the skin and flesh of the striped bass and remove the flesh, leaving the skin on the sheet pan. Shred the fish into 2-inch pieces.
8. Divide the pasta among 4 shallow bowls. Garnish each portion with the shredded fish and serve at once.

PREPARATION:
10 MINUTES

COOKING:
20 MINUTES

YIELD:
4 MAIN-COURSE
SERVINGS

Spaghetti with Broccoli, Garlic, and Pine Nuts

Broccoli is a great source of fiber, calcium, and folic acid. On occasion, we add five chopped anchovies to the sauce, but our kids prefer the meal without them. This simple combination of whole-grain spaghetti, broccoli, and pine nuts makes a quick and nutritious meal any day of the week. Pine nuts provide a heart-healthy protein source in this dish

⅓ cup pine nuts
   Kosher salt
1 pound whole-grain spaghetti
1 tablespoon olive oil
6 cloves garlic, peeled and thinly sliced
2 cups homemade or low-sodium canned chicken broth
1 tablespoon unsalted butter
   Black pepper
1½ pounds broccoli, trimmed florets separated, stems peeled and
      sliced into discs
4 tablespoons grated Romano cheese

1. Bring a large pot of water to a boil.
2. Place the pine nuts in a small skillet over low heat. Sprinkle them
   with kosher salt. Toast them until they are golden, shaking the
   pan occasionally, approximately 8 minutes. Set them aside for a
   moment.
3. Add kosher salt to the water followed by the pasta.
4. While the pasta is cooking, heat the olive oil in a Dutch oven over
   medium heat. When the oil is hot, add the garlic and cook for 45
   seconds, stirring constantly. Raise the heat to high and add the
   chicken broth. Simmer for 2 minutes. Reduce the heat to low and
   add the butter. Season the sauce with kosher salt and black pepper. Keep the sauce over low heat.
5. After the pasta has cooked for 5 minutes, add the broccoli to
   the pot and cover the pot. When the water returns to the boil,
   uncover the pot. When the pasta and broccoli are tender,
   approximately 5 minutes, drain them. Add them to the sauce.
   Cook the pasta and sauce together for 2 minutes, stirring
   occasionally.
6. Divide the pasta among 4 shallow bowls. Garnish each serving
   with a tablespoon of Romano cheese and a sprinkling of pine
   nuts and serve at once.

PREPARATION:
10 MINUTES

COOKING:
30 MINUTES

YIELD:
4 MAIN-COURSE
SERVINGS

Spaghetti with Balsamic Chicken and Chard

With an abundance of complex carbohydrates, calcium, and iron, pasta with braised Swiss chard is a very nutritious meal. When we prepare it, we either garnish the pasta with toasted pine nuts or pan-seared chicken. In this recipe, we have sprinkled the quickly cooked chicken with a bit of sugar and glazed it with balsamic vinegar. Your children are certain to enjoy the slightly sweet-tasting chicken and earthy chard.

CHICKEN

  2 tablespoons olive oil
  2 boneless and skinless chicken breasts (approximately 1 pound), trimmed, halved, and flattened to ⅓-inch thickness
     Kosher salt
     Black pepper
  1 tablespoon sugar
  ¼ cup balsamic vinegar

CHARD AND PASTA

  1 tablespoon olive oil
  6 cloves garlic, peeled and thinly sliced
1½ pounds Swiss chard, trimmed, washed, and drained
     Kosher salt
     Black pepper
  1 pound whole-grain spaghetti
  4 tablespoons Romano cheese, grated

1. Bring a large pot of water to a boil.
2. To prepare the chicken, heat the olive oil in a large skillet over medium high heat. Sprinkle the chicken breasts on each side with kosher salt and black pepper. When the oil is hot, carefully place the breasts into the pan. Sear them until golden brown, approximately 1½ minutes. Turn them over and sear them for an additional 1½ minutes. Reduce the heat to low. Sprinkle them with the sugar, and cook for another minute. Raise the heat to

high. Splash them with the vinegar and cook for a final 30 seconds. Transfer them to a cutting board. Set them aside while you complete the recipe.

3. To prepare the chard and pasta, heat the olive oil in a large Dutch oven over medium heat. When it is hot, add the garlic and cook it for 1 minute.

4. Raise the heat to high. Stir in the chard. Cover the pot. When the chard boils, reduce the heat to medium-low. Braise the chard until it is tender, approximately 10 minutes, stirring occasionally. Season the chard with kosher salt and black pepper.

5. While the chard is cooking, add kosher salt to the boiling water followed by the pasta. Cook the pasta according to the package instructions. Just prior to draining the pasta, remove 1 cup of its cooking water and add it to the chard.

6. Drain the pasta and add it to the Dutch oven containing the chard. Cook the ingredients for 2 minutes, stirring occasionally.

7. Divide the pasta among 4 shallow bowls. Slice the chicken into strips. Garnish each portion with the chicken and a sprinkling of the Romano cheese and serve at once.

PREPARATION:
10 MINUTES

COOKING:
20 MINUTES

YIELD:
4 MAIN-COURSE
SERVINGS

Fettuccine with Tomatoes, Cracked Olives, and Blue Cheese

This recipe was initially written to take advantage of leftover braised pork shoulder. But after making it several times, we decided the meal was better without the meat. The olives and blue cheese complement the tomatoes well, and no other flavors or textures are necessary. This lean dish is a great source of vitamin C and complex carbohydrates. As with many pasta recipes, we toss the kids' portions with the sauce and serve their olives on the side. A bold blue cheese is definitely an acquired taste. Unless your children enjoy intense flavors, garnish their meals with Romano or Parmesan instead.

- 1 tablespoon olive oil
- 5 cloves garlic, peeled and thinly sliced
- 1 35-ounce can whole tomatoes, drained
- ½ cup fresh basil, snipped
- Kosher salt
- Black pepper
- 1 pound traditional fettuccine
- 1 cup pasta cooking water
- 16 cracked green or Sicilian olives, pitted and coarsely chopped
- 2 ounces creamy blue cheese such as Blue Castello

1. Bring a large pot of water to a boil.
2. Heat the olive oil in a Dutch oven over medium heat. When the oil is hot, add the garlic and cook for 1 minute.
3. Raise the heat to high and add the tomatoes. Bring the sauce to a boil, reduce the heat, and simmer for 15 minutes, stirring occasionally.
4. Remove the pot from the heat and stir in the basil. Season the sauce with kosher salt and black pepper.
5. Add kosher salt to the water followed by the pasta. Cook the pasta according to the package instructions. Remove 1 cup of its cooking water. Add it to the sauce.

6. Drain the pasta. Transfer it to the Dutch oven. Cook the pasta and sauce over low heat for 2 minutes, stirring often.

7. Divide the pasta among four shallow bowls. Garnish each portion with the olives and blue cheese and serve at once.

Fettuccine with Mushrooms, Tofu, and Pecans

Our son Joe is fond of pan-fried tofu. We often enhance tofu's neutral flavor with a splash of vinegar (balsamic and red wine are tasty) as we have done here; other times we use tamari or orange juice. With meaty mushrooms, sweet tofu, and crunchy nuts, this simple pasta dish features a variety of interesting tastes and textures. It is a great example of using heart-healthy proteins such as tofu and nuts in ways your family will accept.

PREPARATION:
15 MINUTES

COOKING:
30 MINUTES

YIELD:
4 MAIN-COURSE
SERVINGS

1 pound extra-firm tofu
1 tablespoon canola oil
   Kosher salt
1 tablespoon sugar
2 tablespoons plus 2 tablespoons balsamic vinegar
½ cup pecans, coarsely chopped
1 pound whole-grain fettuccine
1 tablespoon olive oil
2 cloves garlic, peeled and thinly sliced
1½ pounds crimini mushrooms, sliced
1 cup dry white wine
⅓ cup light cream
½ cup flat-leaf (Italian) parsley, chopped
   Black pepper
4 tablespoons Romano cheese, grated

1. Bring a large pot of water to a boil.
2. Remove the moisture from the tofu by placing it on a plate and setting a heavy pot on top of it. After approximately 15 minutes, remove the tofu from the plate and discard the accumulated liquid. Cube the tofu.
3. Heat the canola oil in a wok over high heat. When the oil is hot, carefully add the tofu. Sprinkle it with kosher salt. Sear the tofu until golden and crisp, tossing occasionally, approximately 5 minutes. Add the sugar and cook for another minute. Add 2 tablespoons of the vinegar and cook for a final minute. Transfer the tofu to a plate. Set it aside for a moment.
4. Place the pecans in a small skillet and sprinkle them with kosher salt. Toast them over low heat until they are no longer raw tasting, shaking the pan occasionally, approximately 10 minutes.
5. While the pecans are toasting, add kosher salt to the water followed by the pasta. Cook the pasta according to the package instructions.
6. While the pecans are toasting and the pasta cooking, heat the olive oil in a Dutch oven over medium heat. When it is hot, add the garlic and cook for 1 minute.
7. Raise the heat to high and add the mushrooms. Sprinkle them with kosher salt. Cook the mushrooms until soft, stirring often, approximately 5 minutes.
8. Add the wine and simmer for 2 minutes. Add the cream and remaining vinegar and cook for 2 minutes. Reduce the heat to low and add the parsley. Season the sauce with kosher salt and black pepper.
9. Drain the pasta and add it to the sauce. Cook the pasta and sauce together over low heat for 2 minutes, stirring often.
10. Divide the pasta between 4 shallow bowls. Garnish each portion with the tofu, pecans, and Romano cheese and serve at once.

Tagliatelle with Flank Steak and Asparagus

PREPARATION:
10 MINUTES

COOKING:
20 MINUTES

YIELD:
4 MAIN COURSE
SERVINGS

The easiest, most nutritious, and best weekday meals we prepare are pasta dishes that contain one vegetable and a protein source. The vegetable may be broccoli or cauliflower or an earthy-tasting cooking green such as chard, spinach, or mustard greens. The protein source is usually chicken breast, tofu, or flank steak. We try to use whole-grain pasta as much as possible. Occasionally we garnish the dish with toasted nuts, and we always use a robust cheese to tie the elements together. This particular meal stars roasted asparagus and seared flank steak. Flank steak is a lean choice for red meat. To add another layer of flavor, we cook the garlic to a golden stage, making it sweet and nutty. **TIPS:** Be certain the beef is thoroughly dried before cooking it. Moisture will cause it to steam rather than sear. Also, children may find the blue cheese to be too strong tasting.

1½ pounds asparagus,
1 tablespoon plus 1 tablespoon olive oil
　Kosher salt
1 pound whole-grain tagliatelle or fettuccine
　Black pepper
1 pound flank steak, thoroughly dried and thinly sliced across the grain
5 cloves garlic, peeled and thinly sliced
1½ cups homemade or low-sodium canned chicken broth
2 ounces creamy blue cheese such as saga

1. Preheat the oven to 450°F. Bring a large pot of water to a boil.
2. Place the asparagus on a sheet pan. Toss it with 1 tablespoon of the olive oil and sprinkle with kosher salt. Place the tray in the oven and roast the asparagus for 10 minutes.
3. While the asparagus is roasting, add kosher salt to the boiling water followed by the pasta. Cook the pasta according to the package instructions.

4. Meanwhile, heat the remaining tablespoon of olive oil in a Dutch oven over medium high heat. Sprinkle the meat with kosher salt and black pepper. When the oil is hot, add the beef strips. Sear them until a crust forms, approximately 2 minutes. Turn them and sear for an additional minute or two. Transfer the meat to a plate and set it aside for a moment.

5. Reduce the heat to medium and add the garlic. Cook the garlic until it is golden and slightly crisp, approximately 1 minute, stirring constantly.

6. Raise the heat to high. Deglaze the pot by adding the chicken broth and stirring to dissolve the caramelized bits.

7. Reduce the heat to low. Add the cooked pasta and stir thoroughly. Cook the pasta and sauce together for 2 minutes, stirring occasionally. Season with kosher salt and black pepper.

8. Divide the pasta among 4 shallow bowls. Garnish each portion with the blue cheese, flank steak, and asparagus and serve at once.

CHAPTER 16

vegetarian dishes

Vegetarianism is practiced at three levels of strictness. Ovolacto vegetarians are the least strict. In addition to foods of plant origin, these individuals include eggs and dairy products in their diets. Since these foods supply a variety of important nutrients, this type of diet is generally nutritionally sound. Lacto vegetarians eat foods of plant origin and dairy products but abstain from eggs. Followers of this regimen need to pay special attention to their diets to be certain they are ingesting adequate amounts of iron and zinc. The strictest vegetarians are vegans. They exclude all animal foods, including eggs and dairy products, from their meals. This diet lacks vitamin B_{12} (found only in animal products). It may also be deficient in iron, zinc, vitamin D, and calcium. The best vegetarian diet is a varied one. Focus your meals on nutrient-dense foods such as dried peas and beans, whole-grain breads and pastas, vegetables (especially antioxidant-rich leafy greens, tomatoes, and deep-orange-fleshed ones) nuts, seeds, and soy products.

The diets of vegetarian children require special attention. Vegetarian children may have a difficult time ingesting sufficient amounts of calcium and iron that their growing bodies need. To boost their calcium consumption, be certain your children consume plenty of soy milk, calcium-fortified fruit juices, tofu, and leafy greens. Iron-rich foods such as dried peas and beans, leafy greens, enriched grain products, and nuts should be a part of their daily diets. Also, to maximize iron absorption, accompany their meals with fruits and vegetables rich in vitamin C.

You don't need to be a vegetarian to prepare and enjoy vegetarian meals. Even if you don't consider yourself a vegetarian, you are probably following the new food pyramid and trying to reduce your intake of fatty meats, saturated fats, and full-fat dairy products, while increasing your intake of fruits, vegetables, nuts, seeds, unsaturated fats, and whole grains. In the past, vegetarian meals were either fat- and calorie-laden affairs or dull and flavorless. With the increasing exposure of the benefits a well-balanced vegetarian diet and the availability of excellent-quality soy foods and meat-mimicking products, vegetarian cooking and eating are now much more exciting and healthful. Vegetarian meals don't need to be complex or elaborate to be healthful. Vegetarian meals are often more economical and practical than meat-based ones. Dried beans, pastas, soy products and vegetables cost a fraction of what meat costs. Many vegetarian meals can be prepared entirely in advance without any loss of flavor or texture; most even taste better the following day.

Lasagna is near the top of everyone's favorite comfort food list. When prepared with beef and an abundance of cheese, it is not something you can enjoy on a regular basis. So why not indulge in our Tofu and Provolone Lasagna (see page 221)? It is a delightful blend of meaty porcini mushrooms, a zesty tomato sauce, and tangy provolone cheese. Most important, though, it is wonderfully nutritious and simple to put together. One of the most healthful and versatile meals one can prepare is rice and beans. Our Stewed Pinto Beans and Brown Rice (see page 225) contains an abundance of fiber, protein, iron, and carbohydrates. It can be served sprinkled with a bit of grated cheddar or Jack cheese and a dollop of plain yogurt. Or the mixture can be rolled into flour or corn tortillas for a delicious Mexican treat. When you have a bit more time and desire an elegant vegetarian meal, try our Acorn Squash Stuffed with Wild Rice, Apples, and Pumpkin Seeds (see page 224). It's a wonderful meal and is certain to win over even the most reluctant of meat eaters.

We should all strive to view vegetarian food as simply another type of meal. Just as you would have chicken or fish for dinner one evening, enjoy a meatless meal based on legumes and whole grains on another. Vegetarian meals offer interesting contrasts of flavors and textures and provide top-flight nutrition.

PREPARATION:
20 MINUTES

COOKING:
30 MINUTES

YIELD:
6 CUPS

Fresh Tomato Sauce

Canned tomatoes are a staple in our kitchen. We use them regularly throughout the year except for six weeks during summer when our garden produces an abundance of great plum tomatoes. Even the very best canned tomatoes don't compare to the deep red gems from your own garden or a local farmer's market. Several times during these six weeks, we either oven-dry the tomatoes or turn them into an irresistible fresh sauce seasoned with nothing more than garlic, fresh basil, kosher salt, and black pepper. We often make a triple batch and freeze the extra to enjoy during the colder months to remind us of a beautiful summer day. This sauce is delightful ladled onto steaming pasta but it also works well with eggplant Parmesan or lasagna. It can serve as a pizza sauce as well or be used to top grilled fish, tofu, or vegetables.

25 plum tomatoes
2 tablespoons olive oil
6 cloves garlic, peeled and thinly sliced
1 cup fresh basil, snipped
Kosher salt
Black pepper

1. Bring a large pot of water to a boil. Carefully drop the tomatoes into the water and simmer for 2 minutes. Drain them and allow to cool for 10 minutes.
2. Slip off their skins and transfer them to a large bowl. Slightly tip the bowl into the sink and drain the tomatoes of any accumulated water. With your hands, crush the tomatoes. Set the bowl aside for a moment.
3. Heat the olive oil in a large Dutch oven over low heat. When the oil is hot, add the garlic. Cook it for 2 minutes, stirring often.
4. Raise the heat to high under the Dutch oven. Carefully add the tomatoes. Bring the sauce to a boil. Reduce the heat and simmer the sauce for 20 minutes, stirring occasionally.
5. Stir in the basil. Season the sauce with kosher salt and black pepper. Allow the sauce to cool before refrigerating.

Tofu and Provolone Lasagna

The traditional American version of lasagna can be a time-consuming affair. It is often made with ground beef and pork and high-fat cheeses. Obviously it cannot be considered healthy fare. Our lasagna can be prepared in a fraction of the time. It features a tofu and dried porcini mushroom sauce and just enough provolone cheese to bind all the elements and enhance the overall taste of the meal. And with plenty of calcium, protein, and complex carbohydrates, it scores high marks for nutrition. Don't tell your kids that it is made with tofu and watch them gobble it up.

TIPS: To prevent the lasagna noodles from sticking together, add them to the boiling water one at a time. Also, the lasagna can be assembled up to two days in advance and popped into the oven thirty minutes prior to serving.

PREPARATION:
40 MINUTES

COOKING:
30 MINUTES

YIELD:
8 MAIN-COURSE
SERVINGS

⅔ cup dried porcini mushrooms
1 cup boiling water
1 pound firm tofu
  Kosher salt
1 pound whole-grain lasagna noodles
1 tablespoon olive oil
6 cloves garlic, peeled and thinly sliced
1 onion peeled and diced
2 heaping tablespoons tomato paste
1 35-ounce can whole tomatoes in juice, chopped
½ cup flat-leaf (Italian) parsley, chopped
¼ cup light cream
  Black pepper
12 ounces provolone cheese, sliced or grated

1. Preheat the oven to 450°F. Have on hand a 10-by-12-inch baking dish with 3-inch-deep sides.
2. Place the mushrooms in a bowl and pour the boiling water over them. Allow them to soak for 20 minutes.
3. Meanwhile, remove the moisture from the tofu by placing it on a plate and setting a heavy pot on top of it. After approximately 15 minutes, remove the tofu from the plate and discard the accumulated liquid. Crumble the tofu and set it aside for a moment.

4. While the mushrooms are soaking and tofu is being pressed, bring a large pot of water to a boil. Add kosher salt to the water. Add the noodles one by one and cook them for 6 minutes, stirring occasionally. Drain them and rinse them under cold water. Set them aside for a moment.

5. Heat the olive oil in a Dutch oven over medium heat. When the oil is hot, add the garlic, and cook for 30 seconds. Add the onion. Sprinkle it with kosher salt and cook for 3 minutes, stirring often.

6. Stir in the tomato paste and cook for 1 minute.

7. Raise the heat to high and add the mushrooms and their soaking water. Add the tomatoes and tofu. Bring the sauce to a boil. Reduce the heat, and simmer for 15 minutes, stirring occasionally. Stir in the parsley and cream. Season the sauce with kosher salt and black pepper.

8. To assemble the lasagna, cover the bottom of the baking dish with 3 or 4 noodles. Cover the noodles with one-fourth of the sauce and one-fourth of the cheese. Repeat the procedure 3 more times, creating 4 layers, using the remaining noodles, sauce, and cheese.

9. Transfer the lasagna to the oven and bake until bubbly and golden, approximately 20 minutes. Allow the lasagna to rest for 10 minutes before slicing and serving,

Tofu

Tofu, or bean curd, comes from soy milk. It is made by adding nigari (a compound from sea water), calcium sulfate, and vinegar to soy milk. The excess moisture is removed, and the remaining curds are pressed into blocks. A 6-ounce serving of tofu provides 12 grams of protein and 720 milligrams of calcium.

Tofu is mildly flavored and requires bold seasonings to transform it into something special. Firm and extra-firm tofu act like sponges in absorbing flavors during cooking. They turn out especially well when paired with full-flavored ingredients such as herbs, spices, vinegars, garlic, and onions. Firm and extra-firm tofu can be baked, grilled, stir-fried, and mashed. Soft tofu works well in spreads, desserts, and dressings. When pureed in a blender or food processor, silken tofu can be used to replace cream in your favorite sauces, dressings, soups, and puddings.

Tofu is sold in the refrigerated section of most markets packed in water in one-pound blocks. Store unused portions of tofu floating in a container of water in your refrigerator. If you change the water daily, the tofu should remain fresh for approximately one week.

PREPARATION:
20 MINUTES

COOKING:
1 ¼ HOURS

YIELD:
6 MAIN-COURSE
SERVINGS

Acorn Squash Stuffed with Wild Rice, Apples, and Pumpkin Seeds

We enjoy this healthful meal most often during the fall when acorn squash are inexpensive and plentiful. At first glance, this recipe appears to be time-consuming. But, like many stuffed vegetable dishes, it can be assembled entirely in advance and baked just prior to serving, making it an ideal meal to add to your weekend cooking menu. Pecans add protein and heart-healthy fats to the dish.

½ cup pecan pieces
   Kosher salt
3 medium acorn squash, halved and seeded
1 cup raisins
1 cup plus 2 ½ cups water
1 ¼ cups wild rice, thoroughly rinsed
1 tablespoon unsalted butter
1 onion, peeled and diced
1 rib celery, finely chopped
2 Cortland apples, cored and diced
⅓ cup roasted pumpkin seeds
   Black pepper
6 ounces cheddar, grated

1. Preheat the oven to 400°F.
2. Place the pecans in a small skillet and sprinkle them with kosher salt. Toast them over low heat until they are no longer raw tasting, shaking the pan often, approximately 5 minutes. Set them aside.
3. Place the squash, skin side up, on a lightly oiled sheet pan. Transfer the tray to the oven and bake the squash until they are tender, approximately 40 minutes. Remove the squash from the oven. Do not turn off the oven.
4. While the squash are baking, place the raisins in a small saucepan and add 1 cup of water. Bring the water to a boil and

remove the pan from the heat. Allow the raisins to soak for 15 minutes. Drain them, reserving their cooking water.

5. In a medium-sized pot, combine the raisin water and the remaining 2½ cups of water. Bring the water to a boil and season with kosher salt. Stir in the wild rice. Return the water to a boil and reduce the heat to a simmer. Cover the pot and cook the rice until it is tender, approximately 40 minutes. Set the rice aside.

6. While the squash and rice are cooking, melt the butter in a large skillet over medium heat. Add the onion and sprinkle it with kosher salt. Cook the onion for 5 minutes, stirring often. Add the celery and apples and cook them until they are tender, stirring often, approximately 10 minutes.

7. Combine the reserved raisins, cooked rice, onion mixture, pumpkin seeds, and pecans in a large bowl. Season the mixture with kosher salt and black pepper. Fill the cavity of each squash half with an equal amount of the rice mixture. Sprinkle the stuffed squash with the cheese.

8. Return the squash to the oven and bake until the cheese has melted, approximately 10 minutes.

Stewed Pinto Beans and Brown Rice

A pot of long-simmered pinto beans accompanied with brown rice is in the Healthful Meals Hall of Fame. The meal provides plenty of protein, fiber, iron, and complex carbohydrates. And with a bag of beans costing a dollar, a bag of brown rice about two, and a recipe yielding eight generous servings, rice and beans are very economical as well. Dried-bean recipes are flexible. This one features bell peppers and a hint of Mexican seasoning. You can vary the types of peppers and spices and can even garnish the meal with your favorite cooked greens and salsa. The leftovers can be layered with corn tortillas and turned into a casserole or used as a burrito filling (see page 228).

BEAN SOAKING:
OVERNIGHT

PREPARATION:
15 MINUTES

COOKING:
2½ HOURS

YIELD:
4 MAIN-COURSE SERVINGS PLUS LEFTOVERS
(SEE PAGE 228)

BEANS

- 1 pound pinto beans
- 1 tablespoon canola oil
- 4 cloves garlic, peeled and thinly sliced
- 2 medium onions, peeled and thinly sliced
    Kosher salt
- 2 red bell peppers, cored and thinly sliced
- 2 jalapeño peppers, cored, seeded, and chopped
- 2 tablespoons spice rub (see page 280) *or* 1 tablespoon cumin and
    1 tablespoon Chili powder
- 3 tablespoons tomato paste
- 7 cups water
    Black pepper

RICE

5½ cups water
    Kosher salt
2½ cups long-grain brown rice

GARNISH

- 4 scallions, thinly sliced
- 2 ounces cheddar cheese, grated
- 4 tablespoons low-fat sour cream

1. The night prior to cooking, rinse, sort, and soak the beans.
2. The following day, preheat the oven to 300°F. Drain the beans of their soaking water.
3. Heat the canola oil in a large Dutch oven over medium heat. When the oil is hot, add the garlic and cook for 1 minute. Add the onions and sprinkle them with kosher salt. Cook the onions for 4 minutes, stirring often. Add the bell peppers and jalapeno peppers. Cover the pot and cook the ingredients for 4 minutes, stirring often.
4. Add the spice blend and stir in the tomato paste. Raise the heat to high and add the water. Add the beans and season them with kosher salt and black pepper. Bring them to a boil. Cover the pot and transfer it to the oven. Braise the beans until tender, approximately 2 hours.

5. While the beans are cooking, prepare the rice. Bring the water to a boil in a medium saucepan. Add kosher salt to the water. Stir in the rice. Cover the pot and bring the rice to a boil. Reduce the heat and simmer the rice until tender and all the water has been absorbed, approximately 45 minutes.

6. To serve, place approximately 1 cup of cooked rice on a plate and top it with 2 cups of beans. Garnish each portion with a sprinkling of scallions, cheese, and low-fat sour cream.

Chilies

Chilies not only provide flavor and heat to a dish, but they are also nutritious. They are high in vitamins A and C and, when consumed in moderation, can increase the flow of gastric juices and aid in the digestive process.

All chilies are hot, but in varying degrees. The habañero, also known as the Scotch Bonnet, is the hottest. This tiny, neon-orange, red, or green lantern-shaped firebomb is many times hotter than the jalapeño. A jalapeño is hot but definitely manageable. Jalapeños, deep-green, finger-shaped peppers, are available fresh or pickled in brine.

Be extremely cautious when working with fresh chilies. They contain oils that can burn your skin. Many people wear plastic gloves or coat their hands with vegetable oil (it acts as a barrier between your skin and the pepper oils) when cutting chilies. If your skin begins to burn, wash the affected area immediately under cool running water. Never touch your face or eyes when working with chilies, and always wash your hands, knife, and cutting board when you are finished. Since much of the heat is concentrated in the seeds and ribs, removing them will lessen the intensity of the peppers, as will soaking them in cold water for forty-five minutes.

PREPARATION:
20 MINUTES

COOKING:
10 MINUTES

YIELD:
4 MAIN-COURSE
SERVINGS

Tofu and Pinto Bean Burritos

Practically any leftover meal can be turned into a sandwich. This quick recipe transforms the leftovers from Stewed Pinto Beans and Brown Rice (see page 225) into tasty burritos that are ideal for a quick lunch or a no-fuss dinner. Kids enjoy burritos almost as much as pizza. And with tofu and avocado slices as garnishes, they are more interesting and nutritious than those from your local taqueria. We often prepare an extra-large batch of beans and enjoy these burritos all week long for lunch. **TIPS:** Be careful not to overfill your children's burritos. If they begin falling apart while they are eating them, it may frustrate them and end a nutritious meal prematurely.

1   pound extra-firm tofu
1   tablespoon canola oil
2   ounces cheddar cheese, grated or sliced
4   whole-grain flour tortillas
2   cups cooked brown rice (see page 226), warmed
2   cups cooked pinto beans (see page 226), warmed
1   ripe avocado, peeled, pitted, and sliced

1. Remove the moisture from the tofu by placing it on a plate and setting a heavy pot on top of it. After approximately 15 minutes, remove the tofu from the plate and discard the accumulated liquid. Cube the tofu.
2. Heat the canola oil in a wok or well-seasoned Dutch oven over high heat. When the oil is hot, add the tofu and sear until golden, tossing occasionally, approximately 5 minutes. Remove the pan from the heat.
3. Divide the cheese among the 4 tortillas. Microwave the tortillas, until the cheese melts and they are warmed, approximately 35 seconds.
4. Place the tortillas on plates and divide the rice, beans, tofu, and avocado among them. Fold in the sides and then roll the tortillas up from the bottom to enclose the filling completely.

Black Bean Burritos

Burritos are a great way to introduce fussy eaters to beans, and black beans are the Cadillac of dried beans and are fabulous in burritos. Not only are they versatile and loaded with flavor and texture, but they are a nutritional star as well. They provide significant amounts of protein, folic acid, fiber, iron, and potassium. These burritos can be made spicy, but some children won't eat them that way—ours eat them very lightly spiced. **TIPS:** The best plan for this recipe is to put the beans up to cook and then proceed with the remainder of the recipe. When the beans are tender, all you will have to do is puree them with the seasonings. You can then assemble the burritos. If desired, both the beans and yogurt-tahini sauce can be prepared 1 day in advance. If canned beans are used, skip step 1; add ¾ cup of water and sea salt to taste.

PREPARATION:
30 MINUTES

COOKING:
1¼ HOURS

YIELD:
4 MAIN-COURSE
SERVINGS

BEANS

1½ cups dried black beans, sorted, rinsed, and soaked overnight,
    or 3 cups canned black beans, drained and rinsed
    Sea salt to taste
    Black pepper to taste
1 tablespoon olive oil
1 medium Spanish onion, peeled and diced
1 Scotch Bonnet *or* jalapeño *or* serrano, finely chopped (optional)
3 cloves garlic, peeled and thinly sliced
1 teaspoon coriander
1 teaspoon cumin
1 teaspoon chili powder
½ cup water
    Juice of 1 lemon
½ cup cilantro, chopped

SAUCE

1 cup nonfat plain yogurt
2 tablespoons tahini
    Juice of ½ lemon
2 tablespoons cilantro, finely chopped
    Sea salt to taste
    Black pepper to taste

BURRITOS

4 medium whole-wheat tortillas
3 ounces Monterey Jack cheese, grated or sliced
2 tomatoes, cored and diced
1 medium cucumber, peeled, seeded, and sliced
1 avocado, peeled, pitted, and cubed

1. To prepare the beans, place them in a Dutch oven and cover them with cold water. Bring the water to a boil. Reduce the heat, and simmer the beans until they are tender, approximately 1 hour. Season them with sea salt and black pepper.
2. While the beans are simmering, heat the olive oil in a skillet over medium heat. Add the onion and chili pepper, and sauté the ingredients, stirring them often, until they are soft. Add the garlic, and sauté it until it is fragrant.
3. Add the coriander, cumin, and chili powder, and sauté them for 1 minute. Add the water, and simmer the ingredients for 2 minutes.
4. Add the sautéed seasonings to the cooked beans and their liquid. Transfer the mixture to the work bowl of a food processor fitted with the metal blade. Process the mixture until it is well combined but still a bit chunky.
5. Transfer the bean mixture to a nonmetal bowl. Add the lemon juice and cilantro and season it with sea salt and black pepper.
6. To make the sauce, combine all the sauce ingredients in a nonmetal bowl.
7. To assemble the burritos, divide the cheese among the tortillas. Place them in a microwave or low oven (275°F) until the cheese is melted. Spread them with the beans. Divide the tomatoes, cucumber, and avocado among the tortillas. Drizzle the sauce onto each tortilla. Roll the tortillas. Divide the burritos among 4 plates and serve at once.

Pan-Fried Tofu Sandwich with Basil Pesto

Thickly sliced tofu seasoned with olive oil and balsamic vinegar makes great sandwiches. The first time we made them, though, they clearly lacked a layer of flavor. We considered spreading them with a bit of mayonnaise, but that seemed like the easy way out and would obviously be a fat overload. Instead, we decided upon our favorite and most healthful basil pesto. Prepared with silken tofu rather than olive oil, it is creamy and deceptively rich and the perfect complement to the neutral-tasting tofu. Use great bread and your taste buds will be delighted with the variety of flavors and textures. **TIP:** The pesto can also be tossed with hot or cold pasta or stirred into a soup. It makes an excellent topping for fish, boneless chicken breasts, or toasted bagel sandwiches as well.

PREPARATION:
20 MINUTES

COOKING:
5 MINUTES

YIELD:
3 MAIN-COURSE
SERVINGS

BASIL PESTO

- 4 cups (packed) fresh basil leaves
- 1 clove garlic, peeled and minced
- ⅓ cup pine nuts
- 4 ounces silken tofu, drained
- ⅓ cup grated Parmesan or Romano cheese
   Kosher salt
   Black pepper

TOFU

- 1 pound extra-firm tofu
- 3 tablespoons balsamic vinegar
- 1 tablespoon olive oil
   Kosher salt
   Black pepper
- 2 teaspoons canola oil
- 2 ounces part-skim mozzarella cheese, sliced or grated
- 6 slices whole-grain rustic sandwich bread
- 6 large lettuce leaves
- 6 slices tomato

1. To prepare the pesto, combine the basil, garlic, pine nuts, and silken tofu in the work bowl of a food processor fitted with the metal blade. Puree the ingredients until a smooth pesto forms. Stir in the Parmesan or Romano cheese and season with kosher salt and black pepper. Set the pesto aside for a moment.

2. Remove the moisture from the tofu by placing it on a plate and setting a heavy pot on top of it. After approximately 15 minutes, remove the tofu from the plate and discard the accumulated liquid. Slice the tofu into thirds, lengthwise, and set aside for a moment.

3. Whisk together the vinegar and olive oil. Set it aside for a moment.

4. Sprinkle the tofu with kosher salt and black pepper. Pour the oil mixture onto the tofu. Turn the tofu several times so the mixture is absorbed.

5. Heat the canola oil in a large skillet over medium-high heat. When the oil is hot, carefully place the tofu into the pan. Sear the tofu for 2 minutes on each side or until golden, turning once.

6. Remove the pan from the heat and top each portion of tofu with an equal amount of cheese. Cover the pan and allow the cheese to melt, approximately 2 minutes.

7. Divide the 6 slices of bread among 3 plates. Place a portion of tofu on 1 slice of the bread on each plate. Top each portion with a tablespoon of pesto, 2 lettuce leaves, and 2 slices of tomatoes. Top the sandwiches with the second slice of bread and serve at once.

Spinach, Zucchini, and Tomato Stuffed Potatoes

You can combine the creamy flesh of a baked potato with a variety of vegetables and a bit of your favorite cheese to create a number of great stuffed-potato recipes. They all can be prepared up to two days in advance making them an ideal choice for a quick lunch or a no-fuss dinner.

4 large russet potatoes, well scrubbed
1 tablespoon olive oil
2 cloves garlic, peeled and thinly sliced
1 large onion, peeled and thinly sliced
  Kosher salt
2 medium zucchini, trimmed and sliced into ½-inch pieces
1½ pounds spinach, trimmed, washed, spun dry, and chopped
1 pint cherry tomatoes, halved
½ cup milk
  Black pepper
2 ounces cheddar cheese, sliced or grated

PREPARATION:
15 MINUTES

COOKING:
1¼ HOURS

YIELD:
4 MAIN-COURSE
SERVINGS

1. Preheat the oven to 400°F. Place the potatoes into the oven and bake them until they are tender, approximately 1 hour.
2. While the potatoes are baking, heat the olive oil in a large Dutch oven over medium heat. When the oil is hot, add the garlic and cook for 1 minute. Add the onion and sprinkle it with kosher salt. Cook for 4 minutes, stirring often.
3. Add the zucchini and cook for 4 minutes, stirring often.
4. Raise the heat to high. Add 3 handfuls of spinach and stir until it begins to wilt. Continue adding the spinach and stirring until all the spinach has wilted.
5. Remove the pot from the heat and stir in the cherry tomatoes. Set the pot aside for a moment.
6. When the potatoes are soft, remove them from the oven. Do not turn off the oven. Carefully slice them in half and allow them to cool for a few minutes. With a spoon, scoop out the potato flesh and transfer it to a mixing bowl. Place the potato jackets on a sheet pan. Add the milk to the flesh. Mash the flesh with a fork or hand-held masher. Season with kosher salt and black pepper.
7. Stir the cooked vegetables into the potato flesh and combine thoroughly.
8. With your hands, form the mixture into 4 tightly packed portions. Place each portion into a jacket. Divide the cheese among the stuffed potatoes.
9. Transfer the pan to the oven. Bake the potatoes until the cheese melts and they are heated through, approximately 15 minutes.

PREPARATION:
35 MINUTES

COOKING:
10 MINUTES

YIELD:
4 MAIN-COURSE
SERVINGS

Tofu, Sweet Pepper, and Broccoli Quesadillas

The filling for these quesadillas can be prepared a day in advance, making them ideal for a quick and simple weekday dinner. With plenty of tofu, broccoli, and bell peppers, they provide an abundance of calcium, fiber, and vitamin C. Children will delight in being able to eat them with their hands, and the variety of tastes and textures is certain to appeal to them as well.

TOFU
- 1 pound extra-firm tofu
- 1 tablespoon canola oil
  Kosher salt
- 1 tablespoon sugar
- 2 tablespoons cider vinegar

FILLING AND TORTILLAS
- 1 tablespoon canola oil
- 4 cloves garlic, peeled and thinly sliced
- 1 onion, peeled and sliced
  Kosher salt
- 1 red bell pepper, cored and thinly sliced
- 1 pound broccoli crowns, florets separated
- 2 teaspoons spice rub (see page 280) *or* 1 teaspoon cumin and 1 teaspoon chili powder
- 4 whole-grain flour tortillas
- 2 ounces Monterey Jack cheese, sliced or grated
- 1 avocado, peeled, pitted, and sliced
- 4 tablespoons low-fat sour cream

1. Preheat the oven to 400°F.
2. To prepare the tofu, first remove its moisture by placing it on a plate and setting a heavy pot on top of it. After approximately 15 minutes, remove the tofu from the plate and discard the accumulated liquid. Cube the tofu.
3. Heat the canola oil in a well-seasoned Dutch oven over high heat.

Season the tofu with kosher salt. Carefully add it to the pot. Sear it until it is golden, tossing occasionally, approximately 5 minutes. Add the sugar and cook for another minute. Add the vinegar and cook for a final 30 seconds. Transfer the tofu to a plate. Set it aside for a moment.

4. To prepare the filling, heat the canola oil in the Dutch oven over medium heat. When the oil is hot, add the garlic and cook for 1 minute. Add the onion and sprinkle it with kosher salt. Cook the onion for 3 minutes, stirring often. Add the bell pepper and cook for 3 minutes, stirring often. Reduce the heat slightly and stir in the broccoli. Cover the pot and cook for 5 minutes, stirring occasionally. Stir in the spice blend and cook for a final minute. Remove the pan from the heat.

5. Place the tortillas on 1 large or 2 small sheet pans. Divide the cheese among the tortillas. Spread an equal amount of filling and tofu on the tortillas. Transfer the pans to the oven and heat the quesadillas until hot, approximately 10 minutes.

6. Divide the quesadillas among 4 plates. Garnish each with avocado slices and sour cream, fold in half, and serve at once.

Vegetarian Baked Beans

Whether it is salt pork or bacon, most baked-bean recipes contain fatty pieces of pork. We prepare ours with no meat. They are hearty, have a slightly sweet flavor, and are very nutritious. During the colder months, we enjoy serving baked beans as the centerpiece to a healthful and hearty supper with a green salad and whole-grain bread. Other times, for a classic New England meal, we accompany the beans with a thick fillet of roasted cod. Endurance athletes who are weary of the traditional carbohydrate-loading regime of pasta with tomato sauce and bread may wish to experiment with one of our favorite prerace meals—baked beans with baked sweet potatoes. The beans provide plenty of protein, fiber, iron, and potassium and the potatoes, of course, are a great source of complex carbohydrates. Just be sure to try out the meal while training prior to race day!

BEAN SOAKING: OVERNIGHT

PREPARATION: 15 MINUTES

COOKING: 3 HOURS

RESTING: 30 MINUTES

YIELD: 6 MAIN-COURSE SERVINGS

1 pound navy or small white beans, sorted, rinsed, and soaked in
    enough water to cover for 8 hours
1 tablespoon canola oil
1 large onion, peeled and diced
  Kosher salt
2½ teaspoons ground ginger
2 teaspoons dry mustard
2 heaping tablespoons tomato paste
½ cup brown sugar
½ cup blackstrap molasses
8 cups water

1. Preheat the oven to 300°F.
2. Drain the beans of their soaking water. Discard the soaking
   water. Set the beans aside for a moment.
3. Heat the canola oil in an ovenproof Dutch oven over medium heat.
   When it is hot, add the onion. Sprinkle it with kosher salt, and
   cook for 5 minutes, stirring often.
4. Reduce the heat to low. Add the ginger and mustard and cook the
   ingredients for 2 minutes, stirring often.
5. Add the tomato paste, brown sugar, molasses, and beans. Raise
   the heat to high and cook for 2 minutes, stirring often.
6. Add the water. Bring the beans to a boil. Season them with
   kosher salt. Cover the pot, and transfer it to the oven. Cook the
   beans for 3 hours, stirring occasionally.
7. Remove the beans from the oven. Carefully uncover the pot, and
   stir them one final time. Allow the beans to rest for 30 minutes
   before serving them.

Barbequed Tofu Sandwiches

After tasting Barbequed Beef (see page 346), we decided to make a vegetarian version starring tofu. The appealing taste of the quickly prepared sweet-and-sour sauce enhances the mild flavor and unique texture of the tofu. You may discover that children who don't enjoy the beef version will find this one delicious. These sandwiches are a great source of calcium, vitamin C, protein, and fiber.

PREPARATION:
20 MINUTES

COOKING:
45 MINUTES

YIELD:
4 MAIN-COURSE
SERVINGS

TOFU

1 pound extra-firm tofu
1 tablespoon canola oil
  Kosher salt
  Black pepper
1 tablespoon white sugar
2 tablespoons cider vinegar

SAUCE

1 tablespoon canola oil
3 cloves garlic, peeled and thinly sliced
1 onion, peeled and diced
  Kosher salt
1 green bell pepper, cored and diced
1 red bell pepper, cored and diced
2 tablespoons cider vinegar
2 tablespoons Worcestershire sauce
2 tablespoons brown sugar
1 28-ounce can whole tomatoes with juice, chopped
4 whole-grain rolls

1. To prepare the tofu, first remove its moisture by placing it on a plate and setting a heavy pot on top of it. After approximately 15 minutes, remove the tofu from the plate and discard the accumulated liquid. Cube the tofu.

2. Heat the canola oil in a well-seasoned Dutch oven over high heat. When the oil is hot, add the tofu. Sprinkle it with kosher salt and black pepper. Sear it until it is golden, tossing occasionally, approximately 5 minutes. Add the white sugar and cook for another

minute. Add the 2 tablespoons of vinegar and cook for a final 30 seconds. Transfer the tofu to a plate. Set it aside for a moment.

3. To prepare the sauce, heat the canola oil in the Dutch oven over medium heat. When hot, add the garlic. Cook it for 1 minute, stirring often. Add the onion and sprinkle it with kosher salt. Cook the onion for 3 minutes, stirring often. Raise the heat to medium and add the bell pepper. Cook it for 2 minutes, stirring often.

4. Cover the pot and sweat the vegetables for 5 minutes.

5. Stir in the vinegar, Worcestershire sauce, brown sugar, and tomatoes. Raise the heat to high and bring the sauce to a boil. Reduce the heat and simmer the sauce for 20 minutes, stirring occasionally. Add the tofu to the sauce and simmer for 10 minutes more.

6. Cut the rolls in half and divide them among 4 plates. Spoon the tofu and sauce onto each roll and serve at once.

Baked Tofu Parmesan

PREPARATION:
15 MINUTES

COOKING:
50 MINUTES

YIELD:
6 MAIN-COURSE
SERVINGS

This recipe is adapted from one of our previous cookbooks, *The Menopause Cookbook*. Since it is a meal we prepare regularly and the entire family enjoys, it warrants repeating here. It is a wonderful way to introduce soy into your family's diet. We have discovered that kids who won't even take a nibble of tofu eventually love it when it is prepared this way. Unlike stir-fried tofu, whose appearance and texture is an acquired taste, breaded tofu is disguised enough to get kids to taste it. **TIPS:** In a pinch, substitute your favorite bottled pasta sauce for the homemade sauce. Also, leftover tofu Parmesan makes a delightful sandwich when reheated and tucked into a whole-grain roll or baguette.

SAUCE

1 tablespoon olive oil
4 cloves garlic, peeled and thinly sliced
1 onion, peeled and diced
  Kosher salt
2 teaspoons dried basil
1 35-ounce can whole tomatoes in juice, chopped
  Black pepper

TOFU AND PASTA

2 pounds extra-firm tofu (2 blocks), drained, each block sliced into
    3½-inch-thick rectangles and patted dry

Kosher salt

Black pepper

2 eggs

½ cup milk

2½ cups store-bought Italian-flavored dry bread crumbs

4 tablespoons olive oil

6 tablespoons grated Parmesan cheese

6 ounces part-skim mozzarella cheese, sliced or grated

1 pound whole-grain penne

1. Preheat the oven to 425°F. Bring a large pot of water to a boil.
2. To prepare the sauce, heat the olive oil in a Dutch oven over low
   heat. Add the garlic and cook for 1 minute. Add the onion and
   sprinkle it with kosher salt. Cook the onion until it is soft, stirring
   often. Add the basil.
3. Raise the heat to high and add the tomatoes. Bring the sauce to a
   boil. Reduce the heat and simmer for 30 minutes, stirring occasionally. Season the sauce with kosher salt and black pepper.
4. While the sauce is cooking, prepare the tofu and cook the pasta.
   Sprinkle the tofu slices on each side with kosher salt and black
   pepper. Whisk the eggs and milk in a pie plate. Place the bread
   crumbs on a large plate.
5. Dip a tofu slice into the egg wash, remove it, and allow the excess
   to drain back onto the plate. Coat the tofu in the bread crumbs,
   patting it to be certain they adhere. Place the breaded tofu on a
   plate. Repeat the procedure with the remaining egg wash, tofu,
   and bread crumbs.
6. Drizzle the olive oil onto a heavy baking tray. Place the tray in the
   oven. Allow the oil to get hot, approximately 5 minutes. Carefully
   remove the tray from the oven. Place the tofu rectangles on the
   tray, flipping them to coat in the oil. Return the tray to the oven.
   Bake the tofu until golden and crisp, approximately 15 minutes,
   turning once.
7. Remove the tray from the oven. Do not turn off the oven. Spoon
   the sauce onto each portion of tofu. Sprinkle each portion with

the Parmesan and mozzarella. Return the tray to the oven. Bake the tofu until the cheese melts and bubbles, approximately 5 minutes.

8. While the tofu is baking, add kosher salt to the boiling water, followed by the pasta. Cook the pasta according to the package instructions.

9. Drain the pasta and divide it among 6 plates. Spoon some of the remaining sauce onto each portion. Place a portion of tofu onto each plate and serve at once.

CHAPTER 17

chicken dishes

The health benefits of eating chicken are well documented. A boneless and skinless chicken breast is a lean protein source that is rich in niacin, riboflavin, and iron. The challenge of cooking with lean chicken breasts is that the absence of fat can often be accompanied by an absence of flavor. However, skinless chicken breasts are to a cook what a canvas is to an artist—something plain that with creativity can be transformed into something wonderful. Searing, stir-frying, and grilling are the simplest and best methods for preparing chicken breasts. These quick cooking techniques seal in the breasts' natural juices and prevent them from drying out and becoming tough. The mild flavor of chicken breasts is enhanced by the robust flavors of red and white wines, earthy-tasting vegetables, and gusty condiments such as mustards and vinegars. Our Chicken with Artichoke Hearts and Mushrooms (see page 248) is an incredibly easy and quick meal that features a light and tasty sauce that everyone will love.

Although skinless chicken thighs contain slightly more fat than breasts, they are still leaner than every cut of beef except the top round. The additional fat naturally makes them more flavorful and ideal for braising. Unlike sinewy cuts of beef and pork that require several hours of slow cooking to become tender, dark-meat chicken is fork tender in just an hour. When you crave a hearty and comforting meal and want it on the table in a reasonable amount of time, prepare our Chicken with Red Wine and Mushrooms (see page 243). The entire family will delight in the tender meat and the deeply flavored sauce.

We all have our favorite roast-chicken recipes. When you include the traditional accompanying dishes, many of the recipes require a lot of work and time. In our Chicken Roasted with Many Vegetables (see page 253), we cook a kosher or brined chicken on an oven rack, directly above a pan of a bell peppers, onions, mushrooms, and fennel. The chicken and vegetables go into the oven at the same time and are done simultaneously. The juices from the chicken season the vegetables and the slow cooking process caramelizes them, creating a delightful side dish that can stand on its own. If there was ever a no-fuss roast-chicken meal, this is the one.

With a bit of creativity and an emphasis on bold flavors you can transform the humble chicken into a delicious and wonderfully nutritious meal that the entire family will enjoy.

Chicken with Red Wine and Mushrooms

This version of a classic French dish is not only delicious but also simple and quick to prepare. Young children may find the sauce to be too rich tasting, but they will love the tender chicken and the accompanying egg noodles.

3 pounds bone-in chicken thighs, skin removed and discarded
  Kosher salt
  Black pepper
1 tablespoon olive oil
4 medium shallots, peeled and chopped (about ⅔ cup)
1 pound white button mushrooms, sliced
1½ cups dry red wine (a Burgundy or Beaujolais are excellent
    choices)
1½ cups homemade or low-sodium canned chicken broth
1 tablespoon unsalted butter
½ cup flat-leaf (Italian) parsley, chopped

1. Sprinkle the chicken thighs on each side with kosher salt and black pepper.
2. Heat the olive oil in a large Dutch oven over medium-high heat. When the oil is hot, add one-half of the chicken thighs to the pot. Sear the thighs on each side, turning once, approximately 3 minutes per side. Transfer the chicken to a plate and set it aside. Repeat the procedure with the remaining chicken.
3. Pour off all but 1 tablespoon of the accumulated drippings in the pot. Reduce the heat to low. Add the shallots and cook for 45 seconds, stirring constantly. Raise the heat slightly and add the mushrooms. Sprinkle them with kosher salt and cook for 3 minutes, stirring often.
4. Raise the heat to high. Add the wine and stock. Bring the sauce to a boil. Reduce the heat to medium and simmer the sauce for 3 minutes.
5. Preheat the broiler.
6. Return the chicken to the pot along with any accumulated juices and cook for 30 minutes, turning occasionally.
7. Transfer the chicken to a sheet pan, bone-side down. Place the

PREPARATION:
15 MINUTES

COOKING:
1 HOUR

YIELD:
4 MAIN-COURSE
SERVINGS

tray in the oven and broil for 5 minutes. Transfer the chicken to a serving platter.

8. Raise the heat to high under the sauce. Add the butter and parsley. Simmer the sauce for another minute. Season to taste with kosher salt and black pepper. Pour the sauce onto the chicken. If desired, accompany the chicken with whole-grain egg noodles.

Chicken with Onions, Tomatoes, and Balsamic Vinegar

PREPARATION:
10 MINUTES

COOKING:
45 MINUTES

YIELD:
4 MAIN-COURSE
SERVINGS

With minimal cooking time and relatively few ingredients, you will be pleasantly surprised with the boldly flavored sauce you will create in this healthful recipe. Children will delight in the slightly vinegary sauce and tender chicken.

3 pounds bone-in chicken thighs, skin removed and discarded
Kosher salt
Black pepper
1 tablespoon olive oil
4 cloves garlic, peeled and thinly sliced
2 medium yellow onions, peeled and thinly sliced
2 cups homemade or low-sodium canned chicken broth
3 tablespoons balsamic vinegar
1 28-ounce can whole tomatoes packed in juice, drained, liquid reserved for another use, tomatoes chopped
½ cup flat-leaf (Italian) parsley, chopped

1. Sprinkle the chicken thighs on each side with kosher salt and black pepper.
2. Heat the olive oil in a large Dutch oven over medium-high heat. When the oil is hot, add one-half of the chicken to the pot. Sear the thighs on each side, turning once, approximately 3 minutes per side. Transfer the chicken to a plate and set it aside. Repeat the procedure with the remaining chicken.
3. Pour off all but 1 tablespoon of the accumulated drippings in the pot. Reduce the heat to low. Add the garlic and cook for 15

seconds. Raise the heat slightly and add the onions. Sprinkle them with kosher salt, and cook for 4 minutes, stirring often.

4. Raise the heat to high. Add the chicken stock and simmer for 3 minutes. Add the vinegar and tomatoes and bring the sauce to a boil.

5. Preheat the broiler.

6. Return the chicken to the pot along with any accumulated juices. Reduce the heat to medium-low and simmer the chicken for 15 minutes, turning occasionally.

7. Transfer the chicken to a sheet pan, bone-side down. Place the pan in the oven and broil the chicken until slightly crisp, approximately 5 minutes.

8. Transfer the chicken to a serving platter. Add the parsley to the sauce. Season the sauce with kosher salt and black pepper.

9. Pour the sauce onto the chicken and serve at once.

Orange-Soy Grilled Chicken Thighs

Chicken thighs are wonderful on the grill and are a good choice to serve to a crowd. For the best taste, we always marinate our chicken thighs for a day and cook them over hardwood charcoal. Our marinades usually consist of a combination of bold ingredients that enhance the mild flavor of the chicken, giving it a complex taste without being too salty or too sweet. This juicy, tender, and subtly flavored chicken will appeal to all your family and friends.

21 (approximately 7 pounds) bone-in chicken thighs, skin removed and discarded
1 cup tamari sauce
1 cup orange juice
4 tablespoons sesame oil
½ cup brown sugar
2 teaspoons ground ginger
6 cloves garlic, peeled and thinly sliced
4 scallions, trimmed and sliced

PREPARATION:
10 MINUTES

MARINATING:
24 HOURS

COOKING:
20 MINUTES

YIELD:
10 MAIN-COURSE
SERVINGS

1. The day prior to grilling, divide the thighs among 3 one-gallon freezer bags.
2. In a large bowl, whisk the tamari sauce, orange juice, sesame oil, brown sugar, ginger, garlic, and scallions.
3. Divide the marinade among the 3 freezer bags. Seal the bags and place them in the refrigerator.
4. The following day, light a hardwood charcoal fire. When the charcoal is mostly white ash, remove the chicken thighs from the bags and place them on the grill. Discard the marinade. Grill the thighs for 20 minutes or until cooked through, flipping and turning them occasionally.

PREPARATION:
10 MINUTES

COOKING:
30 MINUTES

YIELD:
4 MAIN-COURSE
SERVINGS

Chicken with Mushrooms, Spinach, and Marsala

The combination of mushrooms and spinach is a real winner. Whether quickly cooked and tossed with pasta, used in a seafood or meat stuffing, or combined with chicken and marsala wine as we have done here, its sweet and earthy flavor is sure to please. Chicken is a lean, iron-rich protein source and spinach is an excellent nondairy source of calcium.

SPINACH

2 teaspoons olive oil
3 cloves garlic, peeled and thinly sliced
1 pound spinach, trimmed, washed, and drained
   Kosher salt
   Black pepper

CHICKEN

2 boneless and skinless chicken breasts (approximately 1½ pounds), trimmed, halved, and flattened to ⅓-inch thickness
   Kosher salt
⅓ cup all-purpose flour
2 teaspoons plus 2 teaspoons olive oil

2 medium shallots, peeled and chopped
1 pound white button mushrooms, sliced
1 cup marsala wine
1 cup homemade or low-sodium canned chicken broth
1 tablespoon unsalted butter
  Black pepper

1. To prepare the spinach, heat the olive oil in a Dutch oven over medium heat. When it is hot, add the garlic. Cook the garlic for 30 seconds. Raise the heat to high and add 3 handfuls of spinach. Stir the spinach until it begins to wilt, adding more as space becomes available in the pot. When all the spinach has wilted, remove the pot from the heat. Season the spinach with kosher salt and black pepper. Keep the spinach warm while you prepare the chicken.

2. Sprinkle the chicken breasts on each side with kosher salt. Dredge them in the flour and shake off the excess.

3. Heat 2 teaspoons of the olive oil in a skillet over medium-high heat. When it is hot, carefully place 2 pieces of chicken into the pan. Sear them for 2 minutes on each side, flipping once. Transfer them to a plate and keep warm. Repeat the procedure with 2 more teaspoons of olive oil and the remaining chicken.

4. Reduce the heat to low under the pan. Add the shallots and cook for 30 seconds, stirring constantly. Raise the heat to medium and add the mushrooms. Sprinkle them with kosher salt. Cook them until they begin to soften, approximately 4 minutes, stirring often.

5. Raise the heat to high and add the wine. Simmer the wine for 2 minutes. Add the chicken broth and simmer for 3 minutes. Have ready 4 dinner plates.

6. Swirl the butter into the sauce. Reduce the heat to low. Return 2 pieces of chicken to the pan along with any accumulated juices. Cook the chicken for 2 minutes, turning once. Transfer the chicken to a clean plate. Repeat the procedure with the remaining chicken. Season the sauce with kosher salt and black pepper.

7. Divide the spinach among the plates, spreading it to create a bed. Place the chicken onto the spinach. Spoon sauce onto each portion and serve at once.

Pan Sauces

Restaurant sauces are based on concentrated stocks that often require hours or days to prepare. This is obviously not practical for the home cook. Many of our quickly prepared chicken and meat dishes rely on simple pan sauces to enhance their flavor. When you cook food, caramelized bits of juices remain on the bottom of the skillet or roasting pan. When the pan is deglazed, these bits (called fond) are the foundation for great pan sauces. The technique of deglazing is simple and straightforward. After cooking a piece of meat, fish, or poultry, transfer it to a plate and keep it warm. Pour off and discard any accumulated fat in the pan and place the pan over medium-high heat. Add stock, wine, or a combination of both (approximately $1\frac{1}{2}$ cups for four servings), and with a spoon, stir thoroughly to dissolve the particles. Then add the juices that have accumulated on the plate in which the food was resting. Simmer the sauce for several minutes to reduce it and concentrate its flavors. To create a silky smooth sauce and to balance its flavors, whisk in 1 or 2 tablespoons of unsalted butter. Last, season the sauce with kosher salt and freshly ground black pepper.

PREPARATION:
10 MINUTES

COOKING:
20 MINUTES

YIELD:
4 MAIN-COURSE
SERVINGS

Chicken with Artichoke Hearts and Mushrooms

While looking over some of our old restaurant menus, we came across this dish that we recalled as being one of our most popular meals. It is a wonderfully simple and nutritious dish that the entire family will savor. Artichoke hearts, like black olives, are a food that one wouldn't predict children would enjoy, but many do. **TIP:** Be certain to use artichoke hearts packed in water. Those packed in a marinade are too strong tasting for this recipe.

2 boneless and skinless chicken breasts (approximately 1 ½
    pounds), trimmed, halved, and flattened to ⅓-inch thickness
  Kosher salt
  Black pepper
⅓ cup all-purpose flour
2 teaspoons plus 2 teaspoons olive oil
2 medium shallots, peeled and chopped
12 ounces white button mushrooms, sliced
⅓ cup marsala wine
1⅓ cups homemade or low-sodium canned chicken broth
1 14-ounce can artichoke hearts packed in water, drained and
    quartered
1 tablespoon unsalted butter

1. Sprinkle the chicken breasts on each side with kosher salt and
   black pepper. Dredge them into the flour and shake off the
   excess.
2. Heat 2 teaspoons of the olive oil in a skillet over medium-high
   heat. When it is hot, carefully place 2 pieces of chicken into the
   pan. Sear them for 2 minutes on each side, flipping once. Transfer them to a plate and keep warm. Repeat the procedure with
   the remaining oil and chicken.
3. Reduce the heat to low under the pan. Add the shallots. Cook
   them for 30 seconds, stirring constantly. Raise the heat to
   medium and add the mushrooms. Sprinkle them with kosher
   salt. Cook them until they begin to soften, approximately 4 minutes, stirring often.
4. Raise the heat to high and add the wine. Simmer the sauce for 1
   minute. Add the chicken broth and simmer the sauce for 1 ½ minutes. Reduce the heat to medium. Have ready 4 dinner plates.
5. Return 2 pieces of chicken to the pan and cook them for 2 minutes longer, turning once. Divide them between 2 plates. Repeat
   the procedure with the remaining chicken.
6. Add the artichoke hearts and butter to the pan. Simmer the
   sauce for 2 more minutes.
7. Season the sauce with kosher salt and black pepper. Spoon the
   sauce onto the chicken and serve at once.

PREPARATION:
10 MINUTES

COOKING:
10 MINUTES

YIELD:
4 MAIN-COURSE
SERVINGS

Pan-Fried Chicken Sandwich with Avocado and Jack Cheese

When boneless and skinless chicken breasts are on sale at the market, we stock up. We wrap and freeze them in individual portions. Of the many meals we prepare with chicken, these quick and healthful sandwiches are one of our favorites. Thin slices of avocado add texture and a rich taste to the mild chicken. Avocados, like olives, are a food that you probably would not imagine appealing to children, but many seem to crave them. They are an excellent source of potassium and vitamin C.

2   boneless and skinless chicken breasts (approximately 1½
        pounds), trimmed, halved, and flattened to ⅓-inch thickness
    Kosher salt
    Black pepper
½   cup all-purpose flour
4   whole-grain crusty rolls
1   tablespoon plus 1 tablespoon canola oil
2   ounces Monterey Jack cheese, sliced or grated
1   avocado, peeled, pitted, and sliced
1   tomato, cored and sliced

1. Sprinkle the chicken breasts on each side with kosher salt and black pepper. Dredge the breasts in the flour and shake off the excess. Set them aside for the moment.
2. Cut the rolls in half and divide them among 4 plates.
3. Heat 1 tablespoon of the canola oil in a skillet over medium-high heat. When the oil is hot, carefully place 2 breast halves into the pan. Sear them until golden and slightly crisp, approximately 2 minutes. Turn them over, sprinkle them each with ½ ounce of cheese. Continue cooking them until they are just cooked through, approximately 2 more minutes.
4. Place each of them in a roll. Repeat this procedure with the remaining oil, chicken, cheese, and rolls.
5. Garnish each sandwich with avocado and tomato slices and serve at once.

Chicken with Asparagus, Cream, and Balsamic Vinegar

PREPARATION:
10 MINUTES

COOKING:
15 MINUTES

YIELD:
4 MAIN-COURSE
SERVINGS

The mild flavor and firm texture of chicken breasts are enhanced by a variety of robust flavors. In this simple recipe, a quick pan sauce, seasoned with cream and balsamic vinegar and containing small pieces of asparagus, is slightly sweet and deceptively rich. Asparagus is a great source of fiber, calcium, and folate. **TIP:** Choose pencil-sized asparagus for this dish. Thicker ones are wonderful roasted but take too long to cook in this type of recipe.

2 boneless and skinless chicken breasts (approximately 1½ pounds), trimmed, halved, and flattened to ⅓-inch thickness

Kosher salt

Black pepper

⅓ cup all-purpose flour

1 tablespoon plus 1 tablespoon canola oil

1 medium shallot, peeled and finely chopped

2 cloves garlic, peeled and thinly sliced

¾ pound asparagus, trimmed and sliced into 2-inch pieces

1⅓ cup homemade or low-sodium canned chicken broth

⅓ cup light cream

2 tablespoons balsamic vinegar

¼ cup flat-leaf (Italian) parsley, chopped

1. Sprinkle the chicken breasts on each side with kosher salt and black pepper. Dredge them in the flour and shake off the excess.

2. Heat 1 tablespoon of the canola oil in a skillet over medium-high heat. When it is hot, carefully place 2 pieces of chicken in the pan. Sear them for 2 minutes on each side, flipping once. Transfer them to a plate and keep warm. Repeat the procedure with the remaining oil and chicken.

3. Reduce the heat to low under the pan. Add the shallots and garlic and cook for 30 seconds, stirring constantly. Add the asparagus and cook for 1 minute, stirring often.

4. Raise the heat to high and add the chicken broth. Bring the broth to a boil. Reduce the heat and simmer for 3 minutes.

5. Add the cream and 2 pieces of chicken. Simmer the sauce and chicken for 2 minutes. Divide the chicken between 2 plates. Repeat the procedure with the remaining chicken.

6. Add the vinegar and parsley. Simmer the sauce for another minute. Season it with kosher salt and black pepper.

7. Spoon sauce and asparagus onto each portion of chicken and serve at once.

Sesame Chicken and Peanut Noodle Wraps

PREPARATION:
10 MINUTES

COOKING:
30 MINUTES

YIELD:
4 MAIN-COURSE
SERVINGS

Leftover peanut noodles from a picnic inspired this recipe. One afternoon, for a quick lunch, we tossed sesame-coated chicken breasts with the noodles. Although this would have been a fine meal, we chose to roll the ingredients into flour tortillas to create great sandwiches. We weren't certain our children would enjoy them and were pleasantly surprised when the sandwiches were devoured. **TIP:** To save time, you can use a top-quality bottled peanut sauce.

PEANUT SAUCE AND NOODLES
   Kosher salt
8 ounces spaghetti or linguine
¾ cup water
½ cup smooth peanut butter
2 tablespoons tamari
2 tablespoons blackstrap molasses
2 tablespoons cider vinegar
3 scallions, trimmed and thinly sliced
¼ cup cilantro, chopped

REMAINING INGREDIENTS
2 boneless and skinless chicken breasts (approximately 1½ pounds), trimmed, halved, and flattened to ⅓-inch thickness
   Kosher salt
½ cup sesame seeds
1 tablespoon plus 1 tablespoon canola oil
4 whole-grain flour tortillas, warmed
⅓ cup unsalted peanuts, finely chopped

1. Bring a large pot of water to a boil. Add kosher salt to the water followed by the pasta. Cook the pasta according to the package instructions. Drain it and transfer it to a large bowl.

2. While the pasta is cooking, prepare the peanut sauce by first bringing the water to a boil in a small saucepan. Remove the pan from the heat. Whisk in the peanut butter, tamari, molasses, and vinegar. Stir in the scallions and cilantro.

3. Stir the peanut sauce into the noodles and toss well. Set the noodles aside for a moment.

4. Place the chicken breasts on a plate. Sprinkle them on each side with kosher salt. Sprinkle them on each side with the sesame seeds. Press the seeds into the flesh with the heel of your hand.

5. Heat 1 tablespoon of the canola oil in a large skillet over medium high heat. When the oil is hot, place 2 breast halves in the pan. Sear them until the sesame seeds are golden brown and crisp, approximately 3 minutes. Turn them over and cook them for an additional 2 minutes. Transfer them to a cutting board. Repeat the procedure with the remaining oil and breast halves.

6. Divide the tortillas among 4 plates. Divide the noodles among the tortillas. Slice the chicken breasts into strips and place an equal portion on each tortilla. Garnish each tortilla with peanuts and serve at once.

Chicken Roasted with Many Vegetables

Although this meal requires that you first brine the chicken, the extra time is well worth it. It is the simplest and best one-dish roast chicken and vegetable meal we have ever made. Having experimented with a variety of vegetables, we have found that bell peppers, red onions, mushrooms, and fennel offer the best combination of taste and texture. Children will love the tender meat, and at least one of the vegetables is certain to appeal to them. We accompany the meal only with great bread but, occasionally, make the kids egg noodles as well. **TIPS:** Reserve the fennel tops and chicken bones to make a stock the following day. Also, since the juices from the brined chicken will flavor the vegetables, they don't need much additional salt. The dish can be prepared several hours in advance and reheated or served at room temperature.

BRINING:
20 HOURS

PREPARATION:
20 MINUTES

COOKING:
1¼ HOURS

YIELD:
4 MAIN-COURSE
SERVINGS

½ gallon cool water

½ cup kosher salt

¼ cup sugar

1 4–5 pound chicken, giblets removed (reserve the neck for stock)

2 red onions, peeled and sliced into eighths

1 red bell pepper, cored, seeded, and sliced into 2-inch pieces

1 yellow bell pepper, cored, seeded, and sliced into 2-inch pieces

1 green bell pepper, cored, seeded, and sliced into 2-inch pieces

2 heads of fennel, trimmed, cored, and sliced into 2-inch pieces

1 pound button mushrooms, quartered

2 heads of garlic, loose skin removed and ¼ inch sliced off the stem
   side to expose the raw cloves

2 tablespoons olive oil

1. The night prior to roasting the chicken, place the water in a large pot and stir in the kosher salt and sugar. Rinse the chicken and place it in the pot. Set a plate on top of it and refrigerate the chicken.

2. The following day, remove the chicken from its brine, rinse well, and dry thoroughly. Set it aside for a moment.

3. Preheat the oven to 350°F.

4. Place the onions, bell peppers, fennel, mushrooms, and garlic in a large roasting pan. Drizzle the vegetables with the olive oil.

5. Transfer the chicken to the oven, placing it directly on a rack in the middle of the oven. Position the vegetables in the roasting pan directly below the chicken.

6. Roast the chicken and vegetables until a thermometer inserted in the thickest part of a thigh registers 170°F, approximately 1¼ hours. During the roasting, stir the vegetables 3 or 4 times.

7. Transfer the chicken to a cutting board and allow to rest for 10 minutes. Stir the vegetables thoroughly. Transfer them to a serving bowl. Carve the chicken. Accompany the vegetables and chicken with whole-grain rustic bread and serve at once.

Are All Chickens Created Equal?

The answer to this question is a resounding no! Both genetic and environmental factors play a significant role in a chicken's appearance and, more important, how it tastes. Some producers may breed their birds to have a high yield of breast meat and low amount of fat, while another's goal may be a high yield of meat to bone. What the chicken eats, where it lives, how old it is, and how it is processed also influence its flavor.

If the label on a chicken reads organic, all natural, minimally processed, or free range, it may be more healthful, but it does not guarantee that it will taste better than your average supermarket bird. We believe kosher chickens have the best flavor and texture. If they are not available to you, brining is a simple procedure, which will transform an ordinary chicken into something special.

Essentially, kosher chickens are brined before packaging. They are buried in salt for 1 hour and then rinsed off in cold water. This process enhances the flavor of the bird by encouraging the fibers in the meat to open and trap the salt and water, which results in a juicier and tastier chicken. At home, by soaking a chicken in a solution of water, kosher salt, and sugar for twelve hours in the refrigerator, it is possible to duplicate the qualities of a kosher chicken (see page 254).

Roast Chicken with Kale, Mushrooms, and Bread Salad

BRINING:
20 HOURS

PREPARATION:
15 MINUTES

COOKING:
1¼ HOURS

YIELD:
4 MAIN-COURSE
SERVINGS

We never tire of eating roast chicken. When we prepare one, we try to keep it simple and make it as much of a one-pot meal as possible. There is nothing more disconcerting than roasting a chicken and having to spend an hour in the kitchen afterwards cleaning the numerous pots and pans used in the preparation of the accompaniments. With kale and whole-grain bread as the primary ingredients, this unique salad boasts great flavor and texture and is full of fiber and calcium. Toasted pine nuts add another layer of taste and a pleasant crunch. Rather than stuff the bird with the salad, it is cooked alongside it to keep the cooking time to a manageable 1 1/4 hours. Best of all, the majority of the cleaning can be accomplished while the chicken is roasting, leaving you and your family time to enjoy a leisurely meal.

CHICKEN

- ½ cup kosher salt
- ¼ cup sugar
- ½ gallon water
- 1 4–5 pound chicken, giblets removed (reserve the neck for a stock)

SALAD

- ⅓ cup pine nuts
- 1 tablespoon olive oil
- 2 cloves garlic, peeled and thinly sliced
- 1 onion, peeled and diced
  Kosher salt
- 1 pound button mushrooms, sliced
- 1 pound Dinosaur or other nonornamental kale, washed and drained
- ½ cup water
- 1 cup raisins
- 4 cups cubed crusty day-old whole-grain bread
  Black pepper

1. The night prior to roasting the chicken, place the water in a large pot and stir in the kosher salt and sugar. Rinse the chicken and place it in the pot. Set a plate on top of it and refrigerate the chicken.
2. The following day, remove the chicken from its brine, rinse well, and dry thoroughly.
3. Preheat the oven to 350°F.
4. Transfer the chicken to the oven, placing it directly on a rack set in the middle of the oven. Roast the chicken until a thermometer inserted into the thickest part of a thigh reads 170°F, approximately 1¼ hours. Transfer the chicken to a cutting board and allow to rest for 10 minutes.

5. While the chicken is roasting, prepare the salad. Place the pine nuts in a small skillet over low heat and toast them until they are golden, shaking the pan often, approximately 10 minutes. Remove the pan from the heat.

6. Heat the olive oil in an ovenproof Dutch oven over medium heat. When the oil is hot, add the garlic. Cook it for 30 seconds. Add the onion and sprinkle it with kosher salt. Cook the onion for 2 minutes, stirring often.

7. Raise the heat to high and add the mushrooms. Cook the mushrooms for 3 minutes, stirring often. Add the kale and water. Cover the pot and bring the vegetables to a boil. Reduce the heat to medium. Braise the vegetables until the kale is tender, stirring occasionally, approximately 20 minutes.

8. Stir in the raisins and bread. Season the salad with kosher salt and black pepper.

9. Place the pot in the oven. Bake the salad uncovered for 20 minutes.

10. Carve the chicken. Divide the chicken and salad among 4 plates and serve at once.

Herb-Braised Chicken and Vegetables

A common cool weather meal in our home is a braised chicken. Unlike tough cuts of beef that require three or four hours of slow cooking to become palatable, chicken is mouthwateringly tender in just an hour. Occasionally, we braise a cut-up chicken in red wine, tomatoes, and bell peppers and accompany it with pasta. Often, though, we slowly cook a chicken in white wine with a variety of vegetables to create a favorite one-pot meal. The gentle cooking process causes the potatoes in the sauce to release their starch, creating a natural thickener. The braising mellows the strong flavors of the garlic and fennel and their now-sweet flavors enhance the herb-laced sauce. We are certain your children will love the taste of the vegetables and will relish the challenge of identifying them.

PREPARATION:
15 MINUTES

COOKING:
1 HOUR

YIELD:
4 MAIN-COURSE
SERVINGS

2 tablespoons olive oil
1 4-pound chicken, cut into 4 pieces and skinned
  Kosher salt
  Black pepper
16 cloves garlic, peeled and trimmed
1 onion, peeled and thinly sliced
2 red bell peppers, seeded and sliced
2 bulbs fennel, trimmed and sliced
1 pound button mushrooms, halved
4 Yukon Gold potatoes, quartered
3 sprigs fresh rosemary
3 sprigs fresh tarragon
2 cups white wine
3 cups water or low-sodium canned chicken broth

1. Preheat the oven to 450°F. Have ready a sheet pan.
2. Heat the olive oil in a large ovenproof Dutch oven over medium-high heat. Sprinkle the chicken pieces on each side with kosher salt and black pepper.
3. When the oil is hot, carefully place the chicken pieces into the pot. Sear them for 5 minutes on each side, turning once. Remove them from the pot and set aside.
4. Reduce the heat to low. Add the garlic cloves and cook for 2 minutes, stirring often. Raise the heat slightly. Add the onion and sprinkle it with kosher salt. Cook the ingredients for 2 minutes, stirring often.
5. Add the bell peppers, fennel, and mushrooms. Cook the ingredients for 5 minutes. Add the potatoes, rosemary, and tarragon. Return the chicken to the pot. Cover the pot and raise the heat to high. When the ingredients begin to simmer, reduce the heat to low. Sweat the ingredients for 5 minutes, stirring occasionally.
6. Raise the heat to high and add the wine. Simmer the wine for 5 minutes. Add the water and bring the sauce to a boil.
7. Place the pot in the oven. Cook the chicken, uncovered, for 30 minutes.
8. Remove the pot from the oven and place on the stove. Turn on the broiler. Transfer the chicken to the sheet pan. Place the sheet

pan in the oven and broil the chicken for 5 minutes. Simmer the sauce over medium heat while the chicken is broiling.

9. Distribute the vegetables, sauce, and chicken among 4 plates and serve at once.

Smoky Backyard Chicken

Once a year we like to have a picnic at our home for neighbors and friends. We roll out our homemade smoker and delight in a classic barbeque. The incredible flavor and tenderness of slow-cooked beef, pork, and turkey are to die for. Barbequing requires low temperatures (220°F) and a lot of time. When we crave that smoky flavor but don't want to spend hours stoking the smoker, we turn to our kettle grill and cook a whole chicken over an off-set fire. The smoky-flavored chicken is an excellent substitute for a barbeque. Accompany it with the traditional sides (coleslaw, baked beans, and corn bread) and you will be in for a real treat.
TIP: Add a handful of smoking chips every 30 minutes to enhance the smoky flavor of the chicken.

BRINING:
20 HOURS

COOKING:
1¾ HOURS

YIELD:
4 MAIN-COURSE
SERVINGS

½ gallon water
½ cup kosher salt
¼ cup sugar
1 4–5-pound chicken, giblets removed (reserve the neck for stock)

1. The night prior to roasting the chicken, place the water in a large pot and stir in the kosher salt and sugar. Rinse the chicken and place it in the pot. Set a plate on top of it and refrigerate the chicken.
2. The following day, set both the bottom and top vents of your grill ¾ open. Light a hardwood charcoal fire. When the charcoal is mostly white ash, carefully pile the coals on one side of the grill. Place the chicken on the side of the grill with no coals. Cover the grill. Cook the chicken for 45 minutes in this manner.
3. Remove the cover and rotate the chicken so the opposite side is now facing the hot coals. If your fire has burned too low, add

more hardwood charcoal. Cover the grill once again and continue cooking the chicken until a meat thermometer inserted into the thickest part of the thigh reads 170°F, approximately 1 hour more.

4. Transfer the chicken to a cutting board and allow it to rest for 15 minutes before carving.

Hardwood Charcoal

Like many other people, we used to grill with charcoal briquettes. Briquettes add an off flavor to your food and are very unhealthful. There is now a widely available alternative: hardwood charcoal. Hardwood charcoal enhances the flavor of your grilled food and is much better for the environment and your health. Hardwood charcoal is the pure residue of burned and seasoned hardwood. It is free of additives, burns hotter and more evenly than briquettes, and is easily ignited using a charcoal chimney or newspaper.

CHAPTER 18

beef and pork dishes

Although we are proponents of a diet rich in fruits, vegetables, whole grains, legumes, and exceptionally lean protein sources, such as chicken and seafood, it is perfectly healthful to enjoy an occasional meat-based meal. You do not need to be extreme and entirely eliminate beef from your diet in order to have a heart-healthy diet. You can serve beef approximately once a week. It is important, though, that when you do indulge, you are conscious of portion size. A three-ounce serving of cooked meat, which is approximately the size of a deck of cards, is the ideal serving. Keep in mind that if you view meat as an accompaniment and fill out the remainder of the plate with whole grains and vegetables, you will be practicing healthful nutrition.

The nutritional benefits of meat cannot be overlooked. Meat is a tremendous source of high-quality protein. The protein in meat is a "complete" protein because it supplies all the essential amino acids needed to build and repair muscle. Meat also provides impressive amounts of vitamin B₁₂, iron, and zinc, nutrients difficult to get elsewhere, especially in vegetables. The iron in meat is better absorbed than the iron in vegetables and legumes.

To prepare a succulent meat meal it is helpful to know which cuts are suited for a particular cooking method. When we were children, our parents could rely on the neighborhood butcher for this information. Now, with most of us shopping in large markets and choosing prepackaged cuts of meat, we need to be more knowledgeable. All meat is muscle. The muscles the animal uses most frequently will be the toughest but also the most tasty. These are the cuts from the legs, shoulder, and rump. They turn out incredibly tender and flavorful when stewed or braised. The rib and loin sections are the least exercised and therefore the leanest, and most tender. This is where the finest steaks and roasts hail from. These cuts are best grilled, pan-fried, and sautéed. Leaner choices for beef include tenderloin, sirloin, flank steak, first-cut brisket, and hamburger with less than 12 percent fat.

The recipes in this chapter are certain to become family favorites. They combine healthful portions of meat with other delicious ingredients. Beef Stew (see page 270) is definitely a crowd pleaser. With wonderfully tender meat and plenty of vegetables, it is a meal that tastes great and is also good for you. And when you easily transform the leftovers into Cottage Pie (see page 272), your kids will be in heaven savoring the delectable mashed-potato crust. On the other hand, children often find pork too strong tasting. We find it is best to serve them small portions of pork combined with other foods. Our Spice-Rubbed Pork Shoulder with Black Beans and Brown Rice (see page 279) fits the bill. The meat is savory and tender and the beans and rice so tasty and satisfying they can be a meal in themselves.

Meat can still have a place on your dinner table. If you select the appropriate cooking method for the cut and are conscious of portion size, you will be able to create meals that deliver great flavor and first-rate nutrition.

Braciolette

Braciola is the Italian word for chop or cutlet. In Italy you often find braciola prepared with lamb or pork chops. Braciolette refers to stuffed meat rolls that are often braised in a tomato sauce. We have prepared a version with a garlicky spinach and Romano cheese filling. Rather than the usual tough cut of beef, which requires 2 1/2 hours to become tender, we have used lean flank steak. Flank steak is more healthful and cooks in about an hour. Spinach and beef are both excellent sources of iron. And with plenty of vitamin C from the tomato sauce, the iron from the beef is particularly well absorbed.

PREPARATION:
20 MINUTES

COOKING:
1 HOUR

YIELD:
6 MAIN-COURSE
SERVINGS

FLANK STEAK AND FILLING

1¾ pounds flank streak
1 tablespoon olive oil
6 cloves garlic, peeled and thinly sliced
2½ pounds spinach, trimmed, washed, drained, and chopped
1½ cups fresh bread crumbs
1 cup grated Romano cheese
   Kosher salt
   Black pepper

SAUCE

1 tablespoon olive oil
3 cloves garlic, peeled and thinly sliced
1 medium onion, peeled and diced
   Kosher salt
1½ cups dry red wine
1 28-ounce can whole tomatoes in juice, chopped
½ cup flat-leaf (Italian) parsley, chopped
   Black pepper

1. To prepare the flank steak, place it in between two pieces of plastic wrap. With the flat side of a mallet, and beginning from the center and working your way toward the edges, pound the meat so that it is very thin, without tearing it. Set the meat aside for a moment.

2. To prepare the filling, heat the olive oil in a large Dutch oven over medium heat. When the oil is hot, add the garlic. Cook it for 45 seconds. Raise the heat to high and add 4 handfuls of the spinach. Cook it, stirring constantly, until it begins to wilt, adding more to the pot when there is room. When all the spinach has wilted, remove the pot from the heat.

3. Stir in the bread crumbs and Romano. Season the filling with kosher salt and black pepper.

4. Spread the filling over the surface of the meat. Roll the meat, jellyroll fashion, and tie it in 3 or 4 places with kitchen twine. Sprinkle the meat on all sides with kosher salt and black pepper.

5. To prepare the sauce, heat the olive oil in the Dutch oven over medium-high heat. When the oil is hot, carefully place the meat in the pot. Sear the meat, turning occasionally, until it is a deep brown, approximately 7 minutes. Transfer the meat to a plate. Set it aside for a moment. Reduce the heat to low.

6. Add the garlic to the pot and cook it for 30 seconds, stirring constantly. Add the onion and sprinkle it with kosher salt. Cook the onion for 3 minutes stirring often.

7. Raise the heat to high and add the wine. Simmer the wine for 2 minutes. Stir in the tomatoes and bring the sauce to a boil. Return the meat to the pot. Bring the sauce to a boil once again. Cover the pot. Reduce the heat to low. Braise the meat for 45 minutes, turning occasionally.

8. Transfer the meat to a cutting board and allow it to rest for a moment. Raise the heat to high under the sauce. Add the parsley. Reduce the sauce for 5 minutes, stirring occasionally. Season it with kosher salt and black pepper.

9. Have ready 6 plates. Remove and discard the strings from around the meat. Slice the meat into 6 portions and divide them among the plates. Spoon sauce onto each portion. Accompany the meat and sauce with crusty whole-grain bread and serve at once.

Grilled Tuscan Steak

When warm weather arrives, we grill more often. Although we usually grill chicken thighs, whole chickens, and vegetables, occasionally we will cook a great piece of beef. We want the beef flavor to star, so we don't fuss over it. We cook it as they do in Tuscany–simply. We sprinkle it with kosher salt and freshly ground black pepper and set it on the grill. A drizzle of fruity olive oil is the only adornment. For a once-a-week beef treat, this one is hard to beat.

PREPARATION:
30 MINUTES

COOKING:
10 MINUTES

YIELD:
4 MAIN-COURSE
SERVINGS

2 14-ounce rib or sirloin steaks
   Kosher salt
   Black pepper
   Extra-virgin olive oil for drizzling

1. Light a hardwood charcoal fire.
2. Sprinkle the steaks liberally on each side with kosher salt and black pepper.
3. When the fire is mostly white ash, place the steaks onto the grill. Sear the steaks until a deep brown crust forms, approximately 5 minutes. Flip them and cook for an additional 5 minutes for a medium-rare steak. For more well-done steaks, move them to a cooler portion of the grill and cook until desired doneness.
4. Transfer the steaks to a cutting board and allow them to rest for 5 minutes. Slice the steaks in half and divide them among 4 plates. Drizzle each portion with olive oil and serve at once.

Balsamic Grilled Flank Steak

PREPARATION:
10 MINUTES

MARINATING:
24 HOURS

COOKING:
10 MINUTES

YIELD:
4 MAIN-COURSE
SERVINGS

Flank steak is lean and versatile. It is an excellent source of protein, iron, and vitamin B_{12} and is practically as lean as beef tenderloin. It cooks quickly, making it ideal to use in pasta dishes and stir-fries. It also absorbs flavors well, so it is wonderful to marinate and grill. In this recipe we have marinated the meat in a combination of olive oil and balsamic vinegar. The result is a savory piece of meat that is tender and subtly smoky.

1½ pounds flank steak
½ cup balsamic vinegar
¼ cup olive oil
2 teaspoons kosher salt
¼ cup brown sugar
3 cloves garlic, peeled and thinly sliced
1 onion, peeled and diced

1. Place the flank steak in a one-gallon freezer bag.
2. Whisk together the vinegar, oil, salt, brown sugar, garlic, and onion.
3. Pour the marinade into the freezer bag. Seal the bag and place it in the refrigerator.
4. The following day, light a hardwood charcoal fire. When the fire is mostly white ash, remove the meat from the bag and place it on the grill. Discard the marinade. Sear the meat until a deep brown crust forms, approximately 5 minutes. Flip it and cook for an additional 5 minutes for a medium-rare steak. For more well-done meat, move it to a cooler portion of the grill and cook until desired doneness.
5. Transfer the beef to a cutting board and allow it to rest for 5 minutes. Slice it across the grain and serve at once.

Grilling Tips: Dry Rubs and Marinades

All foods taste better on the grill when they are coated with a dry rub or marinated in a flavorful liquid. Dry rubs are most often associated with barbeque, but they are equally important in grilling. Dry rubs were originally developed as a method to preserve food, but we now employ them to add a complex layer of flavor and enhance and develop a savory crust on grilled food. Paprika and chili powder are often the main ingredients in dry rubs. Ground chilies, dry mustard, onion powder, and garlic powder in varying quantities round out the ingredients list of most rubs. Sugar and salt are controversial ingredients. Some people believe that salt draws the moisture out of the food, and we all know that sugar will burn at high temperatures. When we add them to our rubs, we do so in moderation and in quantities only to enhance the flavor of the rub, not to star in it.

Most foods benefit from a liberal and thorough coating of dry rub. Some, though, most notably fish and vegetables, benefit from a lighter touch. Chicken and turkey turn out wonderfully when the rub is applied both on and under the skin. After massaging the rub into the food, place it in a Ziploc bag or glass or plastic container and refrigerate for eight to twenty-four hours.

Marinades are essentially a liquid bath that enhances the natural flavor of foods. They generally consist of a strongly flavored oil (sesame and olive are great), an acid (vinegars and citrus juices are top choices), and other intensely flavored ingredients such as tamari, ginger, garlic, scallions, and onions.

A common misconception is that marinades tenderize meat. The liquid does soften the tissue, but it does not actually make it more tender. If a food is marinated for too long a period, it becomes spongy and unappetizing. Since marinades don't penetrate far beyond the surface of the food, the additional time does nothing for the flavor of the food.

Don't reuse marinades with other foods. Once the food is on the grill, discard the marinade.

PREPARATION:
10 MINUTES

COOKING:
20 MINUTES

YIELD:
4 MAIN-COURSE
SERVINGS

Flank Steak with Tomatoes and Olives

Pan-seared flank steak is perfect for a midweek supper. It cooks quickly and needs little more than a simple pan sauce to round out its great flavor. One of the primary ingredients in the sauce is olives, but don't balk at serving this dish to your children. Many kids find the salty and strong taste of olives appealing. Olives are rich in heart-healthy oils.

1½ pounds flank steak
    Kosher salt
    Black pepper
1 tablespoon olive oil plus 1 teaspoon
3 cloves garlic, peeled and thinly sliced
1 cup red wine
¼ cup red wine vinegar
1 tablespoon unsalted butter
3 plum tomatoes, diced
12 kalamata olives, pitted and chopped

1. Preheat the oven to 450°F.
2. Sprinkle the steak on each side with kosher salt and black pepper.
3. Heat the olive oil in a large ovenproof skillet over high heat. When the oil is hot, carefully place the steak in the pan. Sear the steak for 3 minutes. Turn it over and sear for an additional 3 minutes.
4. Place the skillet in the oven. For a medium steak, roast it for 3 minutes. Adjust the final cooking time to your desired tastes.
5. Remove the steak from the oven. Place it on a cutting board and allow it to rest for 5 minutes. Remove and reserve any juices from the pan.
6. Place the pan on the stove over low heat. Add the remaining teaspoon of olive oil. Add the garlic and cook for 30 seconds. Raise the heat to high. Add the wine, vinegar, and reserved pan juices. Simmer the liquid for 3 minutes.
7. Reduce the heat to medium. Swirl in the butter. Simmer the sauce for 1 minute. Add the tomatoes and olives. Simmer the sauce for a final minute. Season the sauce with kosher salt and black pepper.
8. Slice the steak on the bias into thin strips. Divide the steak among 4 plates. Spoon on the sauce and serve at once.

Open-Faced Steak Sandwiches with Onions and Mushrooms

Steak-and-cheese sandwiches are an institution in Philadelphia where every corner sandwich shop has their own take on the original. Most are prepared with lean beef but contain too much oil and processed cheese to be considered healthful. We make ours with lean flank steak and plenty of sweet onions and earthy mushrooms. A touch of Worcestershire sauce and a sprinkling of provolone cheese complement the star ingredients. Served open faced on whole-grain bread, it elevates the mundane "cheese steak" to new levels. Lean beef is an excellent source of protein and iron. **TIP:** Some children will prefer to have their meat, vegetables, and bread served separately. Before adding the cheese in step four, plate their meals.

PREPARATION:
10 MINUTES

COOKING:
20 MINUTES

YIELD:
4 MAIN-COURSE
SERVINGS

1 tablespoon olive oil
1 pound flank steak
    Kosher salt
    Black pepper
1 clove garlic, peeled and thinly sliced
2 medium onions, peeled and thinly sliced
12 ounces white button mushrooms, sliced
1 tablespoon Worcestershire sauce
2 ounces Provolone cheese, sliced or grated
4 thick slices of whole-grain rustic bread sliced from a round loaf

1. Heat the olive oil in a Dutch oven over medium-high heat. Sprinkle the flank steak on each side with kosher salt and black pepper. When the oil is hot, carefully place the flank steak in the pan. Sear it for 3 minutes on each side, turning once. Transfer it to a plate and set aside for a moment.

2. Reduce the heat to low. Add the garlic and cook for 1 minute. Raise the heat to medium. Add the onions and sprinkle them with kosher salt. Cook the onions for 4 minutes, stirring often. Add the mushrooms and cook for 5 minutes, stirring often.

3. Thinly slice the meat on the bias. Add it to the pot and cook for 2 minutes, stirring occasionally. Add the Worcestershire sauce and

cook for another minute. Season the ingredients with kosher salt and black pepper.

4. Reduce the heat to low and scatter the Provolone onto the meat and vegetables. Cover the pot and cook until the cheese melts, approximately 2 minutes.

5. Divide the bread among 4 plates. Place a portion of steak and vegetables onto each slice of bread and serve at once.

Beef Stew

PREPARATION:
15 MINUTES

COOKING:
3½ HOURS

YIELD:
6 MAIN-COURSE
SERVINGS PLUS
LEFTOVERS
(SEE PAGE 272 FOR
RECIPE)

Like many popular and traditional meals, there are probably as many beef stew recipes as there are cooks. The basic ingredients are usually the same though: a tough cut of beef, root vegetables, and red wine. Rather than the usual chunks of sinewy beef that are so often used, we prefer to braise large pieces of brisket, a leaner choice, and slice them just prior to serving. This step improves the texture of the meat and enhances the consistency of the gravy. With full-flavored, yet mild-tasting meat and rich gravy, kids love beef stew. And with plenty of iron and a mélange of tender and vitamin-rich fresh vegetables, it is a meal you can feel good about serving regularly. **TIP:** The leftovers can be frozen in a tightly sealed container for up to one month.

1 tablespoon plus 1 tablespoon olive oil
2 pieces beef brisket (approximately 1½ pounds each)
   Kosher salt
   Black pepper
4 cloves garlic, peeled and thinly sliced
2 large onions, peeled and coarsely chopped
1   turnip, peeled and sliced into 2-inch pieces
3 carrots, peeled and sliced into 2-inch pieces
3 parsnips, peeled and sliced into 2-inch pieces
2 cups red wine
2 cups homemade or low-sodium canned chicken broth
1 28-ounce can whole tomatoes in juice, chopped

1. Preheat the oven to 300°F.
2. Heat 1 tablespoon of the olive oil in a large Dutch oven over medium-high heat. Sprinkle 1 piece of brisket on each side with kosher salt and black pepper. When the oil is hot, carefully place the brisket in the pot. Sear for 4 minutes on each side, turning once. Remove the meat and set aside. Repeat the procedure with the remaining oil and brisket.
3. Reduce the heat to low, add the garlic, and cook for 30 seconds. Add the onion and sprinkle it with kosher salt. Cook the onion for 3 minutes, stirring often. Raise the heat slightly. Add the turnips, carrots, and parsnips. Sprinkle the vegetables with kosher salt. Cover the pot and sweat for 5 minutes, stirring occasionally.
4. Raise the heat to high and add the wine. Simmer the wine for 2 minutes. Stir in the chicken broth and tomatoes. Return both pieces of brisket to the pot. Bring the stew to a boil.
5. Cover the pot and transfer the stew to the oven. Braise the stew for 3 hours.
6. Remove the stew from the oven. Carefully uncover the pot and transfer both pieces of brisket to a cutting board. Set one aside and allow the other to rest for 10 minutes.
7. Cut the resting beef across the grain into 2-inch-thick slices. Divide the beef among 6 bowls. Ladle vegetables and sauce into each bowl. Accompany the stew with thick slices of whole-grain rustic bread and serve at once.
8. Transfer the leftover vegetables, sauce, and beef to a container and allow to cool before refrigerating.

PREPARATION:
30 MINUTES

COOKING:
45 MINUTES

YIELD:
4 MAIN-COURSE
SERVINGS

Cottage Pie

Cottage pie is a close relative of the more familiar Shepherd's Pie. Traditionally, Shepherd's Pie contains lamb. It was a meal a shepherd's wife prepared to make mutton more palatable. When beef is substituted for the lamb, it is called a Cottage Pie. We like to make our Cottage Pie the way we would imagine an Irish family would. We prepare a beef stew (see page 270) to enjoy one evening, and several nights later, we thin the leftovers a bit and top them with mashed potatoes. The concoction gets baked in a casserole dish until the potatoes are golden and crusty. With beef and plenty of vegetables, the dish provides excellent all-around nutrition. **TIP:** Children seem to prefer their potatoes fluffy and creamy rather than crusty. So we usually remove their portions before topping the stew and serve them on the side accompanied with the beef and vegetables.

MASHED POTATOES

3 large baking potatoes, peeled and quartered
   Kosher salt
2 tablespoons unsalted butter
1 cup milk
   Black pepper

STEW

5 cups leftover vegetables and gravy
½ cup water
1¼ pounds leftover brisket, sliced across the grain into ⅓-inch-thick
      slices

1. Preheat the oven to 400°F. Have on hand an 8-by-8-inch baking dish with 2-inch-deep sides.
2. To prepare the potatoes, place them in a Dutch oven. Cover them with water and season them with kosher salt. Bring them to a boil. Reduce the heat and simmer them for 25 minutes or until tender.

3. Drain them and return them to the pot. Reduce the heat to low. Stir the potatoes several times so their remaining moisture evaporates. Add the butter and milk. Mash the potatoes with a hand-held masher, adding additional milk if necessary to make creamy potatoes. Season the potatoes with kosher salt and black pepper.

4. To assemble the cottage pie, stir together the vegetables and gravy and water. Add the meat and stir gently. Transfer the mixture to the baking dish. Spread the potatoes onto the meat and vegetables.

5. Transfer the pie to the oven. Bake until bubbly and the potatoes begin to color, approximately 45 minutes. Turn on the broiler. Broil the pie until the potatoes are golden, approximately 3 minutes.

6. Divide the pie among four large plates and serve at once.

Pot Roast with Vegetable Gravy

When the weather turns cool, our bodies instinctively crave heartier fare. Gone are the quick pasta dishes with summer vegetables and herbs and in their place are braised meat and poultry dishes and soul-warming soups. Rump roast is a relatively fatty cut of beef, but when accompanied by root vegetables and rich gravy, it is a nutritious and satisfying one-pot meal. With one-pot, casserole-type meals, you'll tend to eat less meat in total, but do watch your portion sizes. **TIPS:** It is important to slice the vegetables into large pieces so they don't disintegrate during braising. Also, if you make this meal in advance, it is best to slice the meat and reheat it in the gravy over a low flame. It will be necessary to thin the gravy with a bit of chicken stock.

PREPARATION:
30 MINUTES

COOKING:
3½ HOURS

YIELD:
8 MAIN-COURSE
SERVINGS

4½ pounds of rump roast
   Kosher salt
   Black pepper
1 tablespoon canola oil
4 cloves garlic, peeled and thinly sliced
2 onions, peeled and quartered
2 ounces tomato paste
2 cups full-bodied red wine
1½ cups homemade or commercial low-sodium chicken stock
1 pound carrots, peeled and sliced into 2-inch pieces
1 pound parsnips, peeled and sliced into 2-inch pieces
6 ribs celery, sliced into 2-inch pieces
3 medium Yukon Gold potatoes, scrubbed and quartered

1. Preheat the oven to 300°F. Sprinkle the roast on all sides with kosher salt and black pepper.
2. Heat the canola oil in a large Dutch oven over medium-high heat. When the oil is hot, carefully place the roast in the pot. Sear the roast on all sides, turning and rolling it as necessary. Remove the meat from the pot and set aside for a moment.
3. Reduce the heat to low. Add the garlic and onions to the pot and sprinkle them with kosher salt. Cook them for 3 minutes, stirring often.
4. Stir in the tomato paste. Raise the heat to high. Add the wine and stock. Bring the liquid to a boil. Reduce the heat and simmer for 5 minutes.
5. Return the roast to the pot. Bring the roast to a simmer.
6. Cover the pot and transfer it to the oven. Braise the roast for 2 hours. Remove the pot from the oven. Do not turn off the oven. Transfer the meat to a plate and set it aside for a moment.
7. Add the carrots, parsnips, celery, and potatoes to the pot. Return the meat to the pot.
8. Cover the pot and return it to the oven. Continue braising the meat for another 1½ hours or until very tender.
9. Remove the pot from the oven. Place the roast on a cutting board and the pot on the range. Allow the roast to rest for 10 minutes.

While the roast is resting, tilt the pot and skim the fat. Season the gravy with kosher salt and black pepper.

10. Carve one-half of the roast against the grain. Divide the slices among 4 plates. Spoon gravy and vegetables onto each portion and serve at once. Allow the leftovers to cool before refrigerating them. They make great sandwiches the following day or later in the week.

Pan-Fried Pork Chops

One of our favorite midweek dinners is pan-fried chicken thighs. With only olive oil, a sprinkling of kosher salt, a couple of grinds of fresh black pepper, and quick sear in a heavy skillet, this no fuss meal is quick and easy. The same ingredients and technique work well with lean pork chops. **TIP:** To entice reluctant children into a taste, accompany the chops with your favorite homemade or store-bought applesauce.

PREPARATION:
5 MINUTES

COOKING:
15 MINUTES

YIELD:
4 MAIN-COURSE
SERVINGS

1 tablespoon olive oil
4 center-cut boneless pork loin chops, approximately ¾ inch thick
Kosher salt
Black pepper

1. Heat the olive oil in a large skillet (preferably cast iron) over medium-high heat.
2. Sprinkle the pork chops on each side with kosher salt and black pepper.
3. When the oil is hot, carefully place the chops in the pan. Sear them until a golden crust forms, approximately 2 minutes. Flip them and sear them for an additional 2 minutes.
4. Reduce the heat. Continue cooking the chops until they reach an internal temperature of 160°F, approximately 6 minutes, flipping them once.
5. Divide the chops among 4 plates and serve at once.

Cooking Pork

It is very important to cook pork thoroughly. In the past, it was recommended that pork be cooked until it reached an internal temperature of 185°F to kill trichinae, which cause the disease trichinosis. But studies have shown that the trichinae in pork are killed at 150°F. So it is perfectly safe to cook pork to 160°F or 170°F. This lower temperature produces more moist and tender meat.

Pork Chops with Shallots and Marsala

PREPARATION:
10 MINUTES

COOKING:
15 MINUTES

YIELD:
4 MAIN-COURSE
SERVINGS

Deglazing the cooking vessel in a basic pan-seared pork chop recipe creates a delicious pan sauce. By varying the deglazing liquid and seasonings, you can create several meals with different flavors and textures. Shallots, chicken broth, and Marsala wine is our favorite combination of seasoning and liquid. But red or white wine or a mixture of your favorite vinegar and cream, along with chicken broth, can serve as the deglazing liquids. Scallions, garlic, or leeks are great choices to add flavor. Begin with this recipe and then be imaginative and create your own delicious pork chop and quick pan-sauce meals.

1 tablespoon olive oil
4 center-cut boneless pork loin chops, approximately ¾ inch thick
  Kosher salt
  Black pepper
2 medium shallots, peeled and finely chopped
1 cup Marsala wine
1 cup homemade or low-sodium canned chicken broth

1. Heat the olive oil in a large skillet (preferably cast iron) over medium-high heat.
2. Sprinkle the pork chops on each side with kosher salt and black pepper.
3. When the oil is hot, carefully place the chops in the pan. Sear them until a golden crust forms, approximately 2 minutes. Flip them and sear them for an additional 2 minutes.
4. Reduce the heat to low. Transfer the chops to a plate and set them aside for the moment.
5. Add the shallots to the pan. Cook them for 1 minute, stirring constantly.
6. Raise the heat to high and add the Marsala. Simmer the wine for 2 minutes.
7. Add the chicken broth and simmer the sauce for 2 minutes.
8. Return the chops to the pan. Reduce the heat and simmer the chops in the sauce for 5 minutes or until they reach an internal temperature of 160°F, flipping them once.
9. Divide the chops among 4 plates, spoon sauce onto each portion, and serve at once.

PREPARATION:
5 MINUTES

COOKING:
40 MINUTES

YIELD:
4 MAIN-COURSE
SERVINGS

Roasted Pork Tenderloin with Herbs and Garlic

Some children will only eat meat if it is ground and in the shape of a hamburger or meatball. Offering them a taste of tough and flavorless beef will certainly enhance their apprehensions. So why not offer them a taste of pork tenderloin? Since it cooks quickly and needs little embellishment, pork tenderloin is ideal for a midweek meal. A thirty-minute roast in a hot oven produces a juicy and amazingly tender final product with a well-browned exterior. A simple pan sauce, laced with fresh herbs, adds moisture and a burst of intense flavor. **TIPS:** Since they require approximately the same cooking time and their flavors are complementary, we usually accompany this dish with Baked Sweet Potatoes and Apples with Cinnamon and Maple Syrup (see page 306). Also, purchasing four different herbs can be expensive. If you prefer, substitute $1/4$ cup of flat-leaf (Italian) parsley for all the herbs.

1⅓–1½ pounds pork tenderloin
    Kosher salt
    Black pepper
1 tablespoon olive oil
12 cloves garlic, peeled, trimmed, and halved
½ cup red wine
1 cup homemade or low-sodium canned chicken broth
2 tablespoons fresh tarragon
3 sprigs fresh thyme, leaves removed
2 tablespoons fresh rosemary
3 fresh sage leaves
1 tablespoon unsalted butter

1. Preheat the oven to 475°F.
2. Place the pork in an ovenproof skillet (cast iron works well) or a small roasting pan. Sprinkle it on all sides with kosher salt and black pepper. Rub it with the olive oil.
3. Place the pan in the oven. Roast the pork for 15 minutes. Remove

the pan from the oven. Turn the pork over. Return the pan to the oven and roast the pork for an additional 15 minutes or until it reaches an internal temperature of 145°F.

4. Remove the pan from the oven. Transfer the pork to a cutting board and allow it to rest for 10 minutes. It will continue cooking as it rests.

5. Meanwhile, place the pan on the range over low heat. If necessary, add another tablespoon of olive oil to the pan. Add the garlic halves and cook them until they are golden, approximately 5 minutes, turning occasionally.

6. Raise the heat to high and add the wine. Simmer the wine for 3 minutes. Add the chicken broth and simmer for 5 minutes.

7. Meanwhile, place all the herbs on a cutting board and thoroughly chop them together.

8. Remove the pan from the heat. Stir in the butter and herbs. Season the sauce with kosher salt and black pepper.

9. Slice the roast and divide it among 4 plates. Spoon on the sauce and serve at once.

Spice-Rubbed Pork Shoulder with Black Beans and Brown Rice

Although this meal requires advance planning, it is simple to put together and requires minimal attention during cooking. It yields plenty of leftovers for another meal (see page 282) so the extra effort is well rewarded. Pork shoulder is a fatty cut. As long as you trim it thoroughly, it can be a delicious part of a healthful diet. In addition, combining it with beans lowers the saturated fat since you will eat less meat altogether. We love to accompany the pork with black beans because they are so nutritious and our kids love them. But pinto or kidney beans are fine substitutes. **TIP:** The spice rub yields two cups. Store the extra in an airtight container for use in other recipes.

PREPARATION:
15 MINUTES

PORK RESTING AND
BEAN SOAKING:
OVERNIGHT

COOKING:
2¾ HOURS

YIELD:
6 MAIN-COURSE
SERVINGS PLUS
LEFTOVERS
(SEE PAGE 282)

SPICE RUB

6 tablespoons paprika

6 tablespoons kosher salt

5 tablespoons chili powder

4 tablespoons brown sugar

2 tablespoons black pepper

2 tablespoons cumin

2 tablespoons garlic powder

2 tablespoons onion powder

1 tablespoon dry mustard

2 teaspoons cayenne pepper

PORK

4 pounds boneless Boston butt, thoroughly trimmed

3 tablespoons spice rub

1 cup water

BEANS

1 pound black beans

1 tablespoon canola oil

3 cloves garlic, peeled and thinly sliced

1 medium onion, peeled and thinly sliced

1 red bell pepper, cored and thinly sliced

1 green bell pepper, cored and thinly sliced

  Kosher salt

1 tablespoon spice rub

3 tablespoons tomato paste

8 cups water

RICE

4½ cups water

  Kosher salt

2 cups brown long-grain rice

½ cup cilantro, chopped

1. The night prior to cooking, prepare the spice rub by combining all the rub ingredients in a bowl and mixing thoroughly. Rub 4 tablespoons of the mixture onto the entire surface of the pork. Cover the pork with plastic wrap and refrigerate. Sort and rinse the black beans. Place them in a bowl. Cover them with cold water, and refrigerate.
2. The following day, preheat the oven to 300°F. Remove the pork from the refrigerator, place it in an ovenproof Dutch oven, and add the water. Cover the pot and place it in the oven. Braise it for 2½ hours.
3. While the pork is braising, prepare the beans by heating the canola oil over medium heat in another Dutch oven. When the oil is hot, add the garlic and cook it for 1 minute. Add the onion and bell peppers. Sprinkle them with kosher salt and cook them for 3 minutes, stirring often. Cover the pot and sweat them for 3 minutes, stirring often.
4. Stir in the spice rub and tomato paste. Raise the heat to high. Add the water and beans. Season them with kosher salt. Bring the beans to a boil. Cover the pot and transfer it to the oven. Cook the beans for 2 hours.
5. While the pork and beans are cooking, prepare the rice by bringing the water to a boil in a saucepan. Add kosher salt to the water. Stir in the rice. Return the water to a boil. Cover the pot. Reduce the heat to a simmer, and cook the rice for 20 minutes. Remove the pan from the heat and add the cilantro. Fluff the rice with a fork.
6. Remove the pork and beans from the oven. Turn on the broiler. Transfer the pork to a sheet pan. Transfer the liquid from the pot to a container and reserve for a future recipe. Transfer the pork to the oven and broil it until crusty, approximately 7 minutes.
7. Place the pork on a cutting board and allow it to rest for 5 minutes. Shred or slice approximately one-half of the roast. Divide the pork among 6 plates. Accompany the pork with the black beans and rice and serve at once.

PREPARATION:
10 MINUTES

COOKING:
15 MINUTES

YIELD:
4 MAIN-COURSE
SERVINGS

Carnitas and Black Bean Burritos

Carnitas is the Spanish word for pork. These tasty burritos make use of the leftovers from Spice-Rubbed Pork Shoulder with Black Beans and Brown Rice (see page 279). The pork is great on its own but by taking the extra time and sprinkling it with spice rub and broiling it, another layer of texture and flavor is added. Since kids love meals where they use their hands to eat, this one is destined to become a family favorite. **TIPS:** When we prepare chicken stock (see page 173), we sometimes use half of the chicken for a soup and the remainder as a substitute for the pork in this recipe. Also, we suggest microwaving the tortillas to warm them and melt the cheese. If you don't have a microwave, preheat the oven to 350°F, divide the cheese among the tortillas, roll them and wrap them in foil, and heat for 7 minutes.

12 ounces cooked pork shoulder (see page 279), shredded or sliced
 2 teaspoons spice rub (see page 280)
⅔ cup low-sodium canned chicken stock or water
 2 ounces cheddar cheese, grated or sliced
 4 whole-grain flour tortillas
 2 cups cooked brown rice (see page 226), warmed
 2 cups cooked black beans (see page 229), warmed

1. Preheat the broiler. Place the pork in a shallow baking dish. Sprinkle it with the spice rub. Add the stock or water. Transfer the dish to the oven and broil the pork until it is hot and slightly crisp, approximately 7 minutes.
2. Divide the cheese among the 4 tortillas. Microwave the tortillas until the cheese melts, approximately 35 seconds.
3. Divide the tortillas among 4 plates. Divide the rice and beans among them. Garnish each tortilla with the pork. Fold in the sides and roll the tortilla up from the bottom to enclose the filling completely.

The New Pork

The diet fed to pigs has undergone drastic changes in the past twenty years. The result has been a more muscular animal that yields leaner cuts of meat. Pork finally is now a nutritious food. The fat content of a well-trimmed pork loin is comparable to that of a skinless chicken thigh. The confusion in the past has been that pork is available not only in lean cuts but also very fatty cuts, such as spare ribs, bacon, and ham. Pork is a good source of protein, iron, thiamin, and niacin.

Since the entire pig is edible, pork provides variety and lends itself to many preparations. The leanest and most tender cuts come from the loin; they are best pan-fried or grilled. The tenderloin can be roasted whole in a fashion similar to beef tenderloin, or it can be sliced, flattened, and quickly sautéed like veal scallops. Although pork shoulder is relatively fatty, much of that fat can be trimmed away. It is an inexpensive and versatile cut. It can be braised, stewed, or smoked and enjoyed on its own or used as a filling for burritos, sandwiches, casseroles, and even tossed with pasta.

Barbequed Pork Butt

At the beginning of summer, just before our family and friends embark on their warm-weather plans, we like to host an outdoor gathering and treat everybody to a barbeque. We prepare slow-cooked beef, pork, and chicken in our homemade smoker and accompany them with traditional favorites like macaroni and cheese, collard greens, coleslaw, and stewed pinto beans. Everything is delicious, but the pork always garners the most praise. Rubbed with spices and slow-cooked for eight hours, the meat is incredibly tender and flavorful. We shred it and mix it with a slightly sweet and spicy vinegar-based sauce and tuck it into soft rolls to create a favorite southern sandwich. **TIP:** Pork shoulder is generally cut into two large pieces of meat, the Boston butt and the picnic. Since it has less bone, the butt is our favorite cut to barbeque. With a flavor and texture similar to ham, the bony picnic is also delicious.

PORK RESTING:
OVERNIGHT

COOKING:
9 HOURS

YIELD:
20 SERVINGS PLUS
PLENTY OF LEFTOVERS

1 cup spice rub (see page 280)

2 6-pound portions of Boston butt

1. The night before you plan to barbeque, massage the spice rub onto the entire surface of the meat. Place the meat in 2 plastic bags and refrigerate.
2. The following day, remove the meat from the refrigerator. Allow it to rest at room temperature for 1 hour.
3. While the pork is resting, bring your smoker to a temperature between 200°F to 220°F.
4. Transfer the pork to the smoker. Barbeque the pork for 8 hours or until it reaches an internal temperature of 180°F, adding wood as needed to maintain a smoking temperature between 200°F and 220°F.
5. Remove the pork from the smoker and place on a cutting board. Allow it to rest for 30 minutes.
6. Slice off chunks of meat and shred or chop them well. Accompany the pork with Vinegar Sauce (see page 328) or Traditional Red Barbeque Sauce (see page 328).

Barbeque

Mention barbeque, and many people imagine a cookout with family and friends. Most often, the food is grilled in a gas or charcoal cooker. A traditional barbeque, though, such as you would find in the Carolinas, Texas, or Kansas City is a completely different affair. True barbequing involves smoking food, most often pork, slowly, over a low fire of smoldering wood. Grilling, on the other hand, is done with much higher heat. Barbequing is the ideal cooking method for tougher cuts of meat. These cuts contain an abundance of connective tissue that requires a long and slow cooking process to break down the sinewy fibers. Grilling works well with tender cuts of meat such as strip steaks, fillets, and lean chops. Barbequing is a more healthful cooking method than grilling. The intense smoky flavor of great barbeque comes from smoldering wood. It does not come from fat or oil dripping on hot coals or metal and flaming back into the food, as is the case in grilling. The smoke and sizzle produced in grilling contain the carcinogen benzopyrene, which has a tendency to stick to food.

Great barbeque is simple to prepare at home as long as you use the correct equipment and fuel. We are fortunate to have a first-class homemade smoker with an offset firebox on one end and a chimney on the other. But it's not necessary to own such a fine, although rustic, contraption to turn out great barbeque. There are lots of options available at a wide range of prices. The best log-burning smokers cost as much as a similar quality gas grill. They are designed to turn out some serious food and will last a lifetime. Fabricated from thick steel, they are bulky and very heavy. A viable option in terms of size and price are smaller pits. These vessels look similar to their more expensive cousins but are made with thinner metal. Although you can burn logs in them, they are more suitable for burning wood chips and chunks. You can find these smokers at discount clubs, department stores, and from mail-order companies.

Although it is a bit more challenging, you can successfully barbeque on your circular-shaped charcoal grill. With a vented cover, a good thermometer, and a large supply of water-soaked wood chunks, wonderful barbeque can be produced in this humble piece of equipment. The technique is simple and very similar to indirect grilling. You place the food over a pan of water on one side of the grill. On the opposite side, you build a low fire. The vents on the cover remain closed to keep the fire low and smoldering. The cover is only removed when more wood is needed. The bottom vents on the grill are used to adjust the temperature. The probe of a candy thermometer, placed into a vent on the cover, is essential in monitoring the temperature.

The flavor and texture of great barbeque depends on wood smoke. Only hardwoods (oak and apple are good choices) should be used. Softwoods, such as cedar and pine, contain too much sap and will give your food an off-taste. Avoid plywood, treated lumber, and anything you can't identify as a hardwood. Wood chips and chunks are widely available and are an excellent choice for backyard barbequing. They should be soaked in water for an hour before being added to a smoldering fire. You can also barbeque with charcoal. But be certain to choose a natural product. Most charcoal briquettes contain additives such as petroleum products, coal, and sodium nitrate. These products are terrible for the environment and your health, and their acrid smoke will ruin your food. The best charcoal to barbeque with is the lump hardwood variety. This charcoal is left in irregular shapes, so there is no need for binders or fillers. It ignites quickly and burns for a good long time. One disadvantage of this charcoal, though, is that it burns very hot. It may require a bit of practice to be able to maintain a steady and low temperature.

CHAPTER 19

seafood dishes

Many of us no longer consider seafood something to eat only in restaurants. The proliferation of great seafood cookbooks has taken the unknown out of seafood cookery and made it possible to create first-rate, ocean-fresh dishes in our own kitchens. Because overcooking and too many flavors tend to mask the texture and distinctive taste of seafood, seafood recipes are naturally quick and simple to prepare. Roasting, pan-frying, and grilling are the best techniques for seafood. Olive oil, garlic, tomatoes, light wine-based sauces, or simply a squeeze of lemon are all that are needed to enhance the clean and delicate flavor of seafood.

Seafood is health food. It is a lean protein source, very low in saturated fat, and rich in B vitamins, iron, and zinc. Most important, it is one of the richest sources of omega-three fatty acids. Studies have indicated that omega-three fatty acids play a critical role in the prevention of heart disease and breast cancer. Oily-fleshed fish, such as salmon, anchovies, and bluefish, contain the largest quantities of omega-threes. Even seafood not usually considered rich sources of omega-threes, such as scallops, shrimp, mussels, and lean white fish like haddock, cod, and halibut, contain modest amounts. All these versatile fish are a snap to prepare and are enhanced by a variety of seasonings.

Preparing seafood meals that children will enjoy is often a dilemma. To be succinct, many children simply don't like fish and are apprehensive about even trying it. The most frequent comments we hear are that fish "smells terrible" and "tastes fishy." Even youngsters who have only been exposed to truly great fish are still reluctant to eat it. We have devised a couple of strategies that you may find helpful. To open your children's minds to the world of seafood, take them on a field trip to a great fish market. Allow them to look around. Whole fish, live lobsters, and clams always seem to capture a child's imagination. Have them speak with the fishmonger. Let them poke and, of course, smell the fish. Point out that truly fresh fish is virtually odorless and smells of the sea. Then, once you decide to cook fish meals for your children, prepare only the dishes that you are fairly certain they will attempt to taste. It always seems that youngsters are apt to try seafood meals in which the fish is somewhat disguised or combined with a familiar food. Pan-Fried Skate with Tofu Tartar Sauce (see page 289) features mild-tasting fish with a crisp coating. Cod Baked with Tomatoes and Bread Crumbs (see page 292) may appeal to the young ones with its savory sauce and crunchy topping. The combination of olive oil and salt is one that many children find appealing. Our Cod Roasted with Olive Oil and Kosher Salt (see page 291) combines the sweet and briny taste of cod with a rich olive oil and slightly salty flavor. Your children's reactions to this meal may just surprise you.

Pan-Fried Skate with Tofu Tartar Sauce

Creating tasty fish dishes that the entire family will enjoy is challenging. Adults love the clean and briny taste of truly fresh fish; kids don't like their fish to taste too much like fish. The bread-crumb-and-cornmeal coating on the skate wings in this recipe will likely appeal to your reluctant young fish eaters. The meal can be put together quickly, making it ideal for any day of the week. **TIP:** The best bread crumbs for this dish are the dried store-bought variety. Also, sole or flounder can be substituted for the skate. If you choose either one of these, step six can be eliminated. Pan-frying will cook these thinner fillets perfectly.

PREPARATION:
10 MINUTES

COOKING:
20 MINUTES

YIELD:
4 MAIN-COURSE
SERVINGS

TOFU TARTAR SAUCE

- 8 ounces firm tofu
- 4 tablespoons prepared pickle relish
- 1 tablespoon Dijon mustard
- ½ cup low-fat sour cream
- 1 small shallot, finely chopped
- Kosher salt
- Black pepper

FISH

- 1 cup plain dry bread crumbs
- ½ cup yellow cornmeal
- 2 teaspoons kosher salt
- ⅓ cup flat-leaf (Italian) parsley
- 1 egg
- ⅓ cup milk
- 1½ pounds skate wings, sliced into 4 pieces
- 1 tablespoon plus 1 tablespoon canola oil
- 1 lemon, sliced into 4 wedges

1. To prepare the tartar sauce, begin by removing the moisture from the tofu by placing it on a plate and setting a heavy pot on top of it. Set the tofu aside for a moment while you continue with the recipe. Combine the relish, mustard, sour cream, and shallot in the work bowl of a food processor fitted with the metal blade.

After approximately 15 minutes, remove the tofu from the plate and discard the accumulated liquid. Crumble the tofu into the work bowl. Turn the machine on and process the ingredients until smooth. Season the tartar sauce with kosher salt and black pepper. Chill it until the fish is cooked.

2. Preheat the oven to 400°F.

3. To prepare the fish, combine well the bread crumbs, cornmeal, kosher salt, and parsley in a pie plate. In another pie plate, whisk together the egg and milk.

4. Dip 1 piece of fish into the egg wash. Remove it and allow the excess to drip away. Dredge it in the bread-crumb mixture, turning it, and pressing the crumbs into the fish with your fingers. Transfer the fish to a plate. Repeat the procedure with the remaining fish, egg wash, and bread crumbs.

5. Heat 1 tablespoon of the oil in a skillet over medium-high heat. When the oil is hot, add 2 pieces of fish to the pan. Cook the fish for 1½ minutes on each side, or until the coating is golden and crisp, turning once. Transfer the fish to a baking tray. Repeat the procedure with the remaining oil and fish.

6. Transfer the tray to the oven. Cook the fish, until just done, approximately 5 minutes.

7. Divide the fish among 4 plates. Accompany it with the tartar sauce and lemon wedges, and serve at once.

Skate

Once considered a "trash fish," skate is finally becoming popular. The French have always prized skate for its delicate, scalloplike flavor and meaty texture. Only the large pectoral fins are edible. The thick and tough skin is usually removed before the fish reaches market. In the kitchen, skate is versatile. It can be pan-fried, baked, broiled, and grilled. It can even be substituted for the usual haddock and cod in seafood soups. Skate is a moderately fatty fish that is an excellent source of omega-three fatty acids.

Cod Roasted with Olive Oil and Kosher Salt

PREPARATION:
5 MINUTES

COOKING:
15 MINUTES

YIELD:
4 MAIN-COURSE
SERVINGS

On a recent Thanksgiving evening I had a commitment in the city, so Hope and the kids traveled to her parents' house without me; I was going to meet them the following morning. Prior to leaving, Hope told me a colleague from work was going deep-sea fishing and that if he caught more than he could eat, he would drop a fish by the house. Sure enough, at eight in the evening, the bell rings and he presents me with a sparkling cod. I had already eaten supper but was excited about the gorgeous specimen. I cleaned and filleted it immediately. I suppose I could have frozen it but, instead, I decided to cook it. I roasted it with nothing more than extra-virgin olive oil, kosher salt, and black pepper. These simple ingredients allowed the cod's mild flavor and great ocean-fresh taste to shine. Although I had only a small taste that night, it made a memorable breakfast with Vegetarian Baked Beans (see page 233) the following morning. It is now one of our favorite ways to enjoy cod. Our children love the mild flavor of the fish and the rich taste of the olive oil. I'm sure yours will as well.

1½ pounds boneless cod fillet
2 tablespoons excellent-quality olive oil
1½ teaspoons kosher salt
   Black pepper
1 lemon, quartered

1. Preheat the oven to 450°F.
2. Place the cod in a roasting pan. Drizzle it with the olive oil, sprinkle it with kosher salt, and grind black pepper onto it.
3. Transfer the pan to the oven. Roast the fish until just cooked through, approximately 12 minutes.
4. Remove the pan from the oven. Divide the fish among 4 plates. Accompany it with the lemon, and serve at once.

PREPARATION:
15 MINUTES

COOKING:
30 MINUTES

YIELD:
4 MAIN-COURSE
SERVINGS

Cod Baked with Tomatoes and Bread Crumbs

This quick recipe uses the identical sauce as Linguine with Smoky Scallops and Garlicky Tomatoes (see page 205). We often prepare a double batch of sauce and use one-half in this recipe and the other in the pasta dish later in the week. If your children enjoy fish, they are certain to like this meal. The cod is mild tasting, the tomatoes sweet, and the bread-crumb topping adds a delightful texture without being heavy or soggy. **TIP:** Although we prefer the meaty texture of cod fillets in this recipe, haddock, pollock, and hake are fine substitutes.

1 tablespoon olive oil plus extra for drizzling
6 cloves garlic, peeled and thinly sliced
1 cup white wine
1 28-ounce can whole tomatoes in juice, drained and chopped
⅓ cup flat-leaf (Italian) parsley, chopped
   Kosher salt
   Black pepper
2 pounds cod fillets
2 cups homemade bread crumbs (see page 293)

1. Preheat the oven to 450°F.
2. Heat the olive oil in a Dutch oven over medium heat. When the oil is hot, add the garlic. Cook it for 1 minute, stirring often. Raise the heat to high. Add the wine, and simmer for 2 minutes.
3. Add the tomatoes and bring the sauce to a boil. Reduce the heat, and simmer for 10 minutes, stirring occasionally. Add the parsley. Season the sauce with kosher salt and black pepper. Remove the pot from the heat.
4. Place the cod in an ovenproof casserole. Season it with kosher salt and black pepper. Spoon the sauce onto the fish. Top the fish with the bread crumbs. Drizzle the bread crumbs with olive oil.
5. Place the casserole in the oven and bake the fish for 15 minutes or until just cooked through. Turn on the broiler and broil the fish until the bread crumbs are golden, approximately 3 minutes. Remove the casserole from the oven. Divide the fish among 4 plates and serve at once.

Homemade Bread Crumbs

These bread crumbs are wonderful on chicken, fish, and vegetables and can even be used as a topping for pasta. **TIP:** Save your leftover bread and make a double batch. They freeze well.

4 cups tightly packed rustic bread cubes
1 tablespoon extra-virgin olive oil
 Kosher salt
 Black pepper

1. Place the bread cubes in the work bowl of a food processor fitted with the metal blade.
2. Turn on the machine and drizzle in the olive oil. Process the bread until it is finely textured. Season with kosher salt and black pepper. Use immediately or wrap tightly and freeze.

PREPARATION:
10 MINUTES

COOKING:
15 MINUTES

YIELD:
4 MAIN-COURSE
SERVINGS

Pan-Seared Salmon with a Quick Zucchini-Tomato Sauce

Zucchini and tomatoes is a versatile combination. With the addition of garlic and onions, a naturally sweet sauce is created that can be used to top fish or chicken. In this recipe, the sauce is the perfect flavor contrast to the richness of the salmon. Salmon is a rich source of omega-three fatty acids. **TIP:** By increasing the proportions of the zucchini and tomatoes, the sauce can be transformed into a soup, pasta sauce, or side dish. Also, halibut steaks or swordfish can be substituted for the salmon.

1 tablespoon olive oil
2 cloves garlic, peeled and thinly sliced
1 onion, peeled and thinly sliced
  Kosher salt
1 medium zucchini, trimmed and diced
2 plum tomatoes, cored and diced
1 cup dry white wine
¼ cup flat-leaf (Italian) parsley, chopped
  Black pepper
1 tablespoon canola oil
1½ pounds boneless, skin-on salmon fillet (cut from the thick end)

1. Heat the olive oil in a Dutch oven over medium heat. When the oil is hot, add the garlic. Cook it for 1 minute, stirring often. Add the onion and sprinkle it with kosher salt. Cook the ingredients for 3 minutes, stirring occasionally. Add the zucchini and cook for 3 minutes, stirring occasionally.
2. Raise the heat to high. Add the tomatoes and cook for 1 minute. Add the wine and simmer for 1 minute.
3. Reduce the heat to low and add the parsley. Season the sauce with kosher salt and black pepper. Keep the sauce warm while you prepare the fish.
4. Heat the canola oil in a cast-iron skillet over medium-high heat. Sprinkle the fish on each side with kosher salt and black pepper. When the oil is hot, carefully place the fish, skin side down, into

the pan. Sear the fish for 4 minutes on each side, or until just cooked through, turning once.

5. Divide the fish among 4 plates. Spoon sauce onto each portion and serve at once.

Salmon Noodle Casserole

We have fond childhood memories of our mothers' casseroles. It seems, though, that a whole generation of kids didn't grow up dining on a weekly casserole. Now, thanks to cookbooks dedicated to the art of preparing great casseroles, they are as popular as ever. The days of the tuna noodle casserole prepared with canned tuna and condensed soup are over. By using fresh and healthful ingredients in creative combinations, it is possible to transform the mundane casserole into a special meal. Since casseroles can be assembled entirely in advance and popped into the oven just before mealtime, they should be a staple on a busy family's menu. **TIP:** Small lima beans or shelled edamame (fresh soy beans) can be substituted for the peas.

PREPARATION:
30 MINUTES

COOKING:
30 MINUTES

YIELD:
6 MAIN-COURSE
SERVINGS

1 pound skinless salmon fillet
   Kosher salt
   Black pepper
1 tablespoon olive oil
1 pound medium shells
2 tablespoons unsalted butter
2 cloves garlic, peeled and thinly sliced
1 onion, peeled and diced
2 tablespoons all-purpose flour
2 cups low-fat milk
10 ounces frozen peas
2½ cups homemade bread crumbs (see page 293)

1. Preheat the oven to 450°F. Bring a large pot of water to a boil. Have on hand a 10-by-12-inch baking dish with 3-inch-deep sides.

2. Place the salmon on a sheet pan. Sprinkle it with kosher salt and

black pepper. Drizzle it with the olive oil. Place the pan in the oven and roast the salmon for 8 minutes. Remove the pan from the oven and set aside for a moment. Do not turn off the oven.

3. While the salmon is roasting, add kosher salt to the boiling water followed by the pasta. Cook the pasta for 7 minutes. Drain it and rinse it under cold water. Transfer it to the baking dish.

4. Melt the butter in a Dutch oven over medium heat. When it stops foaming, add the garlic and cook for 1 minute. Add the onion, sprinkle it with kosher salt, and cook for 3 minutes, stirring often.

5. Reduce the heat slightly. Add the flour to make a roux. Cook the roux for 3 minutes, stirring often.

6. Raise the heat to high and whisk in the milk, 1 cup at a time. After all the milk has been added, reduce the heat to low. Whisk the sauce until smooth. Add the peas and remove the pot from the heat.

7. Stir the sauce into the baking dish. Slice the salmon into strips and gently stir it into the baking dish. Sprinkle the bread crumbs over the casserole. Press them into the noodles with the back of a large spoon.

8. Transfer the casserole to the oven and bake for 25 minutes. Turn on the broiler and broil until the bread crumbs are golden brown, approximately 5 minutes.

9. Divide the casserole among 6 shallow bowls and serve at once.

Roasted Halibut with Garlic, Tomatoes, and Basil

PREPARATION:
10 MINUTES

COOKING:
20 MINUTES

YIELD:
4 MAIN-COURSE
SERVINGS

Our brother-in-law Alan and our nephew Vinny went deep-sea fishing in Alaska and had great success. They sent back a large amount of pristine halibut fillets. We were easily inspired to create meals featuring this great fish. Halibut is so meaty and wonderfully sweet that the less you do with it the better. A quick pan sauce of garlic, tomatoes, and basil is all that is needed to enhance the fish's briny flavor. Youngsters may prefer their fish with the sauce on the side or simply with a drizzle of olive oil and a sprinkling of kosher salt. **TIP:** We cook the garlic a bit longer in this recipe than we normally do. When garlic is cooked to a golden color it becomes nutty and sweet tasting. Monitor it closely so it doesn't burn.

1½ pounds, 1-inch thick, boneless and skinless halibut fillets, cut into 4 pieces
   Kosher salt
   Black pepper
1 tablespoon plus 1 tablespoon olive oil
8 cloves garlic, peeled and thinly sliced
1 cup dry white wine
1 tablespoon unsalted butter
1 pint cherry or grape tomatoes, halved
⅓ cup fresh basil, snipped

1. Preheat the oven to 450°F.
2. Sprinkle the fish on each side with kosher salt and black pepper.
3. Heat 1 tablespoon of olive oil in a large skillet over high heat. When the oil is hot, carefully place the fillets in the pan. Sear them until a crust forms, approximately 4 minutes. Carefully flip them and sear for 4 minutes longer. Transfer the fillets to a sheet pan. Place the pan in the oven and roast the fish until just cooked through, approximately 6 to 8 minutes.
4. While the fish is in the oven, heat the remaining tablespoon of olive oil in the skillet over medium-low heat. When the oil is hot, add the garlic. Cook it until it is golden and crisp, stirring often, approximately 3 minutes.
5. Raise the heat to high and add the wine. Simmer the wine for 2 minutes. Reduce the heat to medium. Swirl in the butter. Simmer the sauce for another minute. Add the tomatoes and simmer for another minute. Remove the pan from the heat. Add the basil. Season the sauce with kosher salt and black pepper.
6. Divide the fish among 4 large plates. Spoon on the sauce, and serve at once.

PREPARATION:
5 MINUTES

COOKING:
20 MINUTES

YIELD:
4 MAIN-COURSE
SERVINGS

Scallops and Haddock Baked with Cracker Crumbs

Haddock and scallops are two of the most versatile seafoods. Their meaty textures make them ideal for baking, pan searing, or for use in soups and stews. Tomatoes, cream, citrus, and fresh herbs complement their mild taste. As with most seafood dishes, a simple preparation and quick cooking time work best. A simple topping of crushed crackers and a rich-tasting wine-and-cream sauce make this straightforward dish ideal to enjoy anytime. **TIP:** Pollock or cod can be substituted for the haddock.

20 low-fat Ritz crackers
1¼ pounds boneless and skinless haddock filet
1¼ pounds sea scallops, attached muscle removed and discarded
 Kosher salt
 Black pepper
1 cup dry white wine
⅓ cup light cream

1. Preheat the oven to 450°F.
2. Place the crackers in a plastic food storage bag. With a kitchen mallet or heavy pan, smash the crackers until they are the consistency of sand. Set them aside for a moment.
3. Place the haddock and scallops in a baking dish large enough to accommodate them without crowding. Sprinkle the seafood with kosher salt and black pepper. Pour in the wine and light cream. Sprinkle the cracker crumbs onto the seafood.
4. Transfer the baking dish to the oven. Bake the seafood until it begins to bubble, approximately 16 minutes. Turn on the broiler. Broil the seafood until the crumbs are deep brown in color and crisp, approximately 3 minutes.
5. Remove the baking dish from the oven. Allow the seafood to cool for 2 minutes. Divide the seafood among 4 plates. Serve at once.

Lemon Pepper Haddock with Wilted Arugula

PREPARATION:
10 MINUTES

COOKING:
15 MINUTES

YIELD:
4 MAIN-COURSE
SERVINGS

In this easy fish recipe, mild-tasting haddock is enhanced by the tartness of lemons and the mild heat of black pepper. Spicy arugula, dressed with a tangy and slightly sweet balsamic vinaigrette, is the perfect accompaniment. Rather than cook the greens, we prefer to place them on the plate and allow the heat from the fish to slightly wilt them. **TIPS:** Children will likely find the greens too pungent for their still-developing palates. Also, cod or hake can be substituted for the haddock.

FISH

1½ pounds haddock fillet, skinned
    Kosher salt
1 tablespoon black pepper
1 tablespoon olive oil
    Juice of 1½ lemons

ARUGULA

8 cups arugula, washed and trimmed
    Kosher salt
1 tablespoon balsamic vinegar
1 tablespoon olive oil
1 teaspoon sugar
    Black pepper

1. Preheat the oven to 450°F.
2. Place the fish on a sheet pan. Sprinkle it with kosher salt and the black pepper.
3. Drizzle the fish with the olive oil and lemon juice.
4. Transfer the pan to the oven. Roast the fish until it is almost cooked through, approximately 8 to 10 minutes. Turn on the broiler and broil the fish until the top begins to color, approximately 2 minutes.
5. While the fish is cooking, place the arugula in a bowl. Sprinkle it with kosher salt. Whisk together the vinegar, olive oil, sugar, and pepper. Pour the dressing onto the greens and toss well.

6. Divide the greens among 4 plates, spreading them to create a bed. Place an equal portion of fish onto each bed of greens and serve at once.

Scampi

PREPARATION:
15 MINUTES

COOKING:
10 MINUTES

YIELD:
4 MAIN-COURSE
SERVINGS OR 6 SIDE-
DISH SERVINGS

Shrimp is at the top of many people's list of favorite seafood. They are versatile and quick cooking. Large shrimp can be grilled or used in a casserole or soup. Smaller ones can be sautéed and served as a first course with bread as in this recipe or tossed with pasta for a quick dinner. Olive oil, garlic, shallots, tomatoes, and fresh herbs complement shrimp's delicate flavor. Shrimp are a great source of protein and with only approximately one hundred calories and a mere 1.73 grams of fat for a three-ounce serving, are very nutritious as well. You may discover that children who won't consume any other seafood will eat shrimp.

1 tablespoon olive oil
6 cloves garlic, peeled and thinly sliced
1 cup dry white wine
1 tablespoon unsalted butter
2 pounds shrimp, peeled (deveined if they are large)
½ cup flat-leaf (Italian) parsley, chopped
Kosher salt
Black pepper

1. Heat the olive oil in a Dutch oven over medium heat. When the oil is hot, add the garlic. Cook the garlic for 1 minute, stirring often.
2. Raise the heat to high. Add the wine and butter. Bring the sauce to a boil. Simmer it for 2 minutes.
3. Stir in the shrimp and parsley. Cook the shrimp only until they just turn pink.
4. Season the shrimp with kosher salt and black pepper. Divide the shrimp among 4 or 6 shallow bowls. Accompany the shrimp with crusty bread and serve at once.

CHAPTER 20

accompaniments

I t's certainly simple and healthful to accompany meals with steamed broccoli, a green salad, and brown rice. But with slightly more effort, you can serve much more creative and delicious "sides." When we prepare a meal that requires several side dishes, such as a Thanksgiving dinner or a traditional "meat and potatoes" supper, we want the accompaniments to shine. In fact, our children often make a meal from all the trimmings. Our accompaniments are always nutritious and flavorful. This may seem like a challenging combination of characteristics, but it's not. It is easy to make delicious mashed potatoes when you are heavy-handed with the butter and cream. But with a bit more attention to the quantities of those rich ingredients, you can prepare just as delectable mashers with less butter and low-fat milk or even a combination of soy milk and silken tofu. From greens to vitamin-packed deep-orange-fleshed vegetables, you will delight your family's palettes and enhance their health with our tasty accompaniments.

With an abundance of calcium, fiber, and antioxidants, dark leafy greens such as spinach, Swiss chard, broccoli rabe, and kale are nutritious and tasty. Their strong flavors, though, often don't appeal to children. Our strategy has always been to combine the greens with familiar and contrasting ingredients. The earthy flavor of spinach is definitely an acquired taste. Rather than just steam it and attempt to coax your youngsters into a taste, try our Spinach with Raisins and Pine Nuts (see page 314). The combination of sweet and soft raisins and creamy and crunchy pine nuts is a winner and will tempt even the most finicky eaters into a nibble.

Deep-orange-fleshed vegetables such as butternut squash, carrots, and sweet potatoes contain great amounts of fiber and the antioxidant beta-carotene. Many children find their natural sweetness appealing. At first glance, you may believe that the slightly bitter flavor of the broccoli rabe in Roasted Butternut Squash and Red Onions with Broccoli Rabe and Dried Cranberries (see page 307) will lead to apprehension even among daring eaters. But the contrasting tastes of the caramelized butternut squash and slightly tart dried cranberries with the pungent rabe have been a proven winner in our home. Whether they are the main ingredients in a satiny soup or a simply prepared side dish, carrots are a favorite vegetable of many. Plenty of kids eat baby carrots right out of the bag for a snack. For a quick side dish, we often steam baby carrots and glaze them with a combination of orange juice and honey. It is such a simple dish you may find yourself preparing it for your kids for a snack.

Potatoes in your diet can be enjoyed as a once in a while treat. Since potatoes are an unrefined starch, too much in your diet is not good for your health. But you do not need to be extreme about this, especially if you lead an active life. If you eliminate this humble root vegetable entirely from your diet—one that has sustained cultures for centuries—you won't just be missing its nutritional value, but its great taste and versatility as well. Whether you serve "Oven Fried" Potatoes (see page 359), Mashed Potatoes (see page 309), or combine potatoes with parsnips and cabbage in the tasty Irish dish Colcannon (see page 308), your children will look forward to seeing it on their plates.

Since we often prepare hearty soups for dinner, we like to accompany them with a green salad. Our salads range from the ubiquitous Mesclun and Arugula with a Balsamic Vinaigrette (see page 322) to the creative Mixed Greens with Apple, Dried Cranberries, and Goat Cheese (see page 323), a pleasing combination of contrasting flavors and textures. Many of our salads are sprinkled with nuts, a heart-healthy protein source.

So next time you are searching for a side dish to round out a meal, don't make it an afterthought; be creative and make your choices the stars of the meal.

PREPARATION:
10 MINUTES

COOKING:
15 MINUTES

YIELD:
4 SIDE-DISH SERVINGS

A Summer Sauté

During the late afternoon in summer, we love walking through our garden and picking all the vegetables that have ripened that day for use in our evening meal. Our children often do the picking and assist us with the cooking. Whenever they help, they are more likely to try their creations. Many of our best warm-weather meals are improvised from cooking these summer treats quickly and simply so that their natural flavors and textures intensify and unite. The finished product can be served as an accompaniment, tossed with pasta and basil pesto (see page 231), or even tucked into a crusty whole-grain baguette for a delightful sandwich.

1 tablespoon olive oil
3 cloves garlic, peeled and thinly sliced
1 onion, peeled and thinly sliced
  Kosher salt
1 red bell pepper, peeled and diced
3 medium zucchini or crookneck summer squash, trimmed and sliced
1 tablespoon unsalted butter
3 plum tomatoes, diced
¼ cup fresh basil, snipped
  Black pepper

1. Heat the olive oil in a Dutch oven over medium heat. When the oil is hot, add the garlic. Cook it for 1 minute. Add the onion and sprinkle it with kosher salt. Cook the onion until it is soft, stirring often, approximately 3 minutes.
2. Add the bell pepper and cook it for 3 minutes, stirring often.
3. Add the squash and sprinkle it with kosher salt. Cook the vegetables until the squash are tender, stirring often, approximately 5 minutes.
4. Stir in the unsalted butter, tomatoes, and basil. Season the vegetables with kosher salt and black pepper and serve at once.

Coleslaw

Sweet and tangy coleslaw is a must with Pulled Pork and our Barbequed Tofu Sandwich. But many people, especially kids, simply like it as a side salad. Cabbage's modest reputation belies its top-notch nutrition. It is an excellent source of fiber, folic acid, and calcium. **TIP:** The cabbage can be sliced by hand with a sharp chef's knife. But the task can be more easily accomplished in a food processor fitted with its slicing attachment. Also, if possible, prepare the coleslaw a day before you plan to serve it. The extra time will tame the bite of the cabbage and allow all the flavors to develop. Stir the coleslaw thoroughly before serving.

1 head green cabbage, trimmed, cored, and thinly sliced
½ head red cabbage, trimmed, cored, and thinly sliced
3 carrots, peeled and grated
1 cup low-fat commercial mayonnaise
½ cup white vinegar
⅓ cup sugar
   Kosher salt
   Black pepper

1. In a large bowl, toss together the green and red cabbages and carrots. Set the bowl aside for the moment.
2. In a small bowl, whisk the mayonnaise, vinegar, and sugar.
3. Pour the dressing over the cabbage mixture and thoroughly toss. Season the coleslaw with kosher salt and black pepper.
4. Cover the bowl and refrigerate for at least an hour.

PREPARATION:
15 MINUTES

CHILLING:
1 HOUR

YIELD:
10 SIDE-DISH
SERVINGS

PREPARATION:
30 MINUTES

COOKING:
35 MINUTES

YIELD:
6 SIDE-DISH SERVINGS

Baked Sweet Potatoes and Apples with Cinnamon and Maple Syrup

This sweet and slightly tart dish is the ideal accompaniment to Roasted Pork Tenderloin with Herbs and Garlic (see page 278). Many kids are fond of white potatoes but are hesitant to try sweet potatoes. By combining them with a familiar food such as apples and sweetening the mixture with maple syrup, your youngsters will be likely to enjoy this dish. The deep orange flesh of sweet potatoes is an indication of their abundance of the antioxidant beta-carotene. **TIP:** The assertive taste of grade-B maple syrup (also referred to as cooking syrup) works particularly well in this recipe.

1 tablespoon unsalted butter
4 medium apples, peeled, cored, and sliced into 1-inch pieces
1 teaspoon cinnamon
4 medium sweet potatoes, peeled and sliced into 1-inch pieces
Kosher salt
⅓ cup maple syrup

1. Preheat the oven to 450°F.
2. Melt the butter in a large skillet over medium-low heat. Add the apples. Cook them until they begin to soften and caramelize, stirring occasionally, approximately 15 minutes. Sprinkle them with the cinnamon.
3. Meanwhile, place the potatoes in a Dutch oven. Cover them with water and season with kosher salt. Bring the potatoes to a boil. Reduce the heat, and simmer them until they are tender, approximately 15 minutes. Drain them and return to the pot.
4. Add the apples to the potatoes. Stir in the syrup. Transfer the mixture to a 9-inch casserole. Place the casserole in the oven and bake until the top begins to brown, approximately 30 minutes.

Roasted Butternut Squash and Red Onions with Broccoli Rabe and Cranberries

PREPARATION:
10 MINUTES

COOKING:
45 MINUTES

YIELD:
4 SIDE-DISH SERVINGS

Antioxidant-rich butternut squash is a versatile vegetable. It can be the star ingredient in a velvety soup or combined with apples and pureed for a wholesome accompanying dish. Cubed pieces of butternut squash can be roasted and tossed with whole-grain pasta and fresh sage for a hearty cool-weather supper. In this recipe, the squash's natural sweetness proves to be the perfect canvas for the contrasting flavors of pungent broccoli rabe and tart dried cranberries. It's great for Thanksgiving dinner and makes an ordinary dinner special.

1 large butternut squash, trimmed, peeled, seeded, and sliced into 2-inch pieces
2 red onions, peeled and sliced
  Kosher salt
½ cup brown sugar
2 tablespoons canola oil
1 cup water
1 bunch broccoli rabe, trimmed and rinsed
1 cup dried cranberries

1. Preheat the oven to 450°F. Have ready an ice bath.
2. Place the squash and red onions on a heavy sheet pan. Sprinkle them with kosher salt. Toss them with the brown sugar and canola oil. Transfer the pan to the oven. Roast the vegetables until the squash is tender and caramelized, stirring 3 or 4 times, approximately 40 minutes.
3. Meanwhile, bring the water to a boil in a medium saucepan. Add the broccoli rabe. Cover the pot, and steam the rabe until tender, stirring 3 or 4 times, approximately 5 minutes. Drain the rabe and transfer it to the ice bath. When the rabe is cool, drain it. Squeeze it thoroughly to remove any excess moisture. Chop it and transfer to a serving bowl.
4. Remove the tray from the oven. With the back of a metal spatula loosen the vegetables from the tray. Transfer them to the serving bowl. Sprinkle on the cranberries. Toss the ingredients, gently but thoroughly. Serve hot or at room temperature.

PREPARATION:
20 MINUTES

COOKING:
30 MINUTES

YIELD:
4 SIDE-DISH SERVINGS

Colcannon

The only negative thing about this traditional Irish dish is that it uses four different cooking vessels. Fortunately, it can be made entirely in advance and popped into the oven thirty minutes prior to serving, providing you with the necessary cleaning time. Colcannon is the ideal accompaniment to any meat, fish, or poultry main course. For a delightful brunch item, serve the warmed leftovers with poached eggs and toast. Kids who like mashed potatoes will love colcannon. Potatoes, while no longer considered a healthful vegetable, can still be a once-a-week treat. If you are physically active, you can eat them a bit more often.

1½ pounds Yukon Gold or russet potatoes, quartered
    Kosher salt to taste
½ pound parsnips, peeled and sliced into 1-inch pieces
1 small head green cabbage, outer leaves removed, cored and
      thinly sliced
2 tablespoons unsalted butter
2 onions, peeled and diced
1 cup milk
    Black pepper to taste

1. Preheat the oven to 450°F. Have on hand a large ovenproof casserole.
2. Place the potatoes in a large Dutch oven. Cover them with water. Season them with kosher salt. Bring them to a boil. Reduce the heat and simmer them for 10 minutes. Add the parsnips to the pot. Simmer the vegetables until they are tender, approximately 10 minutes.
3. Meanwhile, place the cabbage in another Dutch oven. Cover it with water and season with kosher salt. Bring the cabbage to a boil. Reduce the heat and simmer the cabbage until tender, approximately 15 minutes.
4. While all the vegetables are cooking, heat the butter in a skillet over medium-low heat. Add the onions and sprinkle them with kosher salt. Cook them until they are soft, stirring often, approximately 10 minutes. Remove the pan from the heat.

5. Drain the potatoes and parsnips. Return them to the pot. Add the milk. Mash them until well combined but still a bit lumpy. Season them with kosher salt and black pepper. Add the cabbage and onions. Mix the ingredients thoroughly.

6. Transfer the mixture to the casserole. Place the casserole in the oven. Bake the colcannon until the top is golden, approximately 30 minutes. Remove it from the oven and serve at once.

Mashed Potatoes

Whether baked, roasted, French fried, or mashed, our children are crazy about potatoes. We prize potatoes for their versatility and great taste. And with plenty of carbohydrates and potassium, they are a top choice for people with active lifestyles.
TIP: To make mashers even more healthful and without using dairy products, substitute a combination of one cup of soy milk and six ounces of pureed silken tofu for the unsalted butter and milk. You can fool your children into eating tofu this way.

PREPARATION:
15 MINUTES

COOKING:
30 MINUTES

YIELD:
6 SIDE-DISH SERVINGS

3 pounds russet or Yukon Gold potatoes, peeled and quartered
Kosher salt
2 tablespoons unsalted butter
1 cup milk
Black pepper

1. Place the potatoes in a Dutch oven and cover them with water. Season them with kosher salt. Bring them to a boil. Reduce the heat and simmer them until tender, approximately 25 minutes.

2. Drain them and return them to the pot. Reduce the heat to low. Stir the potatoes several times so the remaining moisture evaporates. Add the butter and milk. Mash the potatoes with a hand-held masher, adding additional milk if necessary to make creamy potatoes. Season the potatoes with kosher salt and black pepper and serve at once.

PREPARATION:
20 MINUTES

COOKING:
20 MINUTES

YIELD:
6 SIDE-DISH SERVINGS

Pan-Fried Potatoes with Onions and Peppers

Fried potatoes are not just a breakfast and brunch dish. They are also a great accompaniment to oven-roasted beef or chicken and pan-fried fish fillets. **TIP:** To make another potato dish using a similar technique, omit the onion, bell pepper, and scallions. Instead, while they are cooking, mince together two-thirds of a cup of flat-leaf (Italian) parsley and two cloves of peeled garlic. When the potatoes are tender and golden, remove them from the heat and immediately toss them with the parsley-garlic mixture.

4 medium Yukon Gold potatoes, scrubbed and cut into ½-inch cubes
2 tablespoons olive oil
1 onion, peeled and diced
   Kosher salt
1 red bell pepper, cored, seeded, and diced
3 scallions, trimmed and thinly sliced
   Black pepper

1. Place the potatoes in a Dutch oven. Cover them with cold water and bring to a boil. Reduce the heat, and simmer them until they are just tender, approximately 15 minutes. Drain them and return them to the pot. Shake them over low heat until all their excess moisture has evaporated, approximately 2 minutes.
2. While the potatoes are cooking, heat the olive oil in a large non-stick or cast-iron skillet over medium heat. When the oil is hot, add the onion and sprinkle it with kosher salt. Cook the onion for 3 minutes, stirring often. Add the bell pepper and cook for another 2 minutes, stirring often.
3. Raise the heat to medium-high and carefully add the potatoes. Season them with kosher salt. Cook the potatoes until they are golden and slightly crisp, tossing often, approximately 12 minutes.
4. Remove the potatoes from the heat and stir in the scallions. Season the potatoes with black pepper and serve immediately.

Grilled Corn on the Cob

During the height of the summer-vegetable season, we make grilled corn the centerpiece of an all-grilled vegetable dinner featuring eggplant, bell peppers, zucchini, and portobello mushrooms. **TIP:** When we grill corn, we always husk it. You need to monitor husked corn on the grill closely, though. It can go from perfectly cooked to burned in a minute's time. With its smoky taste and caramelized exterior, the extra effort is well rewarded.

8 ears corn, husked
4 tablespoons olive oil
  Kosher salt
  Black pepper

1. Light a hardwood charcoal fire.
2. Thoroughly rub the corn with the olive oil. Season it all over with kosher salt and black pepper.
3. When the charcoal is mostly white ash, carefully place the corn on the grill. Cook the corn, turning often, until slightly charred and tender, approximately 7 minutes.
4. Transfer the corn to a plate. Serve the corn hot or at room temperature.

PREPARATION:
5 MINUTES

COOKING:
10 MINUTES

YIELD:
8 SIDE-DISH SERVINGS

Polenta

If your children love mashed potatoes, they are going to enjoy polenta. It is the ultimate side dish to serve with Beef Stew (see page 270) and Braciolette (see page 263). **TIP:** Polenta can also be spread on a cutting board, cooled, and sliced. The slices can be used in place of bread for sandwiches or drizzled with canola oil and baked until golden and crisp. Serve the baked polenta with warmed maple syrup for a breakfast treat.

PREPARATION:
5 MINUTES

COOKING:
45 MINUTES

YIELD:
6 SIDE-DISH SERVINGS

3½ cups low-fat or skim milk
3 cups water
Kosher salt
2 cups stone-ground cornmeal
2 tablespoons unsalted butter
½ cup grated Parmesan cheese
Black pepper

1. Combine the milk and water in a Dutch oven and heat to a simmer. Season the mixture with kosher salt.
2. Slowly add the cornmeal in a thin stream while whisking constantly. Continue whisking until the mixture is smooth, approximately 1 minute longer.
3. Reduce the heat to low. Cook the polenta, stirring often with a wooden spoon, until it pulls away from the sides of the pot and is no longer raw tasting, approximately 40 minutes.
4. Remove the pot from the heat and stir in the butter and Parmesan cheese. Season the polenta with kosher salt and black pepper and serve immediately.

PREPARATION:
5 MINUTES

COOKING:
10 MINUTES

YIELD:
4 SIDE-DISH SERVINGS

Orange-and-Honey-Glazed Baby Carrots

In addition to being a perfect snack, beta-carotene-rich baby carrots are ideal to use in a quickly prepared side dish. To retain their nutrients, we have steamed them in a minimal amount of water and used the water as the base for the sauce.

⅓ cup orange juice
2 tablespoons honey
⅓ cup water
Kosher salt to taste
1½ pounds baby carrots

1. In a small bowl whisk together the orange juice and honey. Set the bowl aside for a moment.
2. Bring the water to a boil in a medium saucepan. Add kosher salt to the water, followed by the carrots. Cover the pot and steam the

carrots until tender, stirring occasionally, approximately 7 minutes. If necessary, add a bit more water to prevent them from sticking.

3. Reduce the heat to low. Whisk the orange juice–honey mixture one more time. Add it to the carrots. Simmer the carrots for 2 more minutes, stirring occasionally. Season them with kosher salt and black pepper.

4. Divide the carrots among 4 plates and serve at once.

Broccoli with Oyster Sauce

PREPARATION:
10 MINUTES

COOKING:
15 MINUTES

YIELD:
4 SIDE-DISH SERVINGS

If your kids are reluctant broccoli eaters, prepare this Asian-influenced dish for them. Our children find the bold and slightly sweet sauce appealing, and yours may as well. **TIPS:** Oyster sauce is a common Chinese condiment found in the international food section of most markets. Also, to create a main course, toss the broccoli with cooked linguine and cubed, pan-fried tofu. Chopped peanuts or cashews are also an ideal garnish, and a heart-healthy protein source.

2½ cups water
   Kosher salt
1½ pounds broccoli, trimmed, florets separated, stems peeled and
      sliced into ¼-inch-thick discs
½ cup broccoli cooking water
1 teaspoon cornstarch
4 tablespoons oyster sauce
1 teaspoon sugar
1 tablespoon tamari
1 tablespoon canola oil
1 1-inch piece gingerroot, peeled and minced
3 cloves garlic, peeled and thinly sliced

1. Bring the water to a boil in a Dutch oven. Add a pinch of kosher salt to the water, followed by the broccoli. Cover the pot and cook the broccoli until tender, stirring occasionally, approximately 5 minutes. Drain the broccoli, reserving ½ cup of its cooking water. Set the broccoli and its cooking water aside for a moment.

2. To prepare the sauce, whisk the cornstarch, oyster sauce, sugar, and tamari into the broccoli cooking water. Set it aside for a moment.

3. Heat the canola oil in the Dutch oven over medium-high heat. When the oil is hot, add the ginger and garlic to the pot. Cook the ingredients for 20 seconds, stirring constantly. Whisk the sauce one more time, and add it to the pot. Cook the sauce until it is thick, approximately 45 seconds. Add the broccoli and stir to coat it in the sauce. Cook the broccoli until just hot, approximately 30 seconds.

4. Divide the broccoli among 4 plates and serve at once.

Spinach with Raisins and Pine Nuts

PREPARATION:
10 MINUTES

COOKING:
15 MINUTES

YIELD:
4 SIDE-DISH SERVINGS

Nutrient-packed spinach is the most recognizable cooking green but is one that many children loathe. We have always had success in getting our children to eat spinach when we combine it with some of their favorite foods, in this case, raisins and pine nuts. If this recipe is a hit, try substituting Swiss chard for the spinach as a second option. Pine nuts are a great way to incorporate nuts into your children's diet.

⅔ cup raisins
1 cup water
⅓ cup pine nuts
Kosher salt
1 tablespoon olive oil
1½ pounds spinach, trimmed, chopped, washed, and spun dry

1. Combine the raisins and water in a small saucepan. Bring the mixture to a boil. Remove the pan from the heat. Set the pan aside while you proceed with the recipe.

2. Place the pine nuts in a small skillet over low heat. Sprinkle them with kosher salt. Toast them until golden, tossing often, approximately 6 minutes. Remove the pan from the heat and set aside.

3. Heat the olive oil in a large Dutch oven over medium-high heat. When the oil is hot, add four handfuls of spinach. Sprinkle the

spinach with kosher salt. Stir the spinach until it begins to wilt. Add two more handfuls and continue stirring. Continue adding spinach and stirring until it has all wilted. Remove the pot from the heat.

4. Drain the raisins of their soaking water.
5. Season the spinach with kosher salt and black pepper. Transfer it to a serving bowl. Garnish it with the pine nuts and raisins and serve at once.

Kimberley Brown's Collard Greens

PREPARATION:
15 MINUTES

COOKING:
3 HOURS

YIELD:
8 SIDE-DISH SERVINGS

During the holidays we had a barbeque for Hope's co-workers at our home. We prepared many traditional barbeque favorites (see A Neighborhood Barbeque for Twenty, page 388) except braised collard greens. Kimberley Brown pointed this out to us. The following week, she sent Hope home with a container of braised collard greens. The greens contained bits of smoked turkey and were out of this world. When I asked Kimberley how long she cooked the greens, she replied: "All day." Generally, when we cook greens we cook them until they are just tender. "All day" goes way beyond just tender. But Kimberley was right on the mark. When we tested the recipe, we tasted the greens throughout the cooking process and we were intrigued by their continually changing taste. The longer they cooked, the more deeply flavored they became. This is now our favorite way to prepare these nutrient-packed greens.

1 tablespoon canola oil
¼ pound lean bacon, diced
2 pounds collard greens, trimmed, washed, and drained
  Kosher salt
4 cups homemade or low-sodium canned chicken broth
  Black pepper

1. Heat the canola oil in a large Dutch oven over medium heat. Add the bacon. Cook the bacon until it is crisp, stirring occasionally, approximately 5 minutes.
2. Drain all but 1 tablespoon of the accumulated drippings.

3. Raise the heat to high. Add the collard greens and season them with kosher salt. Stir the greens until they begin to wilt, approximately 2 minutes.
4. Add the chicken stock. Cover the pot and bring the mixture to a boil.
5. Reduce the heat to low. Braise the greens until they are very tender, stirring occasionally, approximately 2½ hours.
6. Season the greens with kosher salt and black pepper. Serve them hot or at room temperature.

Roasted Sesame Asparagus

PREPARATION:
5 MINUTES

COOKING:
10 MINUTES

YIELD:
4 SIDE-DISH SERVINGS

Asparagus is a favorite vegetable in our home. Our kids love it because they can use their fingers to eat it, and we prize it for its great taste and nutrition. In the past, we steamed our asparagus before drizzling it with a bit of lemon or vinaigrette. We now prefer to roast it in the oven. Roasting produces asparagus with a delightfully smoky taste and an intense flavor. Sesame seeds add heart-healthy oils as well as taste. **TIP:** Dark sesame oil is made from toasted sesame seeds. It has a more intense flavor than traditional sesame oil. If you can't locate it, traditional sesame oil can be substituted.

1½ pounds asparagus, tough ends snapped off and discarded
    Kosher salt
    Black pepper
2 tablespoons dark sesame oil
2 tablespoons tamari sauce
2 tablespoons sesame seeds

1. Preheat the oven to 400°F.
2. Place the asparagus on a heavy sheet pan. Sprinkle them with kosher salt and black pepper. Set them aside for a moment.
3. Whisk together the sesame oil and tamari. Drizzle the mixture onto the asparagus and toss.
4. Transfer the pan to the oven. Roast the asparagus for 5 minutes.

Remove the pan from the oven. Do not turn off the oven. Sprinkle the asparagus with the sesame seeds. Return the pan to the oven. Roast the asparagus until tender, approximately 5 minutes more.

5. Transfer the asparagus to a platter and serve them hot or at room temperature.

Green Beans with Toasted Pecans

Green beans, like asparagus, are a favorite finger food with our children. Just-picked green beans are arguably best when simply steamed and tossed with a bit of unsalted butter, kosher salt, and freshly ground black pepper. They are also wonderful when garnished with nuts, in this case toasted pecans. Nuts contain heart-healthy oils and provide plenty of protein, folic acid, vitamin E, and calcium. They are now considered an important part of a healthful diet.

PREPARATION:
5 MINUTES

COOKING:
10 MINUTES

YIELD:
4 SIDE-DISH SERVINGS

⅔ cup whole pecans, coarsely chopped
   Kosher salt
1 cup water
1 pound green beans, trimmed
   Black pepper
1 tablespoon olive oil

1. Place the pecans in a skillet over low heat. Sprinkle them with kosher salt. Toast them until they are no longer raw tasting, shaking the pan often, approximately 8 minutes.
2. While the nuts are toasting, bring the water to a boil in a large saucepan. Add kosher salt to the water followed by the green beans. Cover the pot and cook the beans until they are tender, stirring occasionally, approximately 8 minutes.
3. Drain the beans and transfer them to a serving platter.
4. Season the beans with kosher salt and black pepper. Drizzle them with the olive oil and garnish them with the pecans. Serve the beans hot or at room temperature.

PREPARATION:
10 MINUTES

COOKING:
30 MINUTES

YIELD:
6 SIDE-DISH SERVINGS

Bulgur with Vegetables and Cashews

Bulgur is prized for its great nutrition, nutty flavor, and ease of preparation. It can be served hot as an accompaniment or chilled as a side salad. When garnished with cubes of seared tofu, it can even be a light main course. Leftovers can be rolled into flour or corn tortillas with melted cheddar for a unique sandwich. Cashews add delicious flavor and heart-healthy protein.

1 tablespoon olive oil
1 onion, peeled and diced
  Kosher salt
1 red bell pepper, cored and diced
1 carrot, scraped and diced
1½ cups bulgur
3 cups water
⅓ cup flat-leaf (Italian) parsley, chopped
  Juice from 1 lemon
  Black pepper
½ cup raw cashews, chopped

1. Heat the olive oil in a Dutch oven over medium heat. When the oil is hot, add the onion. Sprinkle it with kosher salt. Cook it for 3 minutes, stirring occasionally.
2. Add the bell pepper and carrot. Cook the vegetables for 5 minutes, stirring occasionally.
3. Add the bulgur and sprinkle it with kosher salt. Cook the ingredients for 2 minutes, stirring occasionally.
4. Raise the heat to high. Add the water. Bring the bulgur to a boil. Cover the pot and reduce the heat to low. Simmer the bulgur until it is tender, approximately 15 minutes.
5. Add the parsley and lemon to the pot. With a fork, fluff the bulgur. Season the bulgur with kosher salt and black pepper.
6. Divide the bulgur among 6 plates. Garnish each portion with the chopped cashews and serve at once.

Hummus with Horseradish

Hummus, the classic pureed chickpea dish, is a great source of fiber and calcium. A bit of horseradish, added to an otherwise traditional hummus recipe, provides an intense layer of flavor. Try it spread on toasted bagels with sliced tomatoes and arugula or serve it as a dip for raw vegetables. Hummus is a great way to get your family to eat more legumes.

1 small clove garlic, peeled and finely chopped
1 19-ouce can chickpeas, drained and rinsed
⅓ cup sesame tahini
½ cup water
3 tablespoons prepared horseradish
  Juice of 1 lemon
  Kosher salt
  Black pepper

1. Place the garlic, chickpeas, tahini, water, horseradish, and lemon in the work bowl of a food processor fitted with the metal blade. Puree the ingredients. If the spread seems too thick, add a bit more water. Season the spread with kosher salt and black pepper.
2. Transfer the spread to a container and refrigerate until serving time.

PREPARATION:
10 MINUTES

BLENDING:
5 MINUTES

YIELD:
2 CUPS

Mixed Greens with Pecans and Blue Cheese

This simple salad contains a pleasing combination of tastes and textures and is one you will certainly want to accompany many of your meals. With a variety of lettuces, nuts, and a mere tablespoon of olive oil, it contains a minimal amount of saturated fat and provides plenty of calcium, fiber, and protein. We find the addition of nuts to salads makes them more satisfying, and is a great way to consume more heart-healthy proteins and oils.

PREPARATION:
10 MINUTES

COOKING:
10 MINUTES

YIELD:
4 SIDE-DISH SERVINGS

½ cup pecans

Kosher salt

1 medium head Romaine lettuce, trimmed, chopped, washed, and
spun dry

1 medium head red-leaf lettuce, trimmed, chopped, washed, and
spun dry

1 small head radicchio, chopped, washed, and spun dry

3 tablespoons balsamic vinegar

1 tablespoon extra-virgin olive oil

1 teaspoon sugar

2 ounces Blue Castello or a similar creamy blue cheese (room
temperature)

1. Place the pecans in a small skillet over low heat and sprinkle
with kosher salt. Toast them for 10 minutes, tossing occasionally.
Remove the pan from the heat.
2. Combine the Romaine, red leaf, and radicchio in a large salad
bowl.
3. Whisk together the vinegar, oil, and sugar. Sprinkle the greens
with kosher salt. Pour the dressing onto the greens and toss
thoroughly.
4. Divide the greens among 4 plates and garnish each serving with
the toasted pecans and blue cheese.

Greens with Sesame Chicken and Brie

PREPARATION:
10 MINUTES

COOKING:
10 MINUTES

YIELD:
2 MAIN-COURSE
SERVINGS

When we make a salad, we focus on using a few very good ingredients. We dress the salad lightly so all its flavors have a chance to shine and aren't drowning in an overly sweet or pungent dressing. Here is a great main-course salad that needs nothing more than a hunk of crusty bread to make a delightful light lunch. The sesame-crusted chicken provides an interesting flavor and texture contrast to the tender greens and zesty dressing.

1 large boneless and skinless chicken breast (approximately 10 ounces), trimmed, halved, and flattened to ⅓-inch thickness
  Kosher salt
  Black pepper
⅓ cup sesame seeds
1 tablespoon canola oil
10 cups mixed greens (Romaine, red leaf, arugula, and dandelions are great choices), trimmed, washed, drained, and spun dry
2 tablespoons olive oil
3 tablespoons balsamic vinegar
1 teaspoon Dijon mustard
1 teaspoon sugar
2 ounces Brie at room temperature

1. Season the chicken breast halves on each side with kosher salt and black pepper. Sprinkle the halves on both sides with the sesame seeds and press them into the flesh with the heel of your hand.
2. Heat the canola oil in a skillet over medium-high heat. When the oil is hot, carefully place the chicken breast halves in the pan. Sear them until the sesame seeds are deep brown, approximately 2–3 minutes on each side, turning once. Transfer the chicken breast halves to a cutting board. Set them aside for a moment.
3. Place the greens in a large salad bowl and sprinkle them with kosher salt.
4. To prepare the dressing, whisk together the olive oil, vinegar, mustard, and sugar. Pour the dressing onto the greens and toss well.
5. Divide the greens among 4 plates. Slice the chicken into strips. Garnish each portion with chicken strips and Brie and serve at once.

PREPARATION:
10 MINUTES

COOKING:
0

YIELD:
4 SIDE-DISH SERVINGS

Mesclun and Arugula Salad with a Balsamic Vinaigrette

This salad is our top choice when we want something simple, yet bold, to accompany a soup or a quick pasta or chicken dish.

12 ounces mesclun, washed and spun dry
3 cups baby arugula, washed and spun dry
Kosher salt
Black pepper
2 tablespoons olive oil
2 tablespoons balsamic vinegar
½ teaspoon sugar
1 teaspoon Dijon mustard
4 tablespoons grated Parmesan cheese

1. Combine the mesclun and arugula in a large bowl. Season them with kosher salt and black pepper. Set the bowl aside for a moment.
2. Whisk together the olive oil, vinegar, sugar, and mustard. Pour the dressing onto the greens and toss well.
3. Divide the greens among 4 plates. Garnish each portion with the Parmesan cheese and serve at once.

Mesclun

Mesclun is a mixture of seven to ten tender greens. Greens such as arugula, tatsoi, minzuna, cress, and chard are spicy and pungent tasting, while baby lettuces like red and green leaf, Lollo Rosso, Tango, and Little Gem are sweet and mild tasting. Mesclun mix is often available precut and prewashed, either in bulk or small packages. For safety, swirl even prewashed mesclun in a sinkful of cold water and dry it in a salad spinner.

Mixed Greens with Apple, Dried Cranberries, and Goat Cheese

PREPARATION:
10 MINUTES

COOKING:
0

YIELD:
4 SIDE-DISH SERVINGS

Some of the most interesting, delicious, and healthful salads combine a variety of greens with fresh and dried fruits. The greens in this salad are enhanced by the tart and sweet flavors of a Granny Smith apple and dried cranberries. Creamy goat cheese ties everything together. The salad provides plenty of calcium and fiber. **TIP:** As long as each element is kept separate, children seem to love this salad. Before combining the greens and dressing, remove your children's portions. On their plates, arrange separate sections of greens, cranberries, and apple slices.

1   medium head Romaine lettuce, trimmed, chopped, washed, and spun dry
1   medium head red-leaf lettuce, trimmed, chopped, washed, and spun dry
1   small head radicchio, chopped, washed, and spun dry
3   tablespoons red wine vinegar
1   tablespoon extra-virgin olive oil
1   teaspoon sugar
    Kosher salt
1   Granny Smith apple, cored and thinly sliced
1   cup dried cranberries
2   ounces goat cheese at room temperature

1. Combine the Romaine, red leaf, and radicchio in a large salad bowl.
2. Whisk together the vinegar, oil, and sugar. Sprinkle the greens with kosher salt. Pour the dressing onto the greens and toss thoroughly.
3. Divide the salad among 4 plates. Place the apple slices around the perimeter of each plate and garnish each portion with the dried cranberries and goat cheese.

PREPARATION:
10 MINUTES

CHILLING:
30 MINUTES

YIELD:
4 SIDE-DISH SERVINGS

Tomato and Cucumber Bread Salad with Feta and Arugula

During August and September, when our garden produces an abundance of tomatoes, we consume so many that we feel as though we are overloading on vitamin C. Most often, we slice them, sprinkle them with kosher salt, add a dollop of mayonnaise, and enjoy these delicious fruits with crusty bread. Occasionally, we create something more special. With its cool, sweet, spicy, and salty tastes, this simple concoction, inspired by the traditional Tuscan tomato and bread salad, provides great flavor contrasts and is certain to become a regular dish on your summer menu.

1 pound vine-ripened tomatoes, cored and diced
4 small cucumbers, peeled, seeded, and diced
1 clove garlic, peeled and minced
2 tablespoons olive oil
2 cups baby arugula, washed and spun dry
4 cups cubed crusty day-old bread
　Kosher salt
　Black pepper
2 ounces feta, thinly sliced

1. Toss together the tomatoes, cucumbers, garlic, and olive oil in a large bowl.
2. Stir in the arugula and bread. Season the salad with kosher salt and black pepper.
3. Garnish the salad with the feta. Cover the bowl and chill for 30 minutes.

Red Leaf and Arugula Salad with Pine Nuts and Raisins

The best salads are the simplest; this one is a perfect example. Mild and peppery greens combine with sweet raisins and crunchy pine nuts to create a dish with appealing flavors and textures that the entire family will enjoy. Pine nuts are a great addition to your cooking repertoire as they add heart-healthy protein and oils to any recipe.

PREPARATION:
10 MINUTES

COOKING:
10 MINUTES

YIELD:
4 SIDE-DISH SERVINGS

⅓ cup pine nuts
　Kosher salt
½ cup raisins
1 large head red-leaf lettuce, trimmed, chopped, washed, and
　　spun dry
3 cups baby arugula, washed and spun dry
　Black pepper
1 teaspoon Dijon mustard
2 tablespoons red wine vinegar
1 tablespoon extra-virgin olive oil
1 teaspoon sugar

1. Place the pine nuts in a small skillet and sprinkle them with kosher salt. Toast them over low heat until they are golden, shaking the pan often, approximately 7 minutes.
2. Meanwhile place the raisins in a small saucepan and cover them with water. Bring them to a boil. Remove them from the heat and allow them to soften for 5 minutes. Drain them and set them aside.
3. Combine the red leaf and arugula in a large bowl. Sprinkle the greens with kosher salt and black pepper. Whisk together the mustard, vinegar, olive oil, and sugar.
4. Pour the dressing onto the greens and toss well. Divide the salad among 4 plates. Garnish each portion with the pine nuts and raisins and serve at once.

PREPARATION:
10 MINUTES

COOKING:
15 MINUTES

YIELD:
4 SIDE-DISH SERVINGS

"Creamy" Caesar Salad

We have been making this robust and nutritious salad for quite a while, and it is still one of our favorites. The creaminess in the dressing doesn't come from raw eggs or oil but rather pureed silken tofu. This salad will leave your family and friends scratching their heads trying to figure out the "secret" ingredient.

CROUTONS

1 12-inch-long baguette
3 cloves garlic, peeled
2 tablespoons olive oil

DRESSING

Juice from 1 ½ lemons
1 tablespoon Dijon mustard
1 small clove garlic, peeled and chopped
4 ounces silken tofu
Kosher salt
Black pepper

SALAD

1 large head romaine lettuce, trimmed, torn, washed, and spun dry
4 ounces grated Parmesan cheese

1. Preheat the oven to 400°F.
2. To prepare the croutons, cut the bread lengthwise in half. Rub the garlic cloves on the inside of the bread. Drizzle the inside of the bread with the olive oil. Cut the bread into cubes and place on a sheet pan. Bake the croutons until crisp, approximately 10 minutes. Set them aside and allow to cool.
3. Meanwhile, to prepare the dressing, combine the lemon juice, mustard, garlic, and silken tofu in the work bowl of a food processor fitted with the metal blade. Process until a smooth dressing forms. Season with kosher salt and black pepper.
4. To complete the salad, place the lettuce in a large bowl and pour the dressing onto it. Add the croutons to the bowl and toss the salad. Add the Parmesan cheese and toss once more.
5. Divide the salad among 4 plates and serve at once.

Abe and Christy's Yogurt Horseradish Sauce

PREPARATION:
2 HOURS

COOKING;
0

YIELD:
2 CUPS

Abe Faber and Christy Timon are the proprietors of the Clear Flour Bakery in Brookline, Massachusetts. Their bakery consistently produces some of the finest artisan breads in the country. After a gathering at their home one afternoon, Christy brought by some leftovers. She also included smoked salmon and this delicious horseradish-laced yogurt sauce. It was a bold and welcoming change from the cream cheese that we usually serve with the fish and is much more healthful. With the addition of thinly sliced scallions and a bit of chopped cilantro, the sauce also makes a wonderful dip for raw vegetables.

16 ounces nonfat plain yogurt
1 tablespoon prepared horseradish
    Kosher salt
    Black pepper

1. Place the yogurt in a fine mesh strainer over a bowl. Allow the liquid from the yogurt to drip into the bowl, stirring occasionally, for 2 hours.
2. Discard the liquid. Transfer the now-thickened yogurt to a bowl. Add the horseradish. Season the yogurt with kosher salt and black pepper.
3. Cover the bowl and refrigerate until serving time.

Vinegar Sauce

PREPARATION:
5 MINUTES

COOKING:
0

YIELD:
2 CUPS

Before our interest in barbeque intensified, we thought all barbeque sauces were sweet, thick, and tomato based. After reading and experimenting, though, we quickly realized that there are probably as many barbeque sauces as there are barbeque pit masters. We are particularly fond of a sweet and sour vinegar, ketchup-based sauce that is the traditional accompaniment to barbequed pork butt in western North Carolina. **TIP:** This sauce can be substituted for the traditional red sauce in our Barbequed Tofu Sandwich. It is also excellent with rice and bean burritos.

- 1 cup apple cider vinegar
- 1 cup white vinegar
- ⅔ cup ketchup
- ⅓ cup plus 2 tablespoons sugar
- ¼ teaspoon cayenne pepper
- Kosher salt
- Black pepper

1. In a large nonmetal bowl, whisk the cider vinegar, white vinegar, ketchup, sugar, and cayenne pepper. Season the sauce with kosher salt and black pepper.
2. Cover the bowl and refrigerate until serving time.

Barbeque Sauce

PREPARATION:
15 MINUTES

COOKING:
45 MINUTES

YIELD:
APPROXIMATELY 8
CUPS

It is certainly convenient to purchase a commercially prepared barbeque sauce in your local market. But even the tastiest mass-produced variety doesn't rival the quality of a homemade sauce. Here is our version of the thick, sweet, and slightly spicy, tomato-based sauce that is favored by many. Use it on all your favorite meats from brisket to turkey. **TIP:** Leftover barbeque sauce can be frozen for up to two months.

1 tablespoon canola oil
4 cloves garlic, peeled and thinly sliced
2 onions, peeled and diced
   Kosher salt
3 tablespoons chili powder
1 tablespoon cumin
2 tablespoons tomato paste
1 cup water
1 28-ounce can tomato puree
1 28-ounce can crushed tomatoes
1 cup cider vinegar
½ cup ketchup
4 tablespoons Worcestershire sauce
⅓ cup brown sugar
⅓ cup blackstrap molasses
1 teaspoon cayenne pepper
1 tablespoon Dijon mustard
   Black pepper

1. Heat the canola oil in a large Dutch oven over medium heat. When
   the oil is hot, add the garlic. Cook it for 30 seconds. Add the onion
   and sprinkle it with kosher salt. Cook the onion until it is soft,
   stirring often, approximately 3 minutes.
2. Add the chili powder and cumin. Stir in the tomato paste. Cook
   the ingredients for 2 minutes, stirring often.
3. Raise the heat to high and stir in the water. Add the tomato
   puree, crushed tomatoes, vinegar, ketchup, Worcestershire
   sauce, brown sugar, molasses, cayenne pepper, and mustard.
4. Bring the sauce to a boil. Reduce the heat and simmer the sauce
   for 30 minutes, stirring often. If the sauce seems too thick, add a
   bit of water.
5. Season the sauce with kosher salt and black pepper.
6. Allow the sauce to cool. Transfer it to a plastic container and
   refrigerate until serving time.

CHAPTER 21

kids' favorites

Cooking interesting and nutritious meals for children, especially for those who are finicky eaters, is a challenge. Until our younger son, Leo, turned six, he was reluctant to try anything new and preferred only familiar foods. He was your typical fish stick and French fry kid. Our older boy, Joe, has always eaten a variety of foods and is usually willing to taste practically anything we offer him. As Leo gets older, though, his food interests are expanding and his diet is becoming more wide-ranging. The other evening, after watching his brother devour a plate of Spaghetti with Chicken and Broccoli (see page 340), he decided not to just pick through his meal and had a bite of the broccoli. He only had a small nibble, but it was a giant step in the right direction.

It is often difficult to get young children to try new foods and eat healthful meals on a regular basis. Fortunately, there is a strategy to deal with this dilemma. We believe it is important to introduce a variety of foods to kids in their toddler years rather than continually serving them only their favorites. In the best-case scenario, they will find the food appealing, but at the very least, they will be accustomed to seeing it on their plates. When we make a meal that we aren't certain our children are going to enjoy, we serve it to them along with something we know they will eat. We are not advocating cooking separate meals for your children, as this is an easy trap to fall into. But it is important that they do eat food they enjoy. When you prepare something new, explain to your children that you just want them to try it. Tell them that if they don't like it, it's not a big deal. After a sample, they may find it tasty. The next time you prepare it, they are likely to eat more. The important point is to be consistent and insist on one taste. Some children may be reluctant to even take a nibble. In this situation, have the child lick the food.

We have discovered that many children don't like all the elements of their meals combined, such as in a pasta dish. They prefer separate sections of food on their plates. This problem has an easy solution: If you are serving a pasta dish with a variety of vegetables and lean beef, for example, before combining the ingredients in the final step, plate your children's meals first, creating separate sections of noodles, beef, and vegetables. As time passes, and they realize they enjoy all of the flavors and textures of the meal, they won't mind eating in the traditional way.

Hopefully, when you glance through the recipes in this chapter, you will find several meals that even the pickiest eaters will enjoy. Many of the usual suspects are here: chicken fingers, french fries, fish sticks, macaroni and cheese, and pizza. We have altered traditional versions of these recipes, making them more healthful. Also included in this section are meals that we initially thought would be tough sells but turned out to be true favorites. Our Spaghetti and Meatballs (see page 336) is prepared with a combination of tofu and beef, making the meatballs lighter, more nutritious, and just as delicious. Our Oven-Baked Tacos (see page 348) contain the same savory combination of beef and tofu and just may become one of your children's favorite finger foods. Chicken with Sweet Peppers and Rosemary (see page 350) may sound like an adult meal but your kids will delight in the naturally sweet sauce and the tender pieces of boneless chicken breast.

Keep in mind that the goal of raising children with good eating habits is a long-term one. Most kids aren't going to sit down and devour a meal the first time you serve it. But over several years, if repeatedly exposed to healthful and delicious foods, they will develop impressive taste buds, have a true appreciation for good food, and be on their way to a lifetime of healthful eating.

PREPARATION:
10 MINUTES

COOKING:
10 MINUTES

YIELD:
4 MAIN-COURSE
SERVINGS

Chocolate-Chip Pancakes with Peanut Butter and Jam

One morning, our son Joe wanted a chocolate-chip bagel with peanut butter and jelly for breakfast. We did not have any bagels in the freezer, so we suggested a pancake with the same toppings. While eating it, he said: "This should definitely go in the kids' favorites chapter." Many weekday mornings, we use our favorite buttermilk pancake mix, but when we have more time, we prepare this delicious recipe. Pancakes are an excellent source of complex carbohydrates that will keep your body fueled and your mind sharp throughout the morning.

   1 cup unbleached, all-purpose flour
   ½ cup whole-grain flour
   ½ teaspoon kosher salt
   ½ teaspoon baking soda
   1 tablespoon sugar
   1 egg
1 ½ cups buttermilk
   1 tablespoon canola oil
   4 teaspoons butter
   ⅓ cup chocolate chips
   4 teaspoons peanut butter
   4 tablespoons jam
      Maple syrup, warmed

1. In a large bowl, whisk the unbleached flour, whole-grain flour, kosher salt, baking soda, and sugar. Set it aside for a moment.
2. In another bowl, whisk the egg. Whisk in the buttermilk and canola oil.
3. Make a well in the center of the dry ingredients. Pour the wet ingredients into the well. Whisk the batter until smooth.
4. Preheat 2 skillets over medium-low heat. Add 1 teaspoon of butter to each skillet. When it stops foaming, add ½ cup batter to each pan.
5. Cook the pancakes until bubbles appear, approximately

2 minutes. Flip the pancakes and sprinkle with chocolate chips. Cook the pancakes for 2 minutes more.

6. Transfer the pancakes to plates. With a butter knife spread the chocolate chips. Spread a teaspoon of peanut butter and a table-spoon of jam onto each pancake.

7. Repeat this procedure with the remaining butter, batter, choco-late chips, peanut butter, and jam.

8. Accompany the pancakes with the maple syrup and serve imme-diately.

Irish Oatmeal

Oatmeal has always been a breakfast staple in our children's diets. When they were very young, we prepared smooth-textured infant oatmeal for them. As the years passed, they gradually made the transition to rolled oats, and now they enjoy wholesome and hearty steel-cut oats. We lace the oats with dates and raisins to give it a natural sweetness and make it even more nutritious.

PREPARATION:
5 MINUTES

COOKING:
30 MINUTES

YIELD:
4 MAIN-COURSE
SERVINGS

10 cups water
1½ teaspoons kosher salt
2 cups steel-cut oats (Irish oatmeal)
½ cup raisins
8 pitted dates, chopped
4 tablespoons dark brown sugar
Skim milk for serving

1. Bring the water to a boil in a heavy saucepan.

2. Add the salt. Slowly stir in the oats. When the oats return to a boil, reduce the heat. Simmer the oatmeal for 20 minutes, stir-ring often.

3. Stir in the raisins, dates, and brown sugar. Cook the oatmeal for an additional five minutes.

4. Divide the oatmeal among 4 bowls. Thin each portion with skim milk and serve at once.

PREPARATION:
20 MINUTES

COOKING:
1 HOUR

YIELD:
4 MAIN-COURSE
SERVINGS PLUS
ENOUGH FOR 3
MORE MEALS
(SEE PAGES 174
AND 385)

Spaghetti and Meatballs

Spaghetti and Meatballs is an all-time favorite kids' meal. We have always made our meatballs with equal portions of beef and tofu, but when we initially tested this recipe, we decided to mainstream it, substituting pork for the tofu. After several tests, we decided that we prefer the tofu version. Tofu makes the meatballs lighter, moister, and believe it or not, more flavorful. This recipe is a great example of combining beef and tofu in a recipe to decrease the amount of beef, and therefore the saturated-fat content, without compromising taste. We think they taste *better*. **TIPS**: This is a triple recipe, yielding enough meatballs for three meals. They freeze wonderfully and don't need to be defrosted—just drop them into a simmering sauce or soup for a no-fuss midweek supper. Also, depending upon the size of your food processor, the meat may need to be ground in two batches.

2 pounds extra-firm tofu
2½ pounds chuck steak, well trimmed
1 tablespoon olive oil
12 cloves garlic, peeled and thinly sliced
3 medium onions, peeled and diced
   Kosher salt
1 cup dry bread crumbs
½ cup buttermilk
2 eggs
1 cup flat-leaf (Italian) parsley, chopped
   Black pepper
2 tablespoons canola oil
1 35-ounce can whole tomatoes in juice, chopped
1 pound spaghetti
4 tablespoons grated Parmesan cheese

1. To remove the moisture from the tofu, place it on a plate and set a heavy pot on top of it. Set the tofu aside for a moment while you continue with the recipe.

2. Cut the steak into 2-inch pieces. Place it in the work bowl of a food processor fitted with the metal blade. Process the meat for 15 seconds. Set it aside for a moment.

3. Preheat the oven to 400°F.

4. Heat the olive oil in a Dutch oven over medium heat. When the oil is hot, add the garlic. Cook it for 1 minute. Add the onions. Sprinkle them with kosher salt, and cook for 5 minutes, stirring often. Cover the pot and sweat them for 5 more minutes, stirring occasionally. Remove the pot from the heat. Set it aside for a moment.

5. Combine the bread crumbs and buttermilk in a large mixing bowl. Add the beef, eggs, and parsley. Remove the tofu from the plate and discard the accumulated liquid. Crumble the tofu into the bowl. Remove one-half of the onion mixture from the Dutch oven and add it to the bowl. Season the mixture with kosher salt and black pepper.

6. Drizzle the canola oil on 1 large or 2 medium sheet pans, spreading it with a napkin or your fingers.

7. Form the meat-tofu mixture into 36 balls approximately the size of golf balls. Place the balls onto the tray(s). Transfer the meatballs to the oven and bake for 15 minutes.

8. While the meatballs are cooking, return the Dutch oven to the stove over high heat. Add the tomatoes and bring the sauce to a boil. Reduce the heat and simmer the sauce for 15 minutes, stirring occasionally. When the meatballs are cooked, add 12 of them to the sauce. Allow the remainder to cool before dividing them into 2 plastic bags and freezing.

9. Cook the meatballs and sauce together for 30 minutes, stirring occasionally. Season the sauce with kosher salt and black pepper.

10. In the meantime, cook the pasta according to the package instructions. Divide the pasta among 4 plates. Divide the meatballs and sauce among the plates. Garnish each portion with the grated Parmesan and serve at once.

How Safe Is Our Ground Beef?

There have been several well-documented cases of the presence of bacterium Escherichia coli (E. coli) in mass-produced ground beef that have led to the recall of millions of pounds of potentially harmful meat. If you ingest even a small amount of the most dangerous type of E. coli, 0157:H7, you will become extremely sick. It can be fatal to children, the elderly, and people with compromised immune systems.

Ground beef is more difficult to keep safe than steaks or roasts because any contamination is mixed into the meat rather than remaining on the surface. Bacteria on the surface of meat is more easily killed by cooking. Clean meat is most often contaminated at processing plants when it is mixed with meat containing E. coli from fecal matter on the animals' hides or in their intestines. Commercially ground beef comes from a number of different animals. Even if the beef arrives at the processing plant in perfect condition, the grinding equipment can harbor bacteria and pass it on to thousands of pounds of meat.

There are several steps you can take to reduce the risk of contamination. The first is to purchase a piece of beef (for example, a chuck roast) from the market, rinse it thoroughly, and grind it in a food processor. If you do purchase ground beef from the market, be certain to cook it to an internal temperature of at least 160°F. It is best to use an instant-read meat thermometer, since it is not always accurate to judge the temperature of meat by its interior color. Also, clean all spilled juices with paper towels, not sponges. Sponges will harbor the bacteria and contaminate any surface they come into contact with. After you have finished working with meat, wash your hands and all surfaces the meat touched with hot soapy water. These suggestions will not guarantee the meat you consume will not contain harmful bacteria, but they do provide a greater margin of safety.

Rigatoni with Sweet Chicken Sausage

PREPARATION:
15 MINUTES

COOKING:
1¼ HOURS

YIELD:
4 MAIN-COURSE
SERVINGS

Our younger son, Leo, loves hot dogs. We have always been very conscious about cooking him turkey or chicken franks that contain no fillers or chemicals. After serving him this meal several times and impressing upon him that the texture and taste of the sausage was similar to his beloved hot dogs, he started to enjoy it. This meal is now part of our weekly rotation and is one to which we all look forward.

1 tablespoon olive oil
1 pound sweet Italian chicken or turkey sausage, approximately 4 links
4 cloves garlic, peeled and thinly sliced
1 onion peeled and diced
  Kosher salt
2 teaspoons dried basil
1½ cups white wine
1 35-ounce can whole tomatoes in juice, chopped
  Black pepper
1 pound whole-grain rigatoni
4 tablespoons grated Parmesan cheese

1. Heat the olive oil in a Dutch oven over medium-high heat. When the oil is hot, add the sausage links. Sear them on all sides, rolling them occasionally, approximately 5 minutes. Remove the sausages from the pot and set them aside for a moment.
2. Reduce the heat to low. Add the garlic to the pot and cook it for 30 seconds, stirring constantly. Add the onion and sprinkle it with kosher salt. Cook the onion for 2 minutes, stirring often. Add the basil.
3. Return the sausages to the pot. Cover the pot and sweat the ingredients for 5 minutes, stirring occasionally.
4. Raise the heat to high. Add the wine. Simmer the wine for 3 minutes.
5. Add the tomatoes. Bring the sauce to a boil. Reduce the heat and simmer the sauce for 50 minutes, stirring occasionally. Season the sauce with kosher salt and black pepper.

6. Cook the pasta according to the package instructions. Divide the pasta among 4 plates and divvy the sausages and sauce on top of the rigatoni. Garnish each portion with the grated Parmesan and serve at once.

PREPARATION:
20 MINUTES

COOKING:
30 MINUTES

YIELD:
4 MAIN-COURSE
SERVINGS

Spaghetti with Chicken and Broccoli

A version of this dish containing a tofu-basil pesto appears in one of our other books. Since it is such a well-liked meal in our home, we have decided to include a more mainstream version here. When you order this meal in a restaurant, it is often loaded with butter and oil. We enhance our sauce with only a small amount of light cream, making the dish flavorful and rich tasting but considerably lighter. With plenty of lean protein, carbohydrates, and nutrient-dense broccoli, this meal provides great all-around nutrition. **TIP:** Rather than steaming the broccoli in a separate pot or cooking it in the sauce (where it tends to absorb too much of the liquid), we add it to the pasta cooking pot after the pasta has been cooking for approximately four minutes. With this technique, the broccoli will be tender when the pasta is cooked. It can then be drained and tossed with the sauce.

⅓ cup all-purpose flour
1½ pounds boneless and skinless chicken breast, trimmed and
    sliced into strips
  Kosher salt
  Black pepper
3 tablespoons olive oil, divided
1 pound spaghetti
2 cloves garlic, peeled and thinly sliced
1 cup homemade or low-sodium canned chicken broth
1½ pounds broccoli, trimmed, florets separated, stems peeled and
    sliced into discs
⅓ cup light cream
4 tablespoons Romano cheese, grated

1. Bring a large pot of water to a boil. Place the flour in a shallow bowl.
2. Season the chicken strips with kosher salt and black pepper. Place them in the bowl containing the flour and toss. Transfer them to a clean plate, shaking each over the flour bowl to remove any excess flour.
3. Heat 1 tablespoon of the olive oil in a large Dutch oven over medium high heat. When the oil is hot, add one-half of the chicken strips. Sear them for 1½ minutes. Turn them over and sear them for an additional 1½ minutes. Transfer them to a clean plate. Repeat the procedure with another tablespoon of oil and the remaining chicken.
4. Add kosher salt to the boiling water followed by the pasta.
5. While the pasta is cooking, heat the remaining tablespoon of olive oil in the Dutch oven over medium heat. When the oil is hot, add the garlic. Cook the garlic for 1 minute, stirring often. Raise the heat to high and add the chicken broth. Bring the liquid to a boil. Return the chicken to the pot. Reduce the heat and simmer the sauce for 3 minutes.
6. Meanwhile, add the broccoli to the pot containing the pasta.
7. Add the light cream to the Dutch oven. Season the sauce with kosher salt and black pepper.
8. When the pasta and broccoli are tender, drain them. Transfer them to the Dutch oven. Combine the ingredients thoroughly. Cook the pasta and sauce over low heat for 2 minutes, stirring occasionally.
9. Divide the pasta, chicken, and broccoli among 4 plates. Garnish each with a tablespoon of Romano cheese, and serve at once.

PREPARATION:
15 MINUTES

COOKING:
10 MINUTES

YIELD:
6 SIDE-DISH SERVINGS

Rice Noodles with Peanut Sauce and Broccoli

Whether it's mixed into cookie dough, spread on pancakes, or simply slathered onto an English muffin, most children love anything with peanut butter. In this recipe, we have tossed rice noodles and broccoli with a zesty peanut sauce to create a quick and nutritious noodle dish. It can be presented as a main course, but we often serve it as an accompaniment to grilled chicken or flank steak.

1 tablespoon canola oil
1 tablespoon fresh gingerroot, peeled and minced
1 onion, peeled and diced
 Kosher salt
1 cup water
⅔ cup peanut butter
⅓ cup tamari
⅓ cup brown sugar
3 tablespoons cider vinegar
2 tablespoons blackstrap molasses
4 scallions, trimmed and thinly sliced
1 large bunch broccoli, trimmed, florets separated, stems peeled
 and sliced into ¼-inch discs
12 ounces rice noodles
½ cup unsalted peanuts, finely chopped

1. Bring a large pot of water to a boil.
2. Heat the canola oil in a Dutch oven over medium heat. When the oil is hot, add the ginger. Cook it for 1 minute, stirring occasionally. Add the onion and sprinkle it with kosher salt. Cook the onion for 4 minutes, stirring often.
3. Raise the heat to high and add the water. Bring the water to a boil. Remove the pot from the heat. Whisk in the peanut butter, tamari, brown sugar, vinegar, molasses, and scallions. Set the sauce aside for a moment.
4. Add kosher salt to the boiling water followed by the broccoli and rice noodles. Cover the pot and return the water to a boil.

Uncover the pot and cook the ingredients until they are just tender, approximately 5 minutes.

5. Drain the noodles and broccoli. Transfer them to a large serving bowl. Stir in the peanut sauce. Gently but thoroughly toss the ingredients. Garnish the noodles with the peanuts. Serve it hot or at room temperature.

Scallion and Basil Meatballs

At first glance, these meatballs, containing intensely flavored scallions and basil, may seem to be too strong tasting for a child's developing tastes and, while making them, we had the same thought. We anticipated our kids taking one bite and then pushing their plates away. Their appetites for these meatballs certainly surprised us, as did the glowing editorials that followed. Using ground turkey instead of the usual beef gives the meatballs a mild flavor and a light and moist texture. We usually accompany them with Macaroni and Cheese (see page 354). **TIP:** This recipe yields ten generous servings. We generally use half and freeze the remaining portion. To reheat the frozen meatballs, place them in a casserole dish, cover them with foil, and heat in a 350°F oven until they are hot, approximately fifteen minutes.

PREPARATION:
20 MINUTES

COOKING:
20 MINUTES

YIELD:
32 MEATBALLS
(ENOUGH FOR 10
GENEROUS SERVINGS)

3   ½-inch-thick slices whole-grain bread, cubed
¾   cup buttermilk
1   tablespoon olive oil
5   cloves garlic, peeled and thinly sliced
2   onions, peeled and diced
    Kosher salt
2   pounds ground turkey
4   scallions, trimmed and thinly sliced
⅔   cup fresh basil, snipped
2   large eggs
    Black pepper
2   tablespoons canola oil

; 1. Preheat the oven to 400°F.
2. Combine the bread cubes and buttermilk in a large mixing bowl. Set the bowl aside for a moment.
3. Heat the olive oil in a Dutch oven over medium heat. Add the garlic and cook for 1 minute. Add the onion and sprinkle it with kosher salt. Cook the onion for 4 minutes, stirring often. Transfer the mixture to the bowl containing the bread.
4. Add the turkey, scallions, basil, and eggs. Season the mixture with kosher salt and black pepper. With your hands thoroughly combine all the ingredients.
5. Drizzle a large sheet pan with the canola oil. Form the mixture into approximately 32 tightly packed balls, placing them onto the sheet pan.
6. Transfer the pan to the oven and cook the meatballs for 20 minutes, turning them after approximately 10 minutes.
7. Remove the meatballs from the oven and serve at once. When the leftovers are cool enough to handle, divide them between 2 plastic bags and freeze.

A Great Hamburger

PREPARATION:
30 MINUTES

COOKING:
10 MINUTES

YIELD:
4 MAIN-COURSE
SERVINGS

One of our most popular foods has gone upscale. Some restaurants now serve "gourmet" hamburgers, lavishly prepared with high-ticket ingredients such as prosciutto and black truffles. These burgers appeal to some people, but many of us still prefer a homey and simple burger garnished with traditional condiments. Here is our version of the American classic that satisfies children and adults alike.

1¼ pounds chuck steak, trimmed and rinsed
    Kosher salt
    Black pepper
2 teaspoons unsalted butter
2 teaspoons canola oil
4 whole-grain rolls, sliced
4 large leaves Romaine lettuce
1 large tomato, cored and sliced

1. Slice the steak into 2-inch pieces. Place the pieces in the work bowl of a food processor fitted with the metal blade. Turn on the machine and process the meat for 15 seconds.
2. Form the meat into 4 patties. Sprinkle the patties on each side with kosher salt and black pepper.
3. Heat the butter and oil in a cast-iron skillet over medium-high heat. When the oil and butter are hot, carefully place the burgers in the pan. Cook them for 3 to 4 minutes on each side, or until a deep brown crust forms, turning once. Reduce the heat and cook them until they reach an internal temperature of 160°F.
4. Slice the rolls in half and lightly toast them. Divide them among four plates. Place a burger onto each roll. Garnish each with a lettuce leaf and sliced tomatoes. If desired, serve with ketchup, mustard, and low-fat mayonnaise.

Preparing the Perfect Hamburger

Three things need to be considered when preparing a hamburger: the quality of the meat, the forming of the patty, and the cooking. The best cut of meat is a piece of chuck steak. You should grind it yourself. This is easily accomplished in a food processor in fifteen seconds. If you don't have a food processor, select a steak and have the butcher grind it for you. Then take it home and prepare it immediately. Prepackaged ground beef lacks the robust flavor of a freshly ground product and may harbor harmful bacteria (see page 338).

The forming of the patties should be a carefully performed task. Handle the meat as little as possible. Pressing and squeezing it will make the burger tough and rubbery. To achieve a tender and crusty burger, it needs to be cooked over high heat in a small amount of unsalted butter and vegetable oil. A cast-iron skillet is the cooking vessel of choice, but practically any heavy pan will suffice. It is best not to cover the burger while it is cooking since doing so will cause steam that will reduce the heat in the pan and thus toughen the burger. For a delectably moist and tender burger, avoid pressing down on it with a spatula. If you follow these simple guidelines, you will enjoy a burger that will be the envy of any restaurant.

Barbequed Beef

PREPARATION:
20 MINUTES

COOKING:
3½ HOURS

YIELD:
8 MAIN-COURSE
SERVINGS
PLUS LEFTOVERS

The term *barbeque* in this recipe refers to the sauce and not the traditional process of cooking with smoke over a low temperature. The beef brisket is braised in a traditional sweet-and-sour tomato-based sauce. The slow cooking concentrates the brisket's flavor and melts its connective tissue, creating a mouthwatering final product. The first time we tested this recipe, we used a 1½-pound brisket, which was perfect for four people. But since it requires three hours of cooking, we decided to double the amount so there would be plenty of leftovers. The extra can be eaten a couple of days later or frozen for up to a month. With its tender meat and slightly sweet sauce, kids will love these sandwiches. They are an excellent source of iron and vitamin C.

- 3 pounds beef brisket
  Kosher salt
  Black pepper
- 1 tablespoon canola oil
- 3 cloves garlic, peeled and thinly sliced
- 1 onion, peeled and diced
- 1 green bell pepper, cored and diced
- 2 tablespoons cider vinegar
- 2 tablespoons Worcestershire sauce
- 3 tablespoons brown sugar
- 1 35-ounce can whole tomatoes with juice, chopped
- 8 whole-grain rolls

1. Preheat the oven to 300°F.
2. Sprinkle the brisket on each side with kosher salt and black pepper. Heat the canola oil in a large Dutch oven over medium-high heat. When the oil is hot, carefully place the meat in the pot. Sear the meat until a deep brown crust forms, approximately 5 minutes. Turn it over and sear for 5 minutes longer. Transfer the meat to a plate and set it aside for a moment.
3. Reduce the heat to low. Add the garlic and cook it for 45 seconds. Add the onion and sprinkle it with kosher salt. Cook the onion for

3 minutes, stirring often. Raise the heat to medium and add the bell pepper. Cook the pepper for 2 minutes, stirring often.

4. Return the meat to the pot. Cover the pot and sweat the meat and vegetables for 5 minutes. Remove the meat from the pot and set it aside for the moment.

5. Stir in the vinegar, Worcestershire sauce, brown sugar, and tomatoes. Raise the heat to high and bring the liquid to a boil. Return the meat to the pot.

6. Transfer the pot to the oven. Braise the meat for 3 hours. Remove the pot from the oven and place the meat on a cutting board.

7. Cut the rolls in half and divide them among 8 plates. Shred the meat with a fork and knife. Place an equal portion of meat on each roll. Spoon on the sauce and serve at once.

PREPARATION:
45 MINUTES

COOKING:
10 MINUTES

YIELD:
6 MAIN-COURSE
SERVINGS

Oven-Baked Tacos

Tacos are near the top of everyone's list of favorite finger foods. Unfortunately, they are often prepared with an abundance of oil, fatty beef, and stale tortilla shells that are loaded with saturated fat and calories. Our version contains a delicious filling of seasoned beef and tofu. We bake, rather than fry, our shells in a mere two tablespoons of heart-healthy canola oil. Our tacos are fresh tasting, crisp, and healthful. And with all the traditional garnishes as well, they are certain to become a much-anticipated meal in your home.

12 ounces extra-firm tofu
1½ pounds chuck steak, trimmed and rinsed
 1 tablespoon plus 1 tablespoon canola oil
 3 cloves garlic, peeled and thinly sliced
 1 onion, peeled and diced
 1 red bell pepper, cored and diced
 1 yellow bell pepper, cored and diced
    Kosher salt
 2 tablespoons spice rub (see page 280) or 1 tablespoon chili
       powder and 1 tablespoon cumin
 8 ounces prepared tomato sauce
 1 tablespoon Worcestershire sauce
 ½ cup homemade or low-sodium canned chicken broth
12 corn tortillas
 6 ounces Cheddar or Monterey Jack cheese, sliced or grated
 1 avocado, peeled, pitted, and sliced
 ½ head iceberg or Romaine lettuce, cored, washed, spun dry, and
       very thinly sliced
 6 tablespoons nonfat sour cream

1. Remove the moisture from the tofu by placing it on a plate and setting a heavy pot on top of it. After approximately 20 minutes, remove the tofu from the plate and discard the accumulated liquid. Crumble the tofu and set it aside.
2. Cut the steak into 2-inch pieces. Place it in the work bowl of a food processor fitted with the metal blade. Process the meat for 15 seconds. Set it aside for a moment.

3. Preheat the oven to 400°F.

4. Heat 1 tablespoon of the canola oil in a Dutch oven over high heat. When it is hot, add the meat. Sear the meat, stirring occasionally, until cooked, approximately 5 minutes. Reduce the heat to low. Using a slotted spoon, transfer the meat to a bowl, leaving the accumulated drippings in the pot. Pour off all but 1 tablespoon of the drippings.

5. Add the garlic to the pot and cook for 1 minute. Raise the heat to medium and add the onion and bell peppers. Sprinkle the ingredients with kosher salt. Cook the ingredients for 5 minutes, stirring often. Add the spice mixture and cook for an additional minute.

6. Raise the heat to high. Return the meat to the pot. Stir in the tofu, tomato sauce, Worcestershire sauce, and chicken broth. Bring the mixture to a boil. Reduce the heat and simmer for 10 minutes.

7. While the mixture is simmering, divide the remaining tablespoon of canola oil between two sheet pans. Divide the tortillas between the pans. Scatter the cheese onto the tortillas. Transfer the pans to the oven and bake the tortillas for 10 minutes. Remove the trays from the oven.

8. Divide the tortillas among 6 plates. Divide the meat-tofu filling among the tortillas. Garnish each with the avocado, lettuce, and sour cream and serve at once.

PREPARATION:
15 MINUTES

COOKING:
30 MINUTES

YIELD:
4 MAIN-COURSE
SERVINGS

Chicken with Sweet Peppers and Rosemary

One fall afternoon, a frost warning was forecast for the evening, so we decided to harvest all the bell peppers growing in our garden. We roasted a bunch and used others to prepare this delicious and easy meal. Even though it only requires thirty minutes of cooking, it has the richness of a braised dish. Children will love the sweet peppers, and the incredibly tender and flavorful chicken will have them asking for seconds. Tomatoes and bell peppers are top sources of vitamin C. **TIP:** This meal tastes best and is most eye appealing when a variety of colored bell peppers are used. Also, we usually serve this meal with whole-grain pasta, but brown rice, polenta, or crusty whole-grain bread are fine accompaniments as well.

⅓ cup all-purpose flour
1¼ pounds boneless and skinless chicken breasts, trimmed and
      sliced into strips
    Kosher salt
    Black pepper
3 tablespoons olive oil, divided
4 cloves garlic, peeled and thinly sliced
1 onion, peeled and sliced
4 large bell peppers, cored, seeded, and sliced
½ cup Marsala wine
1 28-ounce can whole tomatoes, drained and chopped
1–2 tablespoons fresh rosemary

1. Place the flour on a large plate. Sprinkle the chicken strips with kosher salt and black pepper. Dredge them in the flour, shake off the excess, and transfer them to a plate.
2. Heat 1 tablespoon of the olive oil in a large Dutch oven over medium-high heat. When the oil is hot, add one-half of the chicken strips. Sear them until golden, approximately 1½ minutes. Turn them over and sear them for 1½ minutes more. Transfer them to a clean plate. Repeat the procedure with another tablespoon of olive oil and the remaining chicken.

3. Reduce the heat to low. Add the remaining tablespoon of olive oil to the pot. Add the garlic and cook it for 30 seconds, stirring often. Add the onion and sprinkle it with kosher salt. Cook the onion until it is soft, approximately 3 minutes, stirring often.

4. Raise the heat slightly and add the bell peppers. Cover the pot and sweat the peppers until they are soft, approximately 8 minutes, stirring often.

5. Raise the heat to high and add the wine. Simmer the wine for 3 minutes. Add the tomatoes and bring the sauce to a boil. Reduce the heat and simmer the sauce for 10 minutes.

6. Add the rosemary. Return the chicken to the pot and simmer for 5 minutes. Season the dish with kosher salt and black pepper and serve at once.

"Oven Fried" Chicken Fingers with Honey Mustard

PREPARATION:
30 MINUTES

COOKING:
30 MINUTES

YIELD:
4 MAIN-COURSE
SERVINGS

Children love chicken fingers from fast-food restaurants. They are often deep-fried, though, transforming what is inherently a healthful meal into a grease-laden nightmare. Our chicken fingers feature a crisp and golden exterior and moist and tender meat. And since they are "oven-fried" in a mere two tablespoons of heart-healthy canola oil, they are wonderfully nutritious. Beware: The accompanying sweet and slightly tart dipping sauce is addictive.

HONEY-MUSTARD DIPPING SAUCE
2 tablespoons Dijon mustard
3 tablespoons honey

CHICKEN
1½ cups buttermilk
2 heaping tablespoons Dijon mustard
1½ pounds boneless and skinless chicken breasts, trimmed and sliced
1 cup yellow cornmeal
¾ cup all-purpose flour
1½ teaspoons kosher salt
2 tablespoons canola oil

1. Preheat the oven to 425°F. To prepare the honey-mustard sauce, whisk the mustard and honey. Set it aside for a moment.
2. To prepare the chicken, whisk the buttermilk and mustard. Place the chicken into the mixture and refrigerate for 20 minutes.
3. While the chicken is soaking, combine the cornmeal, flour, and salt on a large plate.
4. After 20 minutes, remove the chicken from the buttermilk. Working with 3 or 4 slices at a time, dredge them in the cornmeal mixture and place them on a clean plate.
5. When all of the chicken has been coated, drizzle the oil onto a heavy sheet pan. Place the sheet pan in the oven for 5 minutes.
6. Remove the pan from the oven. Place the chicken fingers on the pan, turning to coat each side in the oil.
7. Return the pan to the oven and bake the chicken fingers until they are crisp and golden, approximately 20 minutes, turning them over after 10 minutes. Remove the pan from the oven. Divide the chicken fingers among 4 plates and serve at once.

Fish Sticks

PREPARATION:
10 MINUTES

COOKING:
15 MINUTES

YIELD:
4 SIDE-DISH SERVINGS

Our son Leo loves fish sticks. He would be content to have four fish sticks and a slice of bread every night for dinner. His favorite fish sticks, though, are the overly breaded, frozen variety found in every supermarket. They taste fine and provide high-quality protein. But the rest of the family won't touch them. Our solution was to create a healthful version featuring top-quality fish that we would all eat. We discovered that by breading strips of halibut fillet in a combination of store-bought bread crumbs and Romano cheese and baking them in a minimal amount of heart-healthy canola oil in a hot oven, the fish's flavor and texture were not compromised. Fish sticks are now a meal that we all enjoy and prepare often. **TIP:** Cod, haddock, hake, or pollock can be substituted for the halibut.

2 tablespoons canola oil
1 pound of 1-inch-thick halibut fillet, sliced into ½-inch-wide strips
     that are approximately 3–4 inches in length
1 cup milk
1 cup dried bread crumbs
¼ cup grated Romano cheese
¼ cup flat-leaf (Italian) parsley, finely chopped
  Kosher salt
  Black pepper

1. Preheat the oven to 450°F. While the oven is preheating, drizzle the oil onto a heavy sheet pan and place the pan in the oven.
2. Meanwhile, combine the fish strips and milk in a large bowl. Turn the strips to coat them on all sides with the milk. Set the bowl aside for a moment.
3. In a pie plate or similar-sized plate, combine well the bread crumbs, Romano, and parsley. Season the mixture with kosher salt and black pepper.
4. Remove one piece of fish from the milk, allow the excess to drip away, and dredge the strip in the bread crumbs, turning and patting it to be certain the crumbs adhere. Place the strip on a clean plate. Repeat the procedure with the remaining fish and crumbs.
5. Carefully remove the sheet pan from the oven. Place the strips onto the pan, one at a time, turning each to coat in the oil.
6. Return the sheet pan to the oven. Bake the fish sticks until the bottoms are golden and crisp, approximately 7 minutes. Turn them and cook 7 minutes longer.
7. Remove the tray from the oven. Divide the fish sticks among 4 plates and serve at once. If desired, accompany them with Tofu Tartar Sauce (see page 289).

PREPARATION:
10 MINUTES

COOKING:
20 MINUTES

YIELD:
8 SIDE-DISH SERVINGS

Macaroni and Cheese

Working through this simple recipe is not much more difficult or time-consuming than preparing macaroni and cheese from a box. And it tastes like *real* food and not gummy Cheese Wiz tossed with overcooked pasta! Our "mac and cheese" is an excellent source of protein, calcium, and complex carbohydrates. Most important, kids will gobble it up.

2 tablespoons unsalted butter
2 tablespoons all-purpose flour
  Kosher salt
1 pound whole-grain elbow macaroni
2½ cups low-fat milk
6 ounces mild Cheddar cheese, sliced or grated
4 ounces Monterey Jack cheese, sliced or grated
  Black pepper

1. Bring a large pot of water to a boil.
2. Melt the butter in a small Dutch oven over low heat. Stir in the flour to make a roux (see box, page 355). Cook the roux for 5 minutes, stirring often.
3. Add kosher salt to the boiling water followed by the pasta.
4. Raise the heat to medium-high under the roux. Gradually whisk the milk into the roux to make a sauce. Continue whisking the sauce until it is smooth and begins to bubble. Whisk in the cheeses, 2 ounces at a time. Continue whisking the sauce until it is smooth and all the cheese has melted, approximately 1 minute.
5. Remove the sauce from the heat and season it with kosher salt and black pepper.
6. Drain the pasta and return it to the pot. Add the sauce to the pasta and allow the meal to rest for 2 minutes before serving, stirring 2 or 3 times.

Roux

A roux is used to thicken gravies and sauces. Most often, it consists of equal volumes of butter and flour (occasionally oil is substituted for the butter) that have been cooked until the desired color has been attained. The color can vary from light blond (for a white sauce) to dark brown (for a turkey gravy) depending on the flavor desired in the final dish.

Pizza Dough

PREPARATION:
2 HOURS

YIELD:
4 10-INCH PIZZAS
(8 MAIN-COURSE
SERVINGS)

Kids love making pizza almost as much as eating it. Homemade pizza dough is simple to prepare and so much fun to work with that kids of all ages will find it rewarding. Several basic lessons can be learned here. Kids will be taught how to measure ingredients and knead dough. They will recognize that yeast are living organisms and also gain knowledge about yeast's reactions to certain foods and environments. I always treasure a youngster's expression as they watch yeast foam and grow when dissolved in warm water with a bit of sugar.

2 cups warm water (115°F)
1 package active dry yeast (2¼ teaspoons)
3½ cups unbleached, all-purpose flour or bread flour
1 cup whole-wheat flour
2 teaspoons kosher salt

1. Combine the water and yeast in a large bowl. Stir the mixture until the yeast is dissolved.
2. Combine the flours in a large bowl. Begin adding the flour mixture to the yeast mixture, handful by handful, and stirring after each addition with a wooden spoon.

3. After all but 1 cup of flour has been added (this will take approximately 10 minutes), turn the dough out onto a lightly floured work surface. Sprinkle the salt onto the dough. Knead the dough while slowly adding the remaining cup of flour (this will take approximately 5 minutes). The dough should be smooth and moist.

4. Transfer the dough to a large bowl. Cover the bowl with a moistened kitchen towel and let it rise in a warm spot until it has doubled in volume, approximately 1½ hours.

5. Deflate the dough by gently folding the edges toward the center. Allow it to rest for 5 minutes. Turn the dough out onto a lightly floured surface. Divide it into 4 portions. Roll each portion into a ball. Cover the balls with a kitchen towel until you are ready to make the pizza.

Pizza Cooking Equipment

The best restaurant pizzas are cooked in wood-fired or coal-fired brick ovens. These ovens supply a very hot and dry heat (700° to 800°F) and impart a distinctive flavor and texture to whatever is baked in them. Although it is difficult to achieve the exact same flavor at home, you can duplicate the superb texture in your oven. All that is needed are two inexpensive pieces of equipment: a pizza stone and a pizza peel. If you heat a thick, ceramic pizza stone in your oven at 500°F for one hour, your pizzas will cook in approximately 8 minutes and will have a light and crispy crust that is full of a delectable yeasty flavor. A pizza peel is a long-handled, wooden tool used to move pizzas in and out of the oven.

To Peel, Seed, and Chop Tomatoes

Bring a pot of water to a boil. Cut an "x" on the bottom of each tomato. Carefully place each tomato in the boiling water for 30 seconds. Remove the tomatoes and allow them to cool. Slip off their skins, remove their cores, cut each tomato in half, and gently squeeze each half to remove their seeds.

Tomato and Fresh Mozzarella Pizza

Most young children prefer "regular" pizza. For our "regular" pizza, we prefer an uncooked tomato sauce. It is convenient and has a wonderfully fresh tomato taste. During the summer months we always use garden tomatoes. When they are unavailable, imported Italian plum tomatoes from a can are the top choice.

PREPARATION:
10 MINUTES

COOKING:
20 MINUTES

YIELD:
2 10-INCH PIECES
(4 MAIN-COURSE
SERVINGS)

1 28-ounce can whole tomatoes in juice, drained, squeezed, and chopped or 1½ pounds fresh tomatoes, peeled, seeded, and chopped
1 clove garlic, peeled and minced
2 teaspoons sugar
¼ cup fresh basil
Kosher salt
Black pepper
Cornmeal for sprinkling
2 portions pizza dough (see page 355)
6 ounces fresh mozzarella cheese, sliced or grated
Olive oil (optional)

1. Heat a pizza stone in the oven at 500°F for 1 hour.
2. Meanwhile, to make the sauce, combine the tomatoes, garlic, sugar, and basil in a large nonmetal bowl. Season the sauce with kosher salt and black pepper. Set it aside for a moment.

3. Sprinkle a pizza peel with cornmeal. Turn 1 ball of dough onto a floured work surface. Using your fingertips, flatten it into a circle. Gentle pull the edges and stretch it into a 10-inch circle. Transfer the dough to the peel.

4. Ladle approximately 1½ cups of sauce onto the dough and spread it evenly. Scatter 3 ounces of the cheese onto the dough. If desired, drizzle the pizza with olive oil.

5. Slide the dough off the peel and onto the stone. Cook the pizza until the cheese bubbles and the crust is golden brown and slightly crisp, approximately 8 minutes. Transfer the pizza to a wire rack to cool.

6. Repeat the procedure with the remaining dough, sauce, and cheese.

PREPARATION:
5 MINUTES

COOKING:
20 MINUTES

YIELD:
2 10-INCH PIECES
(4 MAIN-COURSE
SERVINGS)

Pea and Onion Pizza

At first glance, a pea and onion pizza topping may seem like an odd combination, but it is absolutely delicious. When Vince was a child, he always came home to eat during lunch hour at school. On certain afternoons, when he opened the porch door and smelled a certain aroma wafting from the kitchen, he instantly knew his grandmother was making pizzas. He would savor a slice of tomato and cheese, a slice of pea and onion, and a tall glass of homemade lemonade. Too bad young kids can't "go home for lunch" any longer.

1 tablespoon olive oil plus extra for drizzling
2 cloves garlic, peeled and thinly sliced
1 Spanish onion, peeled and thinly sliced
  Kosher salt
1 teaspoon paprika
1 15-ounce can of sweet peas, drained
2 portions pizza dough (see page 355)

1. Heat the pizza stone in the oven at 500°F for 1 hour.
2. Meanwhile, heat the olive oil in a Dutch oven over medium heat. When the oil is hot, add the garlic. Cook it for 1 minute. Add the onion and sprinkle it with kosher salt. Cook the onion for 4 minutes, stirring often. Stir in the paprika.

3. Raise the heat to high and add the peas. Bring the mixture to a boil. Reduce the heat and simmer for 10 minutes, stirring occasionally. Season the topping with kosher salt. Set it aside for a moment.

4. Sprinkle a pizza peel with cornmeal. Turn 1 ball of dough onto a floured work surface. Stretch it into a 10-inch circle. Transfer the dough to the peel.

5. Spoon approximately 1½ cups of the pea mixture onto the dough and spread it evenly. Drizzle the pizza with olive oil.

6. Slide the dough off the peel and onto the stone. Cook the pizza until the crust is golden brown and slightly crisp, approximately 8 minutes. Transfer the pizza to a wire rack to cool.

7. Repeat the procedure with the remaining dough and pea mixture.

"Oven Fried" Potatoes

Although French fries can never be part of a healthful diet, here is an alternative that may fool you. These "fries" are crisp and have a real potato flavor. Most important, they are loaded with complex carbohydrates, are low in fat, and kids love them. They are always our accompaniment to "Oven Fried" Chicken Fingers with Honey Mustard (see page 351).

PREPARATION:
10 MINUTES

COOKING:
30 MINUTES

YIELD:
4 SIDE-DISH SERVINGS

4 medium russet potatoes, scrubbed, dried, cut in half, and each half sliced lengthwise into 7 wedges
2 tablespoons olive oil
Kosher salt
Black pepper

1. Preheat the oven to 450°F

2. Spread the potatoes in a single layer on a heavy sheet pan. Drizzle them with the olive oil. Sprinkle them with kosher salt and black pepper.

3. Transfer the pan to the oven. Roast the potatoes for 30 minutes or until golden and slightly crisp.

4. Remove the tray from the oven. With the back of a metal spatula, loosen the potatoes from the sheet pan and serve at once.

PREPARATION:
20 MINUTES

COOKING:
15 MINUTES

YIELD:
4 SIDE-DISH SERVINGS

Onion Rings

Our son Joe always surprises us with his passion for good onion rings. Of the foods he asks us to cook for him, onion rings are one of his most frequent requests. He doesn't care for the heavily breaded frozen ones; he prefers lightly coated thin strips. Since onion rings are almost always deep-fried, they can't be a regular part of a nutritious diet. We have created a healthful version by soaking thin strips of Spanish onions in buttermilk, coating them in a combination of cornmeal and flour, and baking them with a minimal amount of canola oil. They have a delightfully crisp texture and a sweet onion taste. If you don't tell anyone they were baked, they will probably believe they were cooked in a fryolator!

½ cup all-purpose flour
   Kosher salt
½ cup plain bread crumbs
½ cup yellow cornmeal
2 cups buttermilk
2 Spanish onions, peeled and sliced into ½-inch-thick rounds
2 tablespoons canola oil

1. Preheat the oven to 400°F. Have ready a heavy sheet pan.
2. Place the flour in a large pie plate. Season it with kosher salt. Combine the bread crumbs and cornmeal in another pie plate. Pour the buttermilk in a large, shallow bowl.
3. Dredge 5 onion rings in the flour. Dip them into the buttermilk. Remove them from the buttermilk, allowing the excess to drip away. Coat the rings in the bread-crumb mixture. Place the rings on the sheet pan. Repeat the procedure with the remaining onions, flour, buttermilk, and bread-crumb mixture.
4. Drizzle the onion rings with the canola oil and gently toss. Transfer the pan to the oven. Bake the onion rings until golden and crisp, approximately 10 minutes. Carefully flip them and bake for an additional 5 minutes. Remove the tray from the oven and serve at once.

Garlic Bread

You can serve garlic bread with any meal, but it pairs especially well with soups and stews. We prefer to make ours with heart-healthy olive oil rather than butter. If you don't have access to a great baguette, you can still make pretty good garlic bread with a mass-produced supermarket loaf.

PREPARATION:
5 MINUTES

COOKING:
15 MINUTES

YIELD:
4 SIDE-DISH SERVINGS

1 12-inch-long whole-grain baguette
3 cloves garlic, peeled
4 tablespoons olive oil
4 tablespoons grated Romano cheese

1. Preheat the oven to 400°F.
2. Cut the bread in half lengthwise. Rub the garlic cloves on the inside of the bread. Drizzle the inside of the bread with the olive oil. Place the bread on a sheet pan. Bake it until it is crisp and golden, approximately 12 minutes.
3. Transfer the bread to a cutting board. Cut each half into 4 pieces and sprinkle with the Romano cheese.

CHAPTER 22

treats

If your kids are like ours, after dinner, the first words they most likely utter are: "What's for dessert?" In our home, dinner would be incomplete without something sweet at the end. It's easy and convenient to open a package of cookies and hand your youngsters two. We do this often enough. But when our pantry is well stocked and we have the energy, we avoid commercially produced sweets and offer our children a homemade treat. Homemade desserts are always more healthful than mass-produced ones and something you can feel good about serving your family.

You will be pleasantly surprised with the tasty and nutritious sweets that can be crafted when you keep a careful eye on the recipe's fat and sugar content and base your guilt-free desserts on ripe fruits, whole grains, and low-fat dairy products. Your children will be keen for a trip to an orchard for an afternoon of fruit picking and returning home to transform their luscious gems into Blueberry Black Pan Bread (see page 367) or Apple and Almond

Crisp (see page 376). When your kids rush into the house after a hot afternoon of running in the park and crave something cold and sweet, don't give them juice or soda, whip up one of our fruit-and-yogurt-based smoothies. It will satisfy their thirst and craving for sugar while replenishing their energy and providing them with plenty of fiber and a variety of vitamins and minerals. Rather than filling your cookie jar with butter-rich chocolate-chip cookies, keep on hand our Granola–Chocolate-Chip Cookies (see page 378). Made with no butter and a mere two tablespoons of canola oil, these dense delights are chock-full of whole-grain goodness.

Using lower-fat dairy products and intensely flavored seasonings, such as cocoa powder, is also a great way to create luscious desserts that will satisfy your family's sweet tooth and provide a nutritious punch. We all love chocolate pudding. At first glance, it seems to be a guilty pleasure. But when made with low-fat milk and cocoa powder, it is loaded with protein and calcium and can definitely be considered part of a healthful diet. In our Frozen Chocolate-Marshmallow Soy Cream Pie (see page 380), a combination of tofu and low-fat milk replaces the usual cream and egg yolks to create a nourishing frozen treat the entire family will devour.

As parents, it is our job to make these good-for-you treats appetizing and eye appealing and, of course, coax our youngsters into a nibble. As with most other foods, after presenting it several times, they will likely be won over. It is obviously much easier to prod them into tasting a sweet than it is a sea scallop. Plan ahead and keep your pantry stocked with the dry goods needed for wholesome treats, and you will be prepared to whip one up for your family on a moment's notice.

Blueberry-Vanilla Smoothie

Since we planned to include three smoothies in this section, we decided to choose our children's three favorite fruits and make each the focus of a drink. Blueberries are delicious and nutritious (see page 369) and, when combined with vanilla yogurt and a banana, create a luscious and creamy drink with a natural sweetness that can't be beat.

- 2 medium bananas, peeled
- 2 cups frozen blueberries
- 1 cup apple juice
- 1 8-ounce container nonfat vanilla yogurt
- 1 teaspoon vanilla extract
- 3 ice cubes

Place the bananas, blueberries, apple juice, and yogurt into a blender. Blend until smooth. With the machine still running, add the ice cubes one at a time. Continue blending until smooth. Divide the drink between 2 glasses and serve at once.

PREPARATION:
5 MINUTES

BLENDING:
5 MINUTES

YIELD:
2 (10-OUNCE)
SERVINGS

Double Strawberry Smoothie

Besides being a great source of vitamin C, strawberries also contain plenty of fiber, folate, and calcium. When your children tire of eating them by the handful, prepare this smoothie and watch them gulp it down. **TIP:** For a summer outing, take a trip to a "pick-your-own" strawberry farm. Although smaller than the common store-bought berries, the taste of these fresh-picked gems is far sweeter.

- 2 medium bananas, peeled
- 2 cups frozen strawberries
- 1 cup orange juice
- 1 8-ounce container nonfat strawberry yogurt
- 1 tablespoon sugar (optional)
- 3 ice cubes

PREPARATION:
5 MINUTES

BLENDING:
5 MINUTES

YIELD:
2 (10-OUNCE)
SERVINGS

Place the bananas, strawberries, orange juice, yogurt, and sugar into a blender. Blend until smooth. With the machine still running, add the ice cubes one at a time. Continue blending until smooth. Divide the drink between 2 glasses and serve at once.

Pineapple-Orange Smoothie

PREPARATION:
5 MINUTES

BLENDING:
5 MINUTES

YIELD:
2 (10-OUNCE)
SERVINGS

Silken tofu is a unique and healthful ingredient to include in your smoothie recipes. Its neutral taste is the perfect canvas to highlight the prominent sweet and acidic flavors in this smoothie. It creates a delightfully creamy drink that is rich in protein, calcium, iron, and fiber. **TIP:** If using fresh pineapple chunks, place them in a plastic bag and freeze them for 30 minutes.

2 cups fresh or frozen pineapple chunks
2 medium bananas
1 cup orange juice
1 tablespoon orange juice concentrate
4 ounces silken tofu
3 ice cubes

Place the pineapple, bananas, orange juice, orange juice concentrate, and tofu into a blender. Blend until smooth. With the machine still running, add the ice cubes one at a time. Continue blending until smooth. Divide the drink between 2 glasses and serve at once.

Smoothies

It seems as though every corner coffee, ice cream, and sandwich shop has a smoothie menu. The prices charged for these nutritious drinks, which only cost pennies to make, never cease to amaze us.

Smoothies are one of the tastiest ways to incorporate a variety of nourishing foods into your diet. You may discover that children who won't consider eating an apple, banana, or a handful of berries will indulge in these fruits when they are blended into a creamy frozen drink. With a high-quality blender and ripe fruit you can prepare delicious and healthful drinks quickly and inexpensively.

The wide variety of frozen fruit in today's markets makes smoothies convenient to prepare. If you want to save money and use the ripest fruit in your drinks, purchase or pick fruits that are in season, wrap them tightly in individual portions, and freeze them. Even bananas that are past their prime can be frozen. Peel and slice them in half before placing them in your freezer.

Whether you like berries or bananas, pineapple or papaya, a sweet or tart flavor, hopefully, after making the smoothies in this section and realizing how delicious and simple they are to prepare, you will be inspired to create your own mouth-watering concoctions

Blueberry Black Pan Bread

While cycling through the woods during a hot August afternoon in Maine, we came upon a dense area of high bush wild blueberries. We returned the following day with plastic bags and spent an hour picking. On the ride home, we talked about the different things we could make with this prized summer fruit and, of course, blueberry muffins were at the top of our list. Unfortunately, we didn't have a muffin tin but we did have a cast-iron skillet. Borrowing the traditional technique of cooking corn bread in a skillet, we came up with this recipe. Although

PREPARATION:
10 MINUTES

COOKING:
20 MINUTES

YIELD:
1 LOAF

the bread is best with wild Maine blueberries, it is a treat we make regularly with frozen berries. **TIP:** When combining the wet and dry ingredients in quick breads and muffins, stir the ingredients only enough to moisten them. Overmixing the batter will toughen the final product.

TOPPING

2 tablespoons sugar
¼ teaspoon cinnamon

BREAD

  Canola oil for greasing the pan
1 cup unbleached all-purpose flour
1 cup whole-wheat flour
½ cup yellow cornmeal
1 cup sugar
1½ teaspoons baking soda
1 teaspoon cinnamon
¼ teaspoon salt
2 eggs
1⅓ cups buttermilk
2 tablespoons unsalted butter, melted
2 cups blueberries

1. Preheat the oven to 375°F.
2. Prepare the topping by combining the sugar and cinnamon. Set it aside for the moment.
3. Lightly grease a 12-inch cast iron skillet with the canola oil. Set it aside for the moment.
4. In a large bowl whisk the unbleached flour, whole-grain flour, cornmeal, sugar, baking soda, cinnamon, and salt. Set the bowl aside for the moment.
5. In another bowl, whisk the eggs, buttermilk, and butter. Make a well in the center of the dry ingredients and pour the wet ingredients into it. With a spatula, gently fold the ingredients together. Fold in the blueberries.

6. Transfer the batter to the prepared pan. Sprinkle the batter with the topping. Transfer the pan to the oven and bake for 20 minutes.
7. Remove the pan from the oven. Allow the bread to cool for 15 minutes prior to slicing it into wedges.

The Power of Blueberries

Cultivated blueberries are grown all over the world, but wild blueberries are one of the few fruits that are native to North America. Except for a few areas in New Hampshire and Massachusetts, they thrive only in Maine. The season is short, stretching from early August until about the middle of September. Wild blueberries are significantly smaller than the cultivated variety and have a deeper blue color and a more concentrated flavor. Wild and cultivated blueberries are interchangeable in recipes.

Blueberries, wild or cultivated, fresh or frozen, are one of the most versatile fruits. They can be the star ingredient in cakes, pies, syrups, smoothies, and muffins as well as vinegars, salads, and savory sauces.

Besides their wonderful versatility and great taste, blueberries are prized for their incredible nutritional value. Recent studies indicate that blueberries, both wild and cultivated, rank highest among forty other common fruits and vegetables regarding antioxidant activity. That is, they have the ability to neutralize free radicals. Free radicals are the prime suspects that researchers believe cause cancer and heart disease.

Whether you are fortunate enough to pick and indulge in fresh wild blueberries during their brief appearance or purchase cultivated or frozen berries, the flavor and nutrition of this delectable fruit should not be missed.

Irish Soda Bread

PREPARATION:
5 MINUTES

COOKING:
35 MINUTES

YIELD:
1 LOAF

We always try to keep a loaf of Irish soda bread on the counter for healthful snacks and delicious breakfasts. Although the ingredients list is short and the technique simple, several details need to be considered to prepare an outstanding soda bread. Soda bread needs only gentle and minimal mixing (just enough to incorporate the wet and dry ingredients) and has to be baked immediately. The choice of flour is also important. Irish flour is made from spring wheat, giving it a fine and soft texture, but it is difficult to locate in America. Pastry flour is an excellent substitute and produces a light and flavorful soda bread.

2 cups white pastry flour
½ cup whole-grain flour
1 teaspoon kosher salt
1 teaspoon baking soda
3 tablespoons sugar
1 cup currants
1 cup buttermilk

1. Preheat the oven to 350°F. Line a baking sheet with parchment paper.
2. In a large bowl combine well the pastry flour, whole-grain flour, salt, baking soda, sugar, and currants.
3. Make a well in the center of the ingredients. Slowly add the buttermilk, mixing with your hand or a spoon until the dough comes together.
4. Turn the dough out onto a floured surface and with minimal kneading, form the dough into a ball.
5. Transfer the dough to the prepared baking sheet. With a serrated knife cut an "x" into the loaf. Gently prick the loaf with a fork 6 times.
6. Transfer the dough to the oven and bake it for 35 minutes or until it is golden brown and sounds hollow when tapped on the bottom. Allow the bread to cool for 15 minutes before slicing.

Apple-Cinnamon Muffins

Homemade muffins are a perfect accompaniment to whole-grain cereal for breakfast. They are also an energizing snack during or after school. They are quick and simple to prepare and much more healthful than the store-bought variety, which are more akin to cake than anything else. Muffins from your own kitchen are nutrient dense and never too sweet or fat laden. Our apple muffins are fiber-rich and loaded with complex carbohydrates, and with a mere 2 tablespoons of butter, very low in fat to boot. The grated apple provides plenty of moisture and a natural sweetness. If you are like us, you will want to make a couple of batches a week, wrap them individually, and keep them in your freezer to enjoy anytime.

PREPARATION:
10 MINUTES

COOKING:
18 MINUTES

YIELD:
10 MUFFINS

TOPPING

- 2 tablespoons sugar
- ¼ teaspoon cinnamon

MUFFINS

- Canola oil for greasing the muffin tins
- 1 cup unbleached all-purpose flour
- 1 cup whole-grain flour
- ⅔ cup sugar
- ⅓ cup light brown sugar
- 1½ teaspoons baking soda
- 1 teaspoon cinnamon
- ¼ teaspoon kosher salt
- 2 eggs
- 1 cup buttermilk
- 2 tablespoons unsalted butter, melted
- 1 teaspoon vanilla
- 3 apples, grated and squeezed to remove excess moisture

1. Preheat the oven to 375°F.
2. Prepare the topping by combining the sugar and cinnamon. Set it aside for the moment.

3. Lightly grease 10 muffin cups.
4. In a large bowl whisk the unbleached flour, whole-grain flour, sugar, brown sugar, baking soda, cinnamon, and salt. Set the bowl aside for the moment.
5. In another bowl, whisk the eggs, buttermilk, butter, and vanilla. Make a well in the center of the dry ingredients and pour the wet ingredients into it. With a spatula, gently fold the ingredients together. Fold in the apples.
6. Divide the batter among the muffin cups. Sprinkle the batter with the topping. Transfer the muffin tin to the oven and bake for 18 minutes.
7. Remove the tin from the oven. Allow the muffins to cool for 15 minutes.

Corn Muffins

PREPARATION:
10 MINUTES

COOKING:
18 MINUTES

YIELD:
10 MUFFINS

When lightly toasted or grilled and spread with strawberry jam, corn muffins are a delightful snack or a slightly sweet breakfast. They are a must accompaniment with your Neighborhood Barbeque for Twenty (see page 388).

Canola oil for greasing the pan
1½ cups unbleached all-purpose flour
1 cup yellow cornmeal
½ cup sugar
1½ teaspoons baking soda
¼ teaspoon kosher salt
2 eggs
1⅓ cups buttermilk
2 tablespoons unsalted butter, melted
1½ cups frozen corn, thawed

1. Preheat the oven to 375°F.
2. Lightly grease 10 muffin cups.

3. In a large bowl whisk the flour, cornmeal, sugar, baking soda, and salt. Set the bowl aside for a moment.

4. In another bowl, whisk the eggs, buttermilk, and butter. Make a well in the center of the dry ingredients and pour the wet ingredients into it. With a spatula, gently fold the ingredients together. Fold in the corn.

5. Divide the batter among the muffin cups. Transfer the muffin tin to the oven and bake for 18 minutes.

6. Remove the tin from the oven. Allow the muffins to cool for 15 minutes.

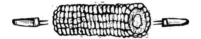

Simple Cinnamon-Raisin Buns

Many recipes for cinnamon buns contain an abundance of butter and are based on a yeast dough, making them unhealthful and impractical to prepare regularly. Our version, made with a mere two tablespoons of butter, is raised with baking powder and baking soda. They can be assembled in forty-five minutes, making them a guilt-free sweet treat to enjoy any time. **TIP:** Pastry flour is low in gluten and gives the buns a softer and slightly dense texture. If you like your buns chewier and crispier, you can substitute all-purpose flour for the pastry flour.

PREPARATION:
15 MINUTES

COOKING:
25 MINUTES

YIELD:
18 BUNS

DOUGH

2½ cups white pastry flour

1 cup whole-grain pastry flour

2 teaspoons baking powder

1 teaspoon baking soda

¼ cup white sugar

1½ teaspoons kosher salt

1½ cups plus 2 tablespoons buttermilk

FILLING

⅓ cup brown sugar, firmly packed

¼ cup white sugar

2 teaspoons ground cinnamon

¼ teaspoon ground nutmeg

2 tablespoons unsalted butter, melted

2 cups raisins

TOPPING

1¼ cups confectioners' sugar

3 tablespoons cream cheese

3 tablespoons buttermilk

1. Preheat the oven to 375°F. Line a sheet pan with parchment paper.

2. To prepare the dough, whisk together the white and whole-grain pastry flours, baking powder, baking soda, white sugar, and salt in a large mixing bowl. Make a well in the center of the dry ingredients. Pour in the buttermilk. With your hands, mix the ingredients until the dough comes together. Knead the dough inside the bowl for about 1 minute. Set the dough aside for a moment.

3. To prepare the filling, combine the brown sugar, white sugar, cinnamon, and nutmeg in a small bowl. Set aside for a moment.

4. Flour a work surface and place the dough on it. Roll the dough into a rectangle measuring approximately 12 by 14 inches. Brush the surface with the melted butter. Scatter on the raisins, gently pressing them into the dough. Sprinkle on the prepared sugar mixture.

5. Beginning with the end nearest you, roll the dough into a log as tightly as possible and seal the seam. Dust the log with flour.

With a serrated knife and using a sawing motion, trim each end of the log. Then cut the log into 18 1½-inch-thick pieces.

6. Transfer the buns to the parchment-lined sheet pan, placing them close together. Transfer the pan to the oven and bake the buns for 20–25 minutes or until they are golden brown.

7. While the buns are baking, prepare the topping by whisking the confectioners' sugar, cream cheese, and buttermilk in a bowl.

8. Remove the buns from the oven and allow to cool for 5 minutes. Drizzle them with the topping and allow to cool for another 10 minutes before serving.

Homemade Granola

PREPARATION:
10 MINUTES

COOKING:
30 MINUTES

YIELD:
4 CUPS

A common misconception is that commercially prepared granola is a "health food." A quick glance at the nutrition information on the label of a mass-produced granola tells a different story. Many of these granolas contain far too much sugar and saturated fat to be even remotely considered healthful. The same can be said about granola bars.

Homemade granola is a snap to make. The ingredients are dry-roasted, which results in a deep toasted flavor. And with plenty of iron, fiber, calcium, and complex carbohydrates, it is highly nutritious. We enjoy homemade granola by the handful, combined with yogurt or milk, or mixed into muffin batter or cookie dough (see page 378). **TIP:** Store the extra granola in an airtight container where it will stay fresh for a week.

2 cups regular (not quick-cooking) rolled oats
⅓ cup raw cashew pieces
⅓ cup pecans, chopped
⅓ cup sesame seeds
⅓ cup sunflower seeds
¼ teaspoon kosher salt
¾ cup toasted wheat germ
⅓ cup brown sugar
1 teaspoon cinnamon
1½ cups raisins

1. Heat a large Dutch oven over medium-low heat. Add the oats, cashews, and pecans. Cook the ingredients, stirring often, until they begin to toast, approximately 10 minutes.
2. Add the sesame seeds and sunflower seeds. Continue toasting the ingredients, stirring often, for another 10 minutes. Add the salt, wheat germ, and brown sugar. Cook the ingredients, stirring constantly, until the sugar has melted, approximately 2 minutes.
3. Add the cinnamon and raisins. Transfer the granola to a large sheet pan to cool.

PREPARATION:
15 MINUTES

COOKING:
45 MINUTES

YIELD:
6 SERVINGS

Apple and Almond Crisp

One of our favorite autumn family activities is apple picking. Once you've tasted an apple directly from a tree, you'll probably be like us and not purchase apples from a market again. Supermarket apples are often a year old by the time they reach the consumer. When we go apple picking, we try to exercise restraint and only pick enough to enjoy as snacks and to make three or four apple-based goodies. But we always lose control, pick too many, and end up giving away a large amount. An easy and scrumptious treat is this healthful crisp. The sliced almond topping is the perfect compliment to the natural sweetness of the apples.

FILLING
6 large apples, peeled, cored, and sliced
Juice from 1 lemon
¼ cup sugar
1 teaspoon cinnamon

TOPPING
1 cup sliced almonds
¾ cup whole-grain flour
¾ cup brown sugar
1 teaspoon cinnamon
3 tablespoons unsalted butter melted

1. Preheat the oven to 375°F.
2. In an 8-inch-by-8-inch casserole, toss together the apples, lemon, sugar, and cinnamon. Set the casserole aside for a moment.
3. To prepare the topping, combine the almonds, flour, brown sugar, and cinnamon in a large bowl. Add the butter. With your hands, thoroughly combine the ingredients.
4. Cover the apples with the topping. Transfer the crisp to the oven. Bake the crisp until the apples are tender, approximately 45 minutes.
5. Allow the crisp to cool for 15 minutes. If desired, accompany the crisp with vanilla frozen yogurt.

Raspberry-Oat Squares

PREPARATION:
10 MINUTES

COOKING:
40 MINUTES

YIELD:
8 SERVINGS

The crust of this healthful treat contains ground flaxseed. Flaxseed, like salmon, swordfish, and mackerel, contains omega-three fatty acids. Omega-three fatty acids have been found to decrease the risk of coronary heart disease. It is thought that they function as natural blood thinners, allowing the blood to flow more freely by not clogging the coronary arteries of the heart. In the kitchen, flaxseed finds its way into crisps, quick breads, yeast breads, cookies, and brownies. It adds an earthy flavor, similar to whole-grain flour, and a pronounced moistness to your baked goods. **TIP:** Flaxseed needs to be ground to release its nutrients.

⅓ cup flaxseed
1 cup all-purpose flour
1 cup rolled oats
⅓ cup packed brown sugar
2 tablespoons white sugar
5 tablespoons unsalted butter, cut into 5 pieces
1 tablespoon canola oil
1 cup raspberry jam

1. Preheat the oven to 350°F.
2. Place the flaxseed in a spice grinder or electric coffee mill. Grind

it until it resembles flour, approximately 10 seconds. Set it aside for a moment.

3. Place the flour, oats, brown sugar, white sugar, and unsalted butter into the work bowl of a food processor fitted with the metal blade. Pulse the mixture 10–15 times or until it resembles coarse meal. Add the ground flaxseed and pulse 3 more times.

4. Lightly coat the bottom of an 8-inch square baking pan with the canola oil. Press two-thirds of the oat mixture into the bottom of the pan. Transfer the pan to the oven and bake for 15 minutes.

5. Remove the pan from the oven. Do not turn off the oven. Spread the jam evenly over the warm crust. Sprinkle on the remaining oat mixture and gently press.

6. Return the pan to the oven and bake until lightly brown, approximately 25 minutes. Remove the pan from the oven and allow to cool completely prior to cutting into squares.

Granola–Chocolate-Chip Cookies

PREPARATION:
30 MINUTES (GRANOLA PREPARATION)

COOKING:
15 MINUTES

YIELD:
1½ DOZEN COOKIES

We often add homemade granola to our basic chocolate-chip cookie recipe. The granola makes the cookies more healthful and adds an interesting texture and taste.

⅔ cup brown sugar
½ cup natural peanut butter
2 tablespoons canola oil
1 egg
1 teaspoon vanilla extract
⅔ cup unbleached, all-purpose flour
¾ teaspoon baking powder
¼ teaspoon kosher salt
1½ cups granola (see page 375)
½ cup chocolate chips

1. Preheat the oven to 350°F. Line a sheet pan with parchment paper. Set the pan aside for the moment.

2. Whisk together the brown sugar, peanut butter, and canola oil in a large bowl. Whisk in the egg and vanilla.

3. Stir in the flour, baking powder, and salt. Stir in the granola and chocolate chips.

4. With your hands, divide the dough into 18 Ping-Pong-sized balls, placing them approximately 2 inches apart on the sheet pan. Transfer the pan to the oven. Bake the cookies until they are just firm, approximately 12 minutes.

5. Remove the pan from the oven and allow the cookies to cool for 5 minutes. Transfer them to a wire rack to cool completely.

Real Chocolate Pudding

Kids love chocolate pudding. And we all know the drill. Open the box, whisk in a couple of cups of milk, and chill. Well, preparing chocolate pudding from scratch is just as simple and not much more time-consuming. Your youngsters will love to help with this one. They will delight in watching the pudding magically thicken after a few minutes of whisking. **TIP:** To make a chocolate cream pie, pour the pudding into a prepared pie crust and top with low-fat whipped cream.

⅓ cup plus 1 tablespoon unsweetened cocoa powder

⅓ cup cornstarch

½ cup plus 2 tablespoons sugar

½ teaspoon kosher salt

2 cups low-fat milk

1 teaspoon vanilla

PREPARATION:
5 MINUTES

COOKING:
10 MINUTES

CHILLING:
1 HOUR

YIELD:
4 SERVINGS

1. In a small bowl, combine the cocoa powder, cornstarch, sugar, and salt. Set it aside for the moment.
2. Combine the milk and vanilla in a medium pot and place it over medium heat.
3. Whisk in the cocoa mixture. Continue whisking until bubbles begin to appear around the edges, approximately 5 minutes.
4. Reduce the heat to low and whisk the pudding until thick, approximately 3 minutes.
5. Divide the pudding among four dessert dishes and refrigerate until chilled, approximately an hour.

PREPARATION:
45 MINUTES

FREEZING:
3 HOURS

YIELD:
8 SERVINGS

Frozen Chocolate-Marshmallow Soy Cream Pie

At first glance, the statement "healthful frozen dessert" seems to be a contradiction in terms. But it isn't. This surprisingly rich-tasting delight, based on low-fat milk and tofu, is an excellent source of calcium, protein, and iron. The lack of cream and egg yolks does not detract from the pie's superb taste. It's decadent and wonderfully satisfying and will win over even the most passionate fans of premium ice cream.

1 pound firm tofu
8 graham crackers
3 tablespoons unsalted butter, melted
1½ cups low-fat milk
1½ cups chocolate chips, divided
¾ cup sugar
2 tablespoons unsweetened cocoa powder
1 teaspoon vanilla extract
¼ teaspoon kosher salt
2 8-ounce containers low-fat frozen whipped topping, defrosted
2 cups mini-marshmallows

1. Preheat the oven to 350°F. Have on hand a 10-inch pie tin and an ice cream maker.
2. Remove the moisture from the tofu by first placing it on a plate. Set a heavy pot on top of it and set aside for 15 minutes.
3. While the tofu is being pressed, combine the graham crackers and butter in the work bowl of a food processor fitted with the metal blade. Process the mixture until the crackers are well ground.
4. Press the cracker mixture onto the bottom and sides of the pie tin. Transfer the tin to the oven and bake for 8 minutes. Remove it from the oven and allow it to cool.
5. Meanwhile, heat the milk in a saucepan over medium-low heat. Whisk in 1 cup of the chocolate chips, sugar, and cocoa powder. Whisk the mixture until the chips have dissolved and the sugar has melted, approximately 5 minutes. Remove the pan from the heat. Whisk in the vanilla and salt. Allow the mixture to cool to room temperature.
6. Place the tofu into the work bowl of the food processor with the metal blade in place. Add the cooled chocolate mixture. Turn on the machine and process the mixture until smooth. Transfer it to a large bowl.
7. Fold in 1 container of whipped topping. Transfer the mixture to the freezer bowl of an ice cream maker. Freeze according to the manufacturer's instructions. During the last 5 minutes, add the remaining ½ cup of chocolate chips and the marshmallows.
8. Transfer the soy cream to the prepared crust, spreading it evenly. Spread the remaining container of whipped topping on the top of the pie. Transfer the pie to the freezer and freeze until firm, approximately 3 hours.

weekend cooking

During busy times, when we know we will be arriving home later that usual, we often spend a couple of hours on Sunday afternoon preparing several meals to enjoy during the week. These meals usually include casseroles, stews, and soups. All these foods taste better after they have sat for a day, can be easily reheated, and offer several options to create quick and interesting meals from their leftovers. Many of the meals can be rounded out by a green salad and a crusty whole-grain baguette. On a typical Sunday we may make a Beef Stew and Spaghetti and Meatballs. On Sunday we will serve the meatballs and on Monday, the stew. On Tuesday, we will use the meatballs in our Meatball and Broccoli Rabe Soup. For Wednesday, we will make a batch of Mashed Potatoes and convert the leftover stew into Cottage Pie. Finally, on Thursday, we will have meatball grinders. At first glance, this may seem as though you are eating a meat-based meal five days in one week. But with a quick look at the recipes, you will realize that the meatballs contain plenty of tofu and that you are really stretching the stew and rounding out the meals with vegetables. When you prepare meals for the week on the weekend, you will be spending a minimal amount of time in the kitchen on workdays, making your evenings more relaxing and enjoyable.

Weekend 1 (Vegetarian)

ON SUNDAY PREPARE

1. Tofu and Provolone Lasagna–page 221
2. Lentil and Barley Soup–page 177
3. Spinach, Zucchini, and Tomato Stuffed Potatoes–page 232

SUNDAY

Tofu and Provolone Lasagna

MONDAY

Lentil and Barely Soup

TUESDAY

Spinach, Zucchini, and Tomato Stuffed Potatoes

WEDNESDAY

Baked Penne with Lentils, Barley, and Feta–page 190

THURSDAY

Tofu and Provolone Baguettes
Slice two medium baguettes in half. Slice open each half lengthwise. Fill the baguettes with leftover Tofu and Provolone Lasagna, garnish with a bit more cheese, and bake in a preheated 400°F oven for 15 minutes.

Weekend 2

ON SUNDAY PREPARE

1. Spice-Rubbed Pork Shoulder with Black Beans and Rice–page 279
2. White Bean, Tomato, and Fennel Soup–page 175
3. Vegetarian Baked Beans–page 235

SUNDAY
Spice-Rubbed Pork Shoulder with Black Beans and Rice

MONDAY
White Bean, Tomato, and Fennel Soup

TUESDAY
Vegetarian Baked Beans accompanied with baked sweet potatoes

WEDNESDAY
Carnitas and Black Bean Burritos—page 282

THURSDAY
Baked Penne with White Beans, Fennel, Tomatoes, and
Provolone—page 189

Weekend 3

ON SUNDAY PREPARE
1. Spaghetti and Meatballs—page 336
2. Beef Stew—page 270

SUNDAY
Spaghetti and Meatballs

MONDAY
Beef Stew

TUESDAY
Meatball and Broccoli Rabe Soup—page 174

WEDNESDAY
Cottage Pie—page 272

THURSDAY
Meatball Grinders
Slice two medium baguettes in half. Slice open each half lengthwise. Fill the baguettes with leftover meatballs, garnish with a bit
of cheese, and bake in a preheated 400°F oven for 15 minutes.

Weekend 4

ON SUNDAY PREPARE

1. Stewed Pinto Beans and Brown Rice—page 225
2. Pot Roast with Vegetable Gravy—page 273
3. Chicken with Red Wine and Mushrooms—page 243

SUNDAY

Chicken with Red Wine and Mushrooms

MONDAY

Stewed Pinto Beans and Brown Rice

TUESDAY

Pot Roast with Vegetable Gravy

WEDNESDAY

Tofu and Pinto Bean Burritos—page 228

THURSDAY

Knife-and-Fork Pot Roast Sandwiches
Toast eight slices of whole-wheat bread. Place two slices of bread on a plate. Place hot sliced beef, vegetables, and gravy on one slice of bread. Place the other slice on top to form a sandwich. Repeat the procedure with the remaining, bread, beef, vegetables, and gravy.

special occasions

Whether you are entertaining friends for a vegetarian dinner, planning a genuine backyard barbeque featuring pulled pork and all the traditional accompaniments, or searching for a simple and comforting soup-and-salad dinner, the menus in this section will steer you in the right direction. Even for an experienced cook, preparing several courses for a large gathering can be a stressful situation requiring a fair amount of intense kitchen work. When we plan an event, we try to choose meals that can be partially prepared in advance so when our guests arrive, we can enjoy their company and not be busy in the kitchen with last-minute tasks. When the food is wonderful and everyone comments on how effortless we made it look, we feel successful. It's not necessary for our visitors to know the effort that went into the execution of the meal.

Dinner at the Shore

Cod Roasted with Olive Oil and Kosher Salt–page 291
Mixed Greens with Apple, Dried Cranberries, and Goat
    Cheese–page 323
A Summer Sauté–page 304
A crusty baguette
Sliced honeydew

A Neighborhood Barbeque for Twenty

Barbequed Pork Butt–page 283
Homemade Barbeque Sauce–page 328
Vinegar Sauce–page 328
Macaroni and Cheese (double recipe)–page 354
Stewed Pinto Beans (double recipe)–page 225
Kim Brown's Collard Greens–page 315
Coleslaw (double recipe)–page 305
Corn Muffins–page 372

The Best Soup and Salad for Dinner

White Bean, Tomato, and Fennel Soup–page 175
Red Leaf and Arugula Salad with Pine Nuts and
    Raisins–page 325
A rich and creamy cheese such as Brie or Camembert
A crusty baguette

A Cold-Weather Meal

Roasted Pork Tenderloin with Herbs and Garlic–page 278
Baked Sweet Potatoes and Apples with Cinnamon and Maple
    Syrup–page 306
Red Leaf and Arugula Salad with Pine Nuts and
    Raisins–page 325
Goat cheese and a whole-grain baguette

A Summer Harvest Supper

Tomato and Cucumber Bread Salad with Feta and
    Arugula–page 324
Penne with Chicken and Summer Vegetables–page 194
A crusty baguette
Fresh raspberries

A Meal to Make with Your Children

Mixed Greens with Apple, Dried Cranberries, and Goat
    Cheese–page 323
Pizza Dough–page 355
Tomato and Fresh Mozzarella Pizza–page 357
Pea and Onion Pizza–page 358

Vegetarians for Dinner

Tofu and Provolone Lasagna–page 221
"Creamy" Caesar Salad–page 326
A crusty baguette
Apple and Almond Crisp–page 376

All-American Meat and Potatoes

Beef Stew–page 270
Mashed Potatoes–page 309
Garlic Bread–page 361
Granola-Chocolate-Chip Cookies–page 378

A Simple Sunday-Evening Dinner

Baked Tofu Parmesan–page 238
Mesclun and Arugula Salad with a
    Balsamic Vinaigrette–page 322
Garlic Bread–page 361

A Family Picnic

Smoky Backyard Chicken–page 259
Chilled Bow Tie Pasta with Asparagus and Spinach–page 199
Coleslaw–page 305
Grilled Corn on the Cob–page 311
Corn Muffins–page 372

A Romantic Dinner

Braciolette–page 263
Polenta–page 311
A crusty baguette
Seasonal fresh fruit

A Weekend Brunch

Broccoli and Cheddar Frittata–page 161
Pan-Fried Potatoes with Onions and Peppers–page 310
Vanilla-Apple French Toast–page 168
Blueberry Black Pan Bread–page 367

index